QuestBusters™
KEYS TO THE
KINGDOMS™ 2

By Shay Addams

Series Editor
Shay Addams

Senior Editor
Willem Knibbe

Design and Production
Schrock & Associates

Vice President and Publisher
Ron Resnick

TO MY MOTHER, LURLINE.
WATCH OUT FOR THAT SNAKE UNDER THE PIANO!

CONTENTS

HOW TO USE THIS BOOK

vii

INTRODUCTION

viii

ALONE IN THE DARK 3

1

BENEATH A STEEL SKY

15

BIOFORGE

23

BUREAU 13

33

DARK SUN: WAKE OF THE RAVAGER

43

DEATH GATE

55

DISCWORLD

67

DRAGON LORE

87

DREAMWEB

99

ECSTATICA

107

Contents

HELL: A CYBERPUNK THRILLER

113

JORUNE: ALIEN LOGIC

127

KING'S QUEST VII

137

KNIGHTS OF XENTAR

153

THE LEGEND OF KYRANDIA 3

163

MENZOBERRANZAN

175

NOCTROPOLIS

191

RAVENLOFT: STONE PROPHET

199

SHADOWS OF CAIRN

211

UNDER A KILLING MOON

217

v

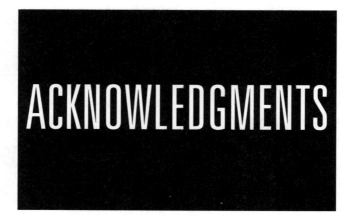

ACKNOWLEDGMENTS

Once again into the dungeon, the stalwart members of the QuestBusters Guild plunged to retrieve the "keys to the kingdoms" found within these hallowed pages. This time around, the Scroll of Honor includes Paul Shaffer, Clancy Shaffer, Fred Philipp, Tracey Portnoy, Jerry Van Horn, Tracy Hicks, Bruce and Peggy Wiley, and ye Guildmaster himself, Shay Addams. May the sun never set on their empires, and if they don't already have empires, may they each get one real soon.

HOW TO USE THIS BOOK

To get the most out of this book, buy a stack of adventure games and play them night and day until hopelessly stuck. (If you're already stuck in a quest, skip to the next paragraph.) Then turn to the Table of Contents and look up the name of your vexing quest. (If the solution is not in this book, please check the contents of the other books in the *QuestBusters* series: *Keys to the Kingdoms*, *The Book of Clues*, and *The Book of Clues 2*.)

Flip to the solution and scan the section headings to find the area of the game where you are stuck. Locate the answer, then get on with the quest.

The most important objects in every quest are listed in each solution's "Orbs & Stuff" table. The objects are in the first column, the name of the section that reveals its location is in the second column, and the "Also See Section" is in the third column. That column refers you to every section of the solution that discusses the object — it's a sort of index to the walk-through. Treasure, equipment, and other items not necessary for completing the game may be simply listed as, for example, "Various Armor" or "Assorted Weapons and Potions." If the answer you find still doesn't work, review the preceding sections; sometimes you must have accomplished a prior feat before a subsequent solution will work, and some have their own peculiarities, which may be pointed out under the General heading at the top of the solution.

Due to the near-universal implementation of automapping, coupled with the relative ease of mapping today's adventures, few maps were deemed necessary. In addition to coordinates and specific directions, we have included maps only for the most maddening areas, such as those with teleports.

If you're *still* stuck after all this, jot down the situation and teleport it to Clue Books Express, Dept. "Why Me?", PO Box 85143, Tucson AZ 85754. Enclose a self-addressed, stamped envelope.

Happy questing!

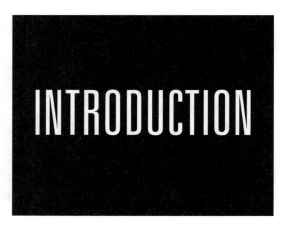

INTRODUCTION

BY
SHAY ADDAMS

Sherlock Holmes, were he still among the living, would be the first to admit that even the World's Most Brilliant Detective sometimes finds himself clueless, baffled, perplexed, and bewildered by the latest turn of events. How did Holmes save the day without a clue book or the steadfast Watson to use as a sounding board in his quest for a logical answer? He turned to his violin, and the music set his mind free from the concentrated thought processes whose very intensity throttled his efforts to penetrate the mystery at hand.

Unfortunately, few adventure gamers play the violin. (Perhaps I should say fortunately — this world would be an unbearable place to live if everyone stumped by an adventure game simultaneously picked up a violin and began playing.) Even fewer of us have such accommodating friends or associates as Watson. That's why we turn to clue books for help.

Often we turn to the books too soon, for all the puzzles in this book were solved by members of the QuestBusters Guild. They're ordinary human beings without violins, friends named Watson, or clue books. Their secret, when confronted by a game-stopping puzzle, is to simply let it go, stop wrangling with it night and day, and let the solution float to the top of their heads. And if that less-than-linear process fails, they call another member of the QuestBusters Guild for help. After all, what are Guilds for, anyway?

So the next time you're stuck in a quest and suddenly realize that you're not Sherlock Holmes, do not play the violin, and don't have a friend named Watson, stop thinking about the puzzle and wait for the answer to rise from your subconscious to the top of your brain. And if that takes too long, call your local software retailer or book store and ask for the latest volume in the never-ending QuestBusters series.

ALONE IN THE DARK 3: SLAUGHTER GULCH

BY
FRED PHILIPP &
CLANCY SHAFFER

TYPE
*Animated
Adventure*

SYSTEM
*IBM PC
(Required:
386DX33+,
4MB RAM,
276KB free
EMS, 35MB
free hard disk
space, mouse,
256-color
VGA,
single-speed
CD-ROM
drive)*

COMPANY
I-Motion, Inc.

EDWARD CARNBY, THE INTREPID SLEUTH OF THE FIRST TWO ALONE IN THE DARK GAMES, IS BACK IN THE SADDLE. THIS TIME CARNBY RIDES OUT TO THE OLD WEST TOWN OF SLAUGHTER GULCH TO INVESTIGATE THE DISAPPEARANCE OF A FILM CREW. AS CARNBY, YOU'LL BATTLE GHOSTS, SOLVE PUZZLES, AND EVEN TURN INTO A COUGAR AS YOU EXPLORE A SPRAWLING ARRAY OF WILD WEST LOCATIONS. THE MUSIC AND SOUND EFFECTS VARY WITH EACH MAJOR LOCATION AND TRANSFORM WHAT MIGHT HAVE BEEN AN ORDINARY ADVENTURE INTO AN ENGROSSING EXPERIENCE. THE GRAPHICS FOLLOW THE SAME STYLE AS ALONE IN THE DARK 2, AND THERE ARE A LOT MORE OF THEM — THIS IS THE BIGGEST GAME OF THE SERIES. YOU CAN ADJUST THE DIFFICULTY SETTING THIS TIME, BUT MOUSE SUPPORT REMAINS UNAVAILABLE. FOR SOME REASON, FEW ADVENTURE GAMES HAVE BEEN SET IN THE OLD WEST. WHILE THIS STORY ISN'T AS FUNNY AS SIERRA'S FREDDY PHARKAS: FRONTIER PHARMACIST, THE PUZZLES AND COMBAT MAKE ALONE IN THE DARK 3 EMINENTLY MORE ENJOYABLE. AMONG THE BEST QUESTS OF THE YEAR, SLAUGHTER GULCH IS A MUST-SEE STOP ON EVERY ADVENTURER'S ITINERARY.

THE SOLUTION ▬▬▬▬▬▬▬▬▬

SALOON

Cross the bridge, which will explode behind you. Walk onto saloon's porch, go behind the water trough, and get gasoline can. Enter saloon.

Go to movie projector and use gasoline can on it. View movie. Pick up oil can behind projector. Get key from table and maraca from stage. Go under stairs into small room left of bar and get matches. Go behind bar.

BEHIND BAR

Ghost will appear and shoot at you. Run out from behind bar and toward projector until ghost is out of bullets and leaves. Return to behind bar.

Pick up lamp from bar, then get healing flask, bottle of wood alcohol, and empty bottle from shelf behind bar. Drink every healing flask (henceforth referred to as "flask") you find. Exit bar and throw empty bottle. Pick up token.

Go to rear of player piano and insert token. Watch enactment. Go to buffalo skull mounted behind bar. Save game. Push right horn. Hide behind left horn until ghost runs out of bullets, then butt him to death. Search and get ace of diamonds and golden Winchester bullet. Jump down the open trapdoor.

CELLAR

Light lamp by using oil, match, and lamp. Walk past three barrels, then to the right. Go behind the last barrel and get cane from wall. Examine poster on wall, then peel away corner and read message.

Use cane on barrel nearest poster. Barrel will open. Step back and use maraca. When snakes exit barrel, enter barrel and save game. Climb stairs.

CELLS

Ghost will follow you through hole. Avoid ghost. Go to bed and search to get stone. Go to cellar door and use cane to get key. Use key to escape cell. Move into corridor. Save.

Throw stone at wall to get the Indian amulet. Enter cell at end of hall and drop wood alcohol directly in front of drunken ghost. Pick up the flask left behind by the ghost and drink it.

SHERIFF'S OFFICE

Go to hall with pentagram on floor and enter sheriff's office. Search desk and get sheriff's badge and box of Winchester bullets. Use key on gun cabinet and get Winchester. Examine three posters on wall relating to Li Tung, Duke and John Elwood, and Jim Burris.

GETTING OUT

Proceed down hall to next area with large cabinet against wall. Go to right side of cabinet and push it to the left to block opening and prevent monster from entering room. Take shotgun from the cabinet, then climb rope ladder.

ON ROOF

Pick up whip. Follow path, turn left at corner, and pick up iron plate. Use plate to protect you. Go past door and around corner to get a Gatling cartridge belt.

The ghost you encounter is the Lone Miner. Load Winchester with golden bullet and shoot him. Pick up the bag of scorpions he drops.

Go north through doorway. Get Gatling gun and flask. Return to trapdoor where you entered. Instead of turning left at first corner, go straight.

A floating object will be shooting out red beams here. Get close to beam and save game. When beam is paused, move forward and pick up voodoo noose. Back up to avoid beam.

HANGMAN

Go to the door you passed earlier. Back up a step and use Gatling gun on door. Enter room and quickly use voodoo noose to remove hangman. Drop bag of scorpions down hole, then push lever to close hole. Walk to the now-closed hole and get dried meat and stick of dynamite.

DYNAMITE

Return to where you found the Gatling gun. Head-butt the ghosts, or shoot them with the Winchester. Enter the north room. The door will close behind you. When the shotgun appears, use the Gatling on the door slot.

Search barrel near crack in wall and get short fuse. Go to crack. Use fuse, then use dynamite, then use match. Back away to avoid explosion. Go through the new hole in the wall.

Alone in the Dark 3: a ghost story filled with western iconography.

●●●●●●●●●●

THROUGH HOLE

Turn right. Use Gatling on ghosts (reload if necessary). Use sheriff's badge on mechanical device, then use whip on lever at top. Enter the opened secret passageway behind you.

Get flask. Step onto plank and take box of bullets. Run from plank to next building, smashing through window.

SALOON: SECOND FLOOR

At window, light lamp on wall near right door (as you look at screen). A vision will appear. Now light opposite wall lamp. Enter first room. Take clothes horse, flask, newspaper cutting (read).

Feed dried meat to vulture and get token. Walk through painting of Arizona Kid into second room. Get perfume spray, pearl, and 30/30 bullet from dresser. Push mirror and take key behind it.

At bed, search Diane's quiver. Take arrow and place in Cupid's bow. See vision. Enter hallway through painting. Pick up cheap ring on floor. Use key on door nearest gaping hole to enter third room.

MORE ROOMS

Take diary and read. Break cheap ring. Use stone from ring on eye socket in statue. Take bullets, flask, and instruction sheet. Read everything you can.

Go out onto balcony and place clothes horse in front of shutter to the left, then back away. Monster will exit and fall through hole. Push open shutter down so you can cross hole. Enter room four.

Get key from table. Examine hanging plates. Get instruction sheet, magnesium flash, and shutter release from floor. Return to hallway.

MONSTER ON BLOCK

Use key on remaining door. Enter. Avoid monster. Move quickly to right behind cabinet with film reel on floor. At the film reel, use bulb on shutter release, use bulb on flash, and use flash to fry monster.

Take oil can from beside piano. Use token on piano. Head-butt the bulls-eye target on cabinet. Get flask and Navajo war stick. The block will slide away, revealing a trapdoor. Jump down.

PILLARS

Light lamp and drop it to divert bats. Move into the pillars room. Save game. Jump across pillars until you confront a mummy blocking the way. Use Navajo war stick. Jump onto platform. Get bullets and small key.

Continue to jump pillars until you are stranded on a pillar in a corner with drawing on wall behind you. (For a better angle from which to jump, spin in place.) Use Indian amulet to escape.

ARCHIVE OFFICE

In hallway, butt the first ghost. Get flask. Butt second ghost. Get top hat and key. Use key on door to enter Archive Office.

Take Ziegler's watch from bust of Jed Stone. Go to table. To read printer's plate, place it in front of mirror. Read Ziegler's watch-making book in the bookcase. Take locked book and unlock it with the key. Read Colonel Walker's book. Go to last row of bookcase.

Take empty book. To read book, use match to light candle on table. Return to hallway and use watch in front of first door. Enter.

MAYOR'S OFFICE

Take storyboard from Morrison. Place top hat on bust of Lincoln. Take two boxes of bullets. Shoot window at top of ladder. Kill any creatures that arrive. Climb ladder and jump through shattered window.

CEMETERY

Place the Navajo war stick at mausoleum in the middle of the cemetery. Watch where lightning strikes — it reveals the grave of One-Eyed Jack. Place the ace of diamonds on his grave. Take message. Climb through window as the ledge stone rises.

KITCHEN

Take pemmican bag from buffet. Chew pemmican. Get can of oil from table. Get film reel from corner. To lift wall, use oil on spit in hearth. Enter ballroom.

BALLROOM

Get bullets from under dress of the paper-mache girl. Go to stage and get guitar string, key for safe, and sheet of music from foot of stage. Head back toward kitchen and get hammer from foot of fat dummy.

To escape the dummies, run into kitchen, open door behind wall to your right, and enter corridor.

MAKE-UP ROOM

Ignore unlocked doors. At locked door, put 30/30 bullet in lock and use hammer on bullet. Enter room and examine model of train station. Take blasting cap, light bulb, and map. Go to adjoining small room.

DARKROOM

Screw light bulb into socket. Place music sheet under magnifying glass of film editor/viewer. Read code: 806. Use guitar string as drive belt. View film reel on editor/viewer. Go through opening in wall to bank.

BANK

Take and read astronomy book on small table in front of teller windows. Hit portrait of Washington to reveal encoding box. Keep pressing against it until 806 flashes. Walk behind teller windows.

Use pearl on safe at end of room. Use safe key. Butt creature as soon as he comes out and steals your Indian amulet. Recover amulet. (If he gets away, follow him and get it.) Take box of bullets and locked suitcase from safe. Go to window and slide down cable to General Store.

GENERAL STORE

After falling through the roof, approach character to get and read message. Get flask on saddle. Go to railway car. Get bullets and detonator box. Enter car to ride to train station.

EXPLORING

Explore area, noting statue and tar. Read storyboard and map. Note that you are back across the bridge and at the saloon, where you first started.

TRAIN STATION

Enter and push "Station" sign to spill paint from can on top of it. Get the suitcase key that falls out. Search the stack of rails. Get the eye bolt. Go to corner near the closed door and use eye bolt three times to open door. Wait until the door is up to the top, then quickly run through the door. Save game.

WATER TOWER

Quickly use the blasting cap near door at the corner of the station. Opposite this, at the hole in the rock wall, use detonator to blow up the station (and kill the monster who, if you wait too long, will arrive and steal the suitcase).

Go to tower. Approach ladder. When requested, drop the suitcase and the suitcase key. You will die but be reincarnated as a cougar.

COUGAR

The Shaman tells you to "Give back to the Earth the Eagle that was stolen." Save game. Time is of the essence now, because the clock is ticking away your life points.

GOLDEN EAGLE

Run to the saloon and climb stairs behind projector. Jump across the gaping hole to the shattered window. Run through window onto plank. Go to hole in wall near statue. Run through hole to statue. You will get the golden eagle and fall onto the ground.

SILVER

Go to the tar barrel you noted earlier and climb onto barrel, which coats your paw with tar. Go to the building next door. The door will now be open. Enter and locate barrel. Walk into the barrel to coat your paw with silver salts.

WEREWOLF

Exit and return to saloon. The werewolf will appear. Kill him with your silver paw. Go to cemetery. Kill second werewolf. Go to cave and walk into fire. After a brief interlude, you are resurrected as Carnby.

DOUBLE

Check your tombstone, then get soap from behind tombstone. Pick up Colt revolver lying on railroad tracks. Go to water tower. Your double is there. Drop the Colt. Walk into double to merge, and you are now dressed as a cowboy! Pick up the Colt.

WATER TOWER AGAIN

To get into the tower, climb the ladder to the top, then walk off the ramp and climb down. Use soap to slay monster. Get the metallic brush it drops. Use brush on peg hole in column in center of tower. Trapdoor opens. Walk behind column and get flask. Enter trapdoor.

THE CAVES

Search wall on your right to view sectional map of caves. Look back the way you came and pick up the dead leaf. To open the door, use the leaf on the Indian bust that is inset into the wall. Pick up notebook near door and read.

EXPLORING CAVES

Climb up ladder. Kill two monsters by butting them. Search recess to left to get the pickaxe. At recess near exit, search to get a flask (drink). Exit through opening.

CHASM

Pick up paper (poem) in corner and read. Save game. Walk into chasm just right (screen right, which is your left) of center. You'll know you're in the right spot when a stone block appears, supporting you. If you're in the wrong spot, you die.

NEEDLESS CHALLENGE

To move the block across the needles, walk in the following directions: west, south, west, west, north, west, north, west, north, west, and west to exit. Use Colt to kill first monster. Enter room beyond. Use pickaxe to kill next monster.

LIBRARY

Pick up scorched book (Don Fernando's journal) from floor and read it. Search room thoroughly to locate and get the water pitcher, book (Jed Stone's sketch book), and candlestick (which opens next door). As you exit the room, you will pick up a needle.

ELEVATOR

To open door, use water pitcher on drawing of man next to elevator door. Enter elevator. Pick up piggy bank. Throw bank. Pick up broken piggy bank and microscope glass slide. Push lever to rise. Exit.

LABORATORY

Note four large, colored buttons hanging around the room. Go to microscope in corner and use glass slide in microscope. Search microscope to view slide. The four colors shown are: grey, green, blue, and red. Push the four buttons in that order to open the next door. Enter door.

SHRINKING

Search table to get vial of poison. Go around corner and use vial on needle. Use vial of poison on distilled water. When you become small, enter the jail cell. Use poisoned needle on old guy. Get piece of straw. Get key to the goal. Get bottle of ammonia.

GOAL

Use key to the goal on goal cell door. Use vial of poison on distilled water again. Walk behind table leg and into small hole in wall. Use straw and run across chasm.

LAVA FLOW

Get vial with a potion. Enter next room and quickly use vial with a potion on lava flow. Get bucket of glue (avoid getting caught in spider web). Step on spider. Use bucket of glue. Climb up light shaft. Quickly get hammer's head. Walk near hole and throw hammer's head. Go down hole.

MR. COBRA

Get lead ingot. Push anvil out of way. Get flask. Get Winchester. Enter next room and kill Mr. Cobra. Get Cobra's wig, get silver dollar, get flask. Use silver dollar on poster. Walk into other room.

ALCHEMY

Use matches on crucible. Use lead ingot on crucible. Get scorched paper, get evil wand with a mineral tip, get Aztec legend parchment, get ammunition. Enter tunnel and kill big guy.

EMILY

Get knife. To awaken Emily, throw bottle of ammonia against door through which you entered. Use Cobra's wig on hook above door, then open it. Run into the other room with the eagle statue in it. Quickly use the evil wand on the statue. Get flask.

ESCAPING

Run into other room. Get rubber glove and use it. Use knife on electrical wires. Use water faucet. Run back into the other room. Get sack of coal. Get on train. Use sack of coal. Use matches. Push lever.

11

ORBS & STUFF

Object	See this Section for Location	Also See Section(s)
Healing flasks	Behind Bar	Cells, On Roof, Through Hole, Saloon: Second Floor, More Rooms, Monster on Block, Archive Office, General Store, Water Tower Again, Exploring Caves, Mr. Cobra, Emily
Key	Saloon, Cells	Location only/Sheriff's Office
Maraca	Saloon	Cellar
Matches	Saloon	Alchemy
Wood alcohol	Behind Bar	Cells
Token	Behind Bar, Saloon: Second Floor	Location only, Monster on Block
Ace of diamonds	Behind Bar	Cemetery
Golden Winchester bullet	Behind Bar	On Roof
Indian amulet	Cells	Pillars, Bank
Sheriff's badge	Sheriff's Office	Through Hole
Winchester and bullets	Sheriff's Office	Location only
Shotgun	Getting Out	Location only
Whip	On Roof	Through Hole
Bag of scorpions	On Roof	Hangman
Voodoo noose	On Roof	Hangman
Gatling gun and bullets	On Roof	Hangman, Dynamite, Through Hole
Dried meat	Hangman	Saloon: Second Floor
Dynamite	Hangman	Dynamite
Perfume	Saloon: Second Floor	Location only
Clothes horse	Saloon: Second Floor	More Rooms
Pearl	Saloon: Second Floor	Bank
30/30 bullet	Saloon: Second Floor	Make-Up Room
Key	Saloon: Second Floor	Location only
Arrow	Saloon: Second Floor	Location only

Object	See this Section for Location	Also See Section(s)
Cheap ring	Saloon: Second Floor	More Rooms
Bullets	More Rooms	Mayor's Office, Ballroom, General Store
Instruction sheet	More Rooms	Location only
Key	More Rooms	Monster on Block
Flash	More Rooms	Monster on Block
Bulb	More Rooms	Monster on Block
Shutter release	More Rooms	Monster on Block
Oil can	Monster on Block	Kitchen
Navajo war stick	Monster on Block	Pillars, Cemetery
Film reel	Kitchen	Darkroom
Can of oil	Kitchen	Location only
Guitar string	Ballroom	Darkroom
Safe key	Ballroom	Bank
Music sheet	Ballroom	Darkroom
Hammer	Ballroom	Make-Up Room
Blasting cap	Make-Up Room	Water Tower
Light bulb	Make-Up Room	Darkroom
Map	Make-Up Room	Exploring
Encoding box	Bank	Location only
Box of bullets	Bank	Location only
Suitcase	Bank	Water Tower
Detonator box	General Store	Water Tower
Suitcase key	Train Station	Water Tower
Eye bolt	Train Station	Location only
Golden eagle	Golden Eagle	Cougar
Tar	Silver	Location only
Silver salts	Silver	Location only
Soap	Double	Water Tower
Colt	Double	Needless Challenge
Pickaxe	Exploring Caves	Needless Challenge

13

Object	See this Section for Location	Also See Section(s)
Pitcher	Library	Elevator
Needle	Library	Shrinking
Candlestick	Library	Location only
Glass slide	Elevator	Laboratory
Vial of Poison	Shrinking	Location only
Straw	Shrinking	Goal
Ammonia	Shrinking	Emily
Lead ingot	Mr. Cobra	Alchemy
Cobra's wig	Mr. Cobra	Emily
Silver dollar	Mr. Cobra	Location only
Evil wand	Alchemy	Emily
Sack of coal	Escaping	Location only
Rubber glove	Escaping	Location only

BENEATH A STEEL SKY

BY
**FRED PHILIPP
& CLANCY SHAFFER**

TYPE
*Animated
Adventure*

SYSTEM
*IBM PC
(Required:
386+, 2MB
RAM, VGA,
CD-ROM
drive.
Supports:
Adlib, Sound
Blaster,
Roland.)*

COMPANY
*Virgin
Interactive
Entertainment
Inc.*

FROM THE DESIGNERS WHO TOOK LURE OF THE TEMPTRESS OUT OF THE FOGGY BRITISH ISLES AND OVER TO THESE SHORES, VIRGIN BRINGS US ANOTHER CARTOON-STYLE QUEST WITH AN ENJOYABLE STORY AND WIDE ASSORTMENT OF PUZZLES. INSPIRED BY THE COMIC BOOK ART OF DAVE GIBBONS, STEEL SKY CATAPULTS YOU TO THE WASTELANDS OF A REMOTE PLANET WHERE YOU WERE RAISED BY NOMADS AFTER YOUR FAMILY'S CRAFT CRASHED THERE. THE LOCAL MAGE SAYS YOU ARE THE ONE AN ANCIENT PROPHECY SAYS WILL SAVE THE CITY, AND RIGHT AWAY YOU KNOW THIS MEANS TROUBLE AS YOU HEAD OUT FOR TOWN. EVENTUALLY YOUR HORIZONS EXPAND AS YOU TRAVEL THROUGH CYBERSPACE IN SEARCH OF OBJECTS (NOT NECESSARILY UNIDENTIFIED OR FLYING). JOEY, IN THE TRADITION OF PLANETFALL'S FLOYD, PROVIDES ENTERTAINMENT AS A ROBOT SIDEKICK; SEVERAL PUZZLES REVOLVE AROUND PUTTING HIM BACK TOGETHER, LIKE THE TIN MAN IN *THE WIZARD OF OZ*. GRAPHICS FILL THE SCREEN, FOR NO MENU OR ICON BARS TAKE UP SPACE. A "SMART CURSOR" NAMES THE THINGS OR PEOPLE OVER WHICH IT'S PLACED, AND YOU CAN CLICK MOUSE BUTTONS TO EXAMINE and get things. Puzzles are logical and fair, but that doesn't necessarily mean easy. Full-voice support and other effects round out 1995's best imported adventure.

THE SOLUTION

SECURITY GUARD

Take the iron rod on the left side of screen. Use it to pry open the security door on the right side. Go through the door. After the guard leaves, go down to the floor. An inventory check reveals that you have the iron bar and a circuit board. On the floor, go through the door to the right. Note the parts in the junk pile that have treads. Click the circuit board on the junk, and Joey will come to life – unhappy but operative. Save game.

HOBBINS

Stand on the elevator and Hobbins will enter and complain about the alarms. As soon as possible, click on the door through which he entered and go into the room. Click on the cabinet on the front wall, then click on the wrench on the lower shelf. This must be timed right or you will have to do it over and over again (you cannot get the wrench while Hobbins is in the room). Talk to Hobbins and find out what is wrong with the Transporter Robot. After he tells you, Joey can fix it. The robot then brings in trash and puts it on the elevator. The elevator descends, and you must click on the elevator shaft to get down the hole. Joey will follow you down.

FURNACE

Click on the door lock and ask Joey to open it. Reich will enter, and the furnace will kill him. Get his ID card and glasses. Go out the door to the right. Go right one screen and enter the door near the Linc Terminal. Talk to the women until Lamb arrives, then tell him you are Security.

After Lamb leaves, go right. Put the wrench in the cogs. After the machine breaks, take the wrench. Walk to the room on the left. Use the wrench to loosen the shell on the robot welder. Give it to Joey. Return to where you broke the cogs and send Joey into the scanner-protected storehouse; ask him to disable the fuse box. You can now enter and click on the grating and it will fold over. Get the putty under it. Don't take anything else; leave the store room. Go back two screens to the left and you will see a bright red cable.

ELEVATOR POWER

Get Joey to cut the red cable, then go as far left as possible and enter the room. Use the wrench to loosen the two buttons on the right side of the screen. Then press the left button and at the same time have Joey press the right button. Steam escapes, and the man in the room leaves.

Go to the left side of center and turn off the switch. Unscrew the light bulb to the left, put the putty in the socket, then turn the switch on. This blows open the door. Inside are two large switches: throw one up and the other down to get power for the elevator.

REICH AND LAMB

Go to the elevator two screens to the right and use the ID card in the slot. It will take you down a level. Exit and go right. Get the red cable, then go to your left and exit the first door into the Reich and Lamb apartments. Use the ID card on the left apartment, enter, and take the magazine from under the pillow. Leave the apartment and the courtyard, go right two full screens, and enter the travel agency. Trade the magazine for a ticket on the Economy Tour. Go back outside the apartments and wait for Lamb; give him the ticket. He will repay you by giving you a tour of the factory.

Go back up the elevator and enter the door to the right of the Linc Terminal. After the tour, you will be able to get into the reactor area. Go to the right and talk to Anita. When the subject of a jammer comes up, click your ID card on her so she can attach it to your card.

BIOSURGERY AND LINC

Return to the apartment level. Be sure Joey is with you. Go all the way to the left of the screens and enter the door marked BioSurgery. Talk to the holograph receptionist. You will have to ask Joey to handle her: tell him to use his natural charm. When you trade with Dr. Burke, settle for your testicles. He gets them after you die. But get the Schribmann Port. Go back to the Linc Terminal one floor up and use the keycard. Enter Security Services, then Special Operations, then File Adjustment. Freeze Lamb assets and make him a D-Link. Leave and search out Lamb, who will want you to feed his cat and will allow you to access his apartment. Get the videotape. Use the Feeding machine next to the VCR for the cat.

Go back to the Doctor's office. Ask about help to get down. He will mention a friend Willy, the insurance agent across from the travel agency. He will leave to contact a friend. Have Joey use his torch on the statue, get the anchor, and put it with the red cable in inventory.

17

PASSWORDS

Go back up to where you started and all the way to the left. Use the anchor and cable on the security sign on the opposite building and go through the locker room window. Go through the next door to the right. Just outside, use the ID card on the slot, then sit in the chair, which moves you into the computer.

On the first screen, collect the ball and move to the screen to the right. Look at your symbol board: you now have an Info, Disconnect, Open, Charon, Computer Data, several documents, and a magnifying glass (after you use the Open icon on the bag). Use the glass on all papers, and the ? will disappear.

Go right. In this room you must use the decompress symbol on the password symbol. Now use the password (green or red) in the following way: In the area you are in, place the green. Now go east and place the red, then go back left and pick up the green. Go north and place the green. Go right and south and pick up the red. Go north, place the red, go left, and pick up the green. Go north, right, south, right, south, and place the green. Then go north and exit. Collect the bust and book, then use the disconnect symbol to exit the interface.

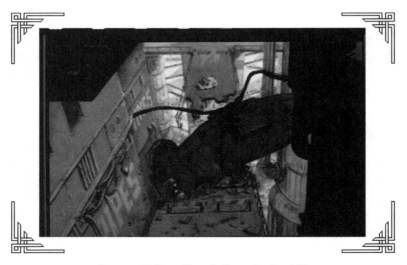

Beware of falling objects in Beneath a Steel Sky.

● ● ● ● ● ● ● ● ●

POOL LEVEL

Use the key card to enter the Linc Terminal. Go to Security Services and look at the new documents. Then go to Special Operations and request a status change, which will give you unlimited access for 48 hours. Descend one level, then go right to the ornate elevator. Take it down to the pool level. Go to the right, then around the pool to the left. Try to open to the door to the storage building. Look at the door. Use keycard on lock to open door. Inside, get cutters.

Go left and talk to the doorman. Ask if he knows anyone who would sponsor you into the club. Talk with Mrs. Piermont, the lady with the dog. Ask if she knows Overman, then ask her to sponsor you. When she invites you up to her apartment, push the button and follow her up. She knows a lot about your parents. Quiz her. Ask again for the sponsorship. When she goes to use the phone, click on the VCR and put the tape from Lamb in it. This will distract the dog. Click on his food bowl until you locate and take the biscuits.

CATHEDRAL AND REACTOR

Leave the apartment and go to the guard standing in front of the Cathedral. Talk with him. Go to the construction on the left side of the screen and put the biscuits on the end of the plank. When a dog goes after them, pull the rope, then release it to create a distraction so you can get into the Cathedral.

Inside the Cathedral, enter the north door. Look in the center locker to find Anita's body. Return to her work station, open the center locker and use her protection suit, then enter the reactor room. Inside you will find Anita's ID card on the floor. Get the card and leave the reactor. Change your clothes and leave the factory; you must go left three screens. Enter the security office, then use the elevator on the right to reach the interface.

THE INTERFACE

Use Anita's ID card on the interface. Check your symbols; you now have two new ones. You must use the Blind symbol on the first eye, then quickly go right and blind the other eye. Go back and exit north, then go north again and get the tuning fork. Exit to the left. Click the playback symbol on the well. Watch the message and the holograph girl, then turn it off. Use the disconnect. Go back down to the pool area and talk with the boy who is playing a computer game. Talk to the gardener, then talk to the boy again. Now talk to gardener three times (he is the person mentioned by the holograph receptionist). Go as far left as you can and enter the Courtroom.

ST. JAMES CLUB

After Hobbins is sentenced, leave and talk to the St. James Club doorman. Enter the St. James Club via the small door beside the doorman. Go down and play a piece on the jukebox, then come up. When one of the men leaves, take his glass. Take the glass to Dr. Burke, who can

19

arrange to transfer the fingerprints from the glass to you, thus giving you a new ID. You must talk to him, then click the glass on him to proceed.

Return to the St. James Club and go to the door on the right back wall. Go to the large box. Use the iron rod to pry the lid off; put the lid on the smaller box. Use the rod to make a hole in the grate. Use the cutters to cut out the grate. Go through the hole into the subway, go to the right, then go north. You will see a hole in the wall. Put the light bulb in the socket. Go to the end of the subway and enter another tunnel (hurry or the roof will fall in on you).

GETTING OUT

After leaving this tunnel, use the rod twice on the plaster above you. A brick will fall out. Use the rod to open the vein, then use the brick as a hammer to complete the opening. A droid will enter soon to repair the wound. Exit through the door. Go north into the room with a pit. At the control panel, lower the temperature. Note that the fire center closes. You can then get on it and pull the rod down over the pit. This opens the grate. Now leave the room. Go two screens to the right and put Joey's circuit board into the Red Cross robot. Use the slot. Go back left twice through the southern door and look through the grill on the wall. Ask Joey to check out the tank room. After his report, have him go back and open the tap. You can now enter the room.

GALLAGGER

Leave via the northeast corner, then go through the top northeast door. Just inside is a terminal. Use your card on the terminal, then access the restricted area. Now open the access door and leave to the left. An android named Gallagger will appear. When Joey attempts to save you, the lights go out. Joey and Gallagger are dead when the lights come back on. Take the circuit board from Joey and the Linc card from Gallagger. Go into the next room on the lower right and get the tongs on the wall next to the door. Go back to the Terminal. Use the Gallagger card to enter the interface.

Inside the interface, go to the right, then north. Be sure to blind the eye. Use Divine Wrath on the Crusader. After he dies, return to the interface, use disconnect. Then reenter and use Anita's card. Go to where the Crusader was and exit right.

TONGS AND STUFF

Use the tuning fork on the ice crystal, then collect the Helix and leave the chambers. Go back to the room with the nitrogen tank and use Anita's card to break into the console monitor. Use the tongs to get a piece of tissue from the tank. Freeze it in the nitrogen tank, and be sure you have a frozen item in the tongs; if they are empty, try again.

Go one screen to the right and open the cabinet below the console to the right of the middle android. Insert Joey's card, then click on the monitor. Choose "Download Character Data," then run the "Startup Program." Rename the new Joey "Ken." To enter the next door, both you and Ken must place your hand on the panel on each side of the door and press them at the same time. Ken's hand will be stuck, so you must proceed to the right alone.

PIPES

Travel along the pipes to the right until they bend downward. Tie the cable to the supports and go down the brackets at the end of the pipe as if they were rungs on a ladder. At the bottom, use the tongs and drop the frozen tissue into the Orifice.

A door will open on the opposite wall. Use the cable to swing over and meet your father. Ask Ken to get into the chair, and the animated conclusion follows.

21

ORBS & STUFF

Object	See this Section for Location	Also See Section(s)
Iron rod	Security Guard	St. James Club, Getting Out
Circuit board	Security Guard	Gallagger
Wrench	Hobbins	Furnace
ID card	Furnace	Reich and Lamb
Glasses	Furnace	Location only
Putty	Furnace	Elevator Power
Red cable	Reich and Lamb	Passwords
Magazine	Reich and Lamb	Location only
Ticket	Reich and Lamb	Location only
Schribmann port	Biosurgery and Linc	Location only
Videotape	Biosurgery and Linc	Pool Level
Anchor	Biosurgery and Linc	Passwords
Bust	Passwords	Location only
Book	Passwords	Location only
Cutters	Pool Level	St. James Club
Biscuits	Pool Level	Cathedral and Reactor
Anita's ID card	Cathedral and Reactor	The Interface, Gallagger
Tuning fork	The Interface	Tongs and Stuff
Glass	St. James Club	Location only
Linc card	Gallagger	Location only
Tongs	Gallagger	Tongs and Stuff, Pipes
Helix	Tongs and Stuff	Location only
Tissue	Tongs and Stuff	Pipes

BIOFORGE

BY
PAUL SHAFFER

TYPE
Animated Adventure

SYSTEM
IBM PC (Required: 486/50+, 8MB RAM 5MB free hard disk space, 29MB recommended, double-speed CD-ROM drive, MSCDEX 2.2+, Microsoft mouse, keyboard, 256-color VGA monitor. Supports: Adlib, Sound Blaster family including AWE32, Wave Blaster, General MIDI.)

COMPANY
Origin Systems, Inc.

LTHOUGH IT BEGINS AS A TYPICAL "WHERE AM I AND HOW DID I GET HERE?" ADVENTURE, BIOFORGE QUICKLY TURNS INTO SOMETHING COMPLETELY DIFFERENT. YOU AWAKEN IN CELL 3 ON A SMALL PLANETOID AT THE EDGE OF THE GALAXY. YOU'RE SHOCKED TO SEE THAT YOU'VE BEEN TRANSFORMED INTO A CYBORG — PART HUMAN, PART ROBOT. EVENTUALLY YOU LEARN THAT THE MAD DR. MASTAFA HAS DISCOVERED AN ALIEN RACE IN SUSPENDED ANIMATION AND IS EXPERIMENTING WITH CYBORGS CREATED FROM COMBINATIONS OF ALIEN PARTS, HUMAN PARTS, AND ROBOTIC ELEMENTS. ONE OF THE ALIEN CYBORGS HAS ESCAPED AND SET OFF A CHAIN REACTION IN THE BASE'S NUCLEAR REACTOR, AND YOUR MAIN GOAL IS TO ESCAPE BEFORE IT GOES OFF. EXPLORATION, SOLVING PUZZLES, AND COMBAT PREFACE THE PLOT'S GRACEFUL UNFOLDING. THE COMBINATION OF VGA GRAPHICS FOR THE FOREGROUND CHARACTERS WITH FINELY DETAILED ILLUSTRATIONS FOR BACKGROUNDS AND OTHER ELEMENTS IS TYPICAL OF ORIGIN GAMES. THE

HALLMARK OF BIOFORGE, HOWEVER, IS ITS INVENTIVE AND SUSPENSE-FILLED PLOT, WHICH DEVELOPS GRADUALLY AND LEADS TO A CREDIBLE AND GRATIFYING CONCLUSION THAT MAKES YOU WANT TO RUN OUT AND GET THE SEQUEL THE MINUTE IT HITS THE SHELF.

THE SOLUTION

CELL 3

Kick drone until it flies into the cell inhibitor field. Pick up logbook and meat (press Enter key). Read journal entries ("J" key). Read logbook by holding it in your hand and using it (space bar). Run through inhibitor field when it's not working.

Go to entrance to Cell 1. Ready meat from inventory. Enter cell by running through field when it flickers. Drop meat (mutant takes it and stays away for awhile). Take Cayana's logbook, photo, and fork. Exit cell. Open large door at end of cell hall (it opens partially). Use fork on control panel beside door. Use panel (press 4, 3, 2, 2, 1 as if the bottom buttons are marked 1-4 from left to right). Open door. Exit.

GUARD ROOM

Push red button on wall to turn off warning. Examine third monitor on lower platform (you see drone in Cell 4). Activate drone by pressing manual. Have drone pick up Dane's logbook and the flute and drop them outside the cell.

Return to cell hall and take Dane's logbook and flute. Read the logbook (noting security code) and play flute. Read journal entries.

Return to guard room and use monitor to make drone pick up severed arm in front of Cell 1. Then move drone into guard room and make it go to hand panel beside closed door (severed hand should be aimed toward panel.) Use first monitor on lower platform. Select Access, then enter access code from Dane's logbook. (Monitor should say, "Need weight on panel.") Exit monitor. Go to panel under drone and stand on it to open door. Save game.

RAPTOR AND CREATURE

Enter Level 2 hallway. Run past guard robot and through southwest door to cryo room. Push red button at far end of room and turn large handle to release coolant for cryo chambers (warning should sound).

Examine monitor on far side of room. Select Container 1 file (when monitor meter begins to rise, exit screen). As raptor breaks out of cryo chamber, run back to handle and turn off coolant. Push red button again (closing floor iris). Fight raptor. When he falls unconscious on top of iris, quickly push red button, dropping him through the floor.

When you hear sounds of combat below, turn coolant on for a few seconds, then turn it off and descend ladder in iris. Follow walkway to end and enter passage up on the right (Cell 2). Fight guard and take his blaster. Return to Cryo Room. Run past guard robot in hall to elevator. Use hand scanner to open elevator door. Enter. Use elevator controls and select Level 1. Save game.

THE TRANSPORTS

Shoot floating droids, using the walls inside and outside elevator to deflect your shots at them. Run around behind elevator to man. Hit man once or twice until he agrees to activate the gun. When he asks you to step back, do so. After he has activated the gun, use it. Aim gun with keyboard arrow keys. Wait for tranports to cross in front of gun and shoot them.

MEETING THE GOOD DOCTOR

Go to Level 3. Enter the med lab. After the animated sequence, examine wall monitor. Select Project Logs and Case Histories and read through them. Exit monitor. Take medical device on the floor. (If you need another battery, you can take the one from the man on the operating table. You can also use the medical device for health boosts, but you should save at least one dose for later in the game.)

REACTOR ROOM ROBOT

Go to the Control Room. Fight guard and take his logbook. Read the logbook, noting the airlock code (this changes with each new game). Walked to the indented area on the upper platform (it encloses you and puts you in a hardsuit). Examine right monitor on upper platform (noting reactor code). Use right monitor on ground platform (shows overhead of forklift). Use controls on monitor to drive forklift to reactor room (doors automatically open for you). Drive forklift into the guard robot, knocking him off the ledge.

THE ICARUS

While still in the control room, walk to the monitors in the area enclosed by the rail. Examine monitors and read files on Icarus. Select Icarus Access (lowers you to Garage Area). Fight guard and get his walkie-talkie. Walk around ship and get alien cube on ground. Return to the control room.

SHUTTING DOWN REACTORS

Exit control room. Fight guard in hall and take his blaster. Go to reactor room. Use controls at far end of ledge, raising light bridge. Save game. Cross bridge and walk close to alien cyborg. Shoot him twice and run back across bridge (if you stood close enough, he will follow you).

Deactivate controls to lower light bridge from under alien (dropping him), or you can fight him on bridge and knock him off. Recross bridge to reactor. Lower levers on both rods on each side of the control panel. Use control panel and enter reactor access code (from monitor in control room). Validate code (reactor should shut down). Go to Level 4. Save game.

THE AIRLOCK

Enter airlock corridor. Avoid fire from guard robot. Shoot him three times. (Your attack strategy should be dodge the first shots, fire one shot at him, and run. There's usually a pause in his motion just after he fires, which is the time to get off a burst at him.) Use airlock panel and enter code indicated in guard's logbook (the pattern on the lock changes with each try). Exit to outside.

THE DOWNED TRANSPORT

Run along deck to elevator. Use panel on elevator to open door. Enter elevator. When it reopens, run along catwalk (avoiding fire from floating drones) and through tunnel.

Continue along catwalk and enter next tunnel (sealed). Read journal entries. Return to the place where the catwalk passed through the first tunnel and jump down onto blocks below catwalk. Continue to climb down to lowest block and use alien cube (which carries you over lake to next cube).

Continue this way across the lake to the inlet where the downed transport sits. Enter transport. Walk to front of transport (Marine should enter through sealed door). Fight Marine (don't bother shooting him), getting key device and big gun when he falls.

CREATURE IN LAKE

Use key device (reopens sealed door). Enter front of transport and use control panel on wall. Press 1 (activates torpedo). Press Fire (torpedo damages column). Press 2. Wait for creature to go beneath damaged column and raise its head. Fire second torpedo (blows off creature's head).

SEALED PASSAGE AND BOMB

Exit transport. Save game. Examine flashing tip of object on ground outside transport (you will discover a bomb and automatically pick it up). Run to other side of inlet (where the beast was) and stand on block. Use alien cube to cross.

Continue across blocks and go back up to the other end of the catwalk. Run into tunnel with sealed passage. Drop cube and bomb (don't waste time putting cube back into inventory). Exit tunnel, moving off to either side. Wait for bomb to go off before returning for cube. Return to inlet and retrieve big gun (which you automatically left there). Return to unblocked passage and continue through. Walk to indentation at end of passage (transports you to other side).

ESCHER AND THE TEMPLE

Walk to Escher at far end of room (bee drone attacks). Shoot bee until he dies (do not shoot at it when curled up because the bee is invulnerable then). Walk back to Escher and use healing device on her (she gives you translator device). Read journal entries.

Go outside and return to blocks at end of catwalk (not the ones by the first tunnel). Go to temple hidden behind tall blocks, using alien cube to cross gaps. In temple, use translator on three stone cubes set against each wall. (Press Scan, then Translate to get translated text.) Return to Escher's room.

27

USING TRANSPORT TUBES

Go through the northern tunnel into the sarcophagus room (alien cyborg arrives). Shoot cyborg several times, then let him hit you once (he will automatically run after hitting you). Follow cyborg (he escapes through tube).

Return to sarcophagus room and open the lid on the cracked sarcophagus. Examine sarcophagus. Read journal entries. Examine sarcophagus again (color puzzle). Match the color combinations of the lower square with those of the topmost square by touching the six bars at the bottom of the screen (three of the bars move the color columns, the other three move the color rows). There is no fixed solution to this puzzle, which is randomized in each new game. When done correctly, you'll get the artifact in the sarcophagus. Return to Escher's room and use artifact on flashing square on transport tube (you'll automatically enter it). Save game.

TUBE ROOM

Walk to center of tube room and use the column (you may have to try it from different angles). Touch cubes on column to activate the three tubes on the ground level. (Do not activate tubes against ceiling or you'll be sorry!)

You must touch combinations of two or three cubes to form patterns that will be shown on the center cube when the pattern is correct. Patterns correspond to the symbols above or below each tube in the room. Once you have the pattern, match the patterns (one at a time) to the ground-level tube symbols and press the central cube to activate each of them. The correct combinations for the ground-level tubes are:

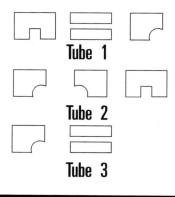

Tube 1

Tube 2

Tube 3

RESURRECTING GEN

Enter the tube on the north wall (which will be to your right when standing with your back facing the door from Escher's room). You arrive in the gravity room. To move around, use the gun, whose momentum pushes you in the opposite direction that you fire. Shoot yourself into the opposite passageway, where you arrive at the pedestal room

Use your translator on the columns to get more background. As you cross the room, the cyborg returns. (Don't shoot him because his reflector suit will ricochet the shots back at you.) Fight him and get his reflective cube. Use reflective cube and walk through force field exit into next room. Walk to control panel and use it. Activate the colors in the following combination: G, Y, O, G, O, Y, O, Y, O, P, G, R, Y, P, B, O, P, R (R = Red, Y = Yellow, O = Orange, B = Blue, G = Green, P = Purple).

Gen arrives and gives you an alien battery. Use alien battery (replacing your own with it). Drop your old battery. Read journal entries. Use reflective cube to pass back through force field exit, but deactivate it before entering the gravity room or you won't be able to use your gun to maneuver. Return to tube room.

GRAVITY RINGS

Enter the south tube to arrive at the gravity rings. Save game. Note the blue outlines on sections of the rings in the distance. You goal is to align the blue outlines on each section of the ring by stepping on the corresponding arrows on the ground. (You must avoid the asteroids flying by while doing this.) It's best to start from the arrow at the far end of the room and work your way back. Once the blue lines are aligned, the gravity rings will clear the room of debris. Return to the tube room.

Technological puzzles and cybernetics keep Bioforge hot.

●●●●●●●●●●

GETTING BACK TO BASE

Return to Escher's room (she'll be gone). Avoid the bee drone and take Escher's logbook. Return to tube room and read her logbook (noting the code for the med lab case history security files). Save game.

Examine the stone ring on the wall by the flashing tube (monitor controls). You'll see an aerial view of the temple, complete now with guards. Touch the top button, raising the sphere in the temple. When a soldier looks in the hole, push the bottom button, lowering the sphere back on top of him.

Raise the sphere once more (guard tosses a hand grenade into the passage). Grab grenade and toss it back into the transport tube (you should hear the guard scream).

Before entering tube, activate reflective cube (environmental suit). Enter tube, which takes you to temple. Return to airlock back at base (fighting guards along the way is optional; you can simply run past them). On the ledge outside base, weave as you run to avoid being knocked off the ledge by laser shots from ship. At the airlock, fight guard and get his logbook. Read guard's logbook, noting new access code for airlock. Use new access code on airlock panel and enter.

ESCAPING THE PLANET

Go to Level 3 and enter med lab. Use wall monitor. Select "Case Histories," then "Secure Data." Enter code from Escher's logbook. Exit file and select Bio Data. Scan through case histories until you find yours (Cell 3).

Exit monitor and read journal entries. Return to Icarus garage. Go to front of Icarus and take flashing battery from ship. Replace your internal alien battery with the ship's depleted battery. Use the alien battery on the ship.

You're off to catch the mad doctor!

ORBS & STUFF

Object	See this Section for Location	Also See Section(s)
Logbook	Cell 3	Location only
Meat	Cell 3	Location only
Photo	Cell 3	Location only
Fork	Cell 3	Location only
Cayana's logbook	Cell 3	Location only
Severed arm	Guard Room	Location only
Dane's logbook	Guard Room	Location only
Dane's flute	Guard Room	Location only
Blaster	Raptor and Creature, Shutting Down Reactors	Locations only
Medical device	Meeting the Good Doctor	Location only
Battery	Meeting the Good Doctor	Resurrecting Gen
Guard's logbook	Reactor Room, Getting Back to Base	The Airlock, Location only
Hardsuit	Reactor Room Robot	Location only
Walkie-talkie	The Icarus	Location only
Alien cube	The Icarus	The Downed Transport, Sealed Passage and Bomb, Escher and the Temple
Key device	The Downed Transport	Creature in Lake
Big gun	The Downed Transport	Sealed Passage and Bomb
Bomb	Sealed Passage and Bomb	Location only
Translator device	Escher and the Temple	Location only
Artifact	Using Transport Tubes	Location only
Reflective cube	Resurrecting Gen	Getting Back to Base
Alien battery	Resurrecting Gen	Escaping the Planet
Escher's logbook	Getting Back to Base	Escaping the Planet
Ship's battery	Escaping the Planet	Location only

BUREAU 13

BY
FRED J. PHILIPP
& CLANCY F. SHAFFER

TYPE
*Animated
Adventure*

SYSTEM
*IBM PC
(Required:
386/33+, DOS
5.0+, 1.5MB
free EMS,
Microsoft-com-
patible mouse,
13MB free hard
disk space.
Recommended:
double-speed
CD-ROM drive
for CD ver-
sion. Supports:
Roland, Adlib,
Sound Blaster,
Sound Master,
Pro Audio, and
compatibles.)*

COMPANY
*Take 2
Software*

BASED ON STALKING THE NIGHT, A PENCIL AND PAPER ROLE-PLAYING GAME WITH A CULT FOLLOWING, BUREAU 13 COVERS THE INTRIGUING PHENOMENON OF PARANORMAL INVESTIGATION. THE BUREAU'S LATEST ASSIGNMENT IS TO TRACK DOWN J.P. WITHERS, A RENEGADE AGENT WHO IS HIGHLY UNSTABLE. YOU MAY CHOOSE YOUR TEAM FROM SEVERAL BUREAU AGENTS, INCLUDING A VAMPIRE, A PRIEST, A COMPUTER SCIENTIST, AND AN ANDROID WARRIOR. DIFFERENT PARTS OF THE QUEST CAN BE SOLVED IN ALTERNATE WAYS DEPENDING ON WHICH CHARACTER YOU'VE SELECTED. THE VAMPIRE, FOR EXAMPLE, CAN TURN INTO MIST TO GAIN ENTRANCE TO A LOCKED ROOM, WHILE THE THIEF CAN PICK THE LOCK. THIS GIVES THE GAME EXCELLENT REPLAY VALUE BECAUSE YOU CAN USE A DIFFERENT SET OF CHARACTERS FOR DIFFERENT RESULTS AS YOU SEEK THE ELUSIVE WITHERS (LAST SEEN IN A COFFEEHOUSE WITH CELLULAR PHONE AND NOTEBOOK COMPUTER). THE POINT-AND-CLICK INTERFACE MAKES IT EASY TO GET RIGHT INTO THE STORY, WHICH IS AMONG THE MOST UNUSUAL EVER SEEN IN AN

ADVENTURE. GRAPHICS AND SOUND EFFECTS ADD TO THE ATMOSPHERE WITHOUT GETTING IN THE WAY.

WITH A SOLID MIX OF PUZZLES THAT VARY WITH REPLAY, BUREAU 13 IS SUITABLE FOR A WIDE RANGE OF

ADVENTURE GAMERS, FROM NOVICE TO EXPERT.

THE SOLUTION

GENERAL

You may play the game with the Thief, Vampire, or the other agents. Choose the Thief and Vampire to follow this solution precisely because it is based on using those two. However, we also provide enough information to solve the quest with either agent acting alone. Many of the numerous items are useless, and you cannot drop an item. For expediency, this solution mentions only those items necessary to complete the game or those that contribute to the story line.

STRATUSBURG CITY

ALLEY

Look closely at the newspaper machine and get quarter from the return chute. Put it in the coin slot and buy a newspaper. (A Thief may simply pick the lock). Read newspaper for update. Go west to hospital.

HOSPITAL

The guard won't let you in now. Continue east to outside the police station and enter.

POLICE STATION

Talk to officer. Get the superglue from the counter and use it on the fire extinguisher case to your left. Push the ashtray (next to the typewriter) into the waste basket to start a fire.

SHERIFF'S OFFICE

Open desk drawer and get a key. Open fuse box, remove good fuse, and turn circuit breaker off. Exit room. Use key to unlock rear door and enter.

EVIDENCE ROOM

Pick up the police report and read it. Exit station. Don't worry about the fire. Head west to outside the gym and messenger service.

MESSENGER SERVICE

Enter and have Thief sneak upstairs to the delivery boys' lockers. (Or have Vampire change into mist and do same.) Open fuse box and put fuse in. Open now-visible locker in corner and get J.P.'s jacket. Search jacket for van keys. Go to gym.

THE GYM

The gym's only purpose is to provide an alternate way to enter the delivery boys' lockers. Have Thief open the outside door and door to women's locker room. Outside gym, change Vampire into mist. As mist, enter locker room. The Vampire can now climb through rear window to arrive at delivery boys' lockers. Return to outside police station and go east to Rick's Electronics.

RICK'S ELECTRONICS

Have Thief pick lock on door and enter. Pick up tapes on floor and play in answering machine for information. Get the wire cutters. Exit and go east to AI Headquarters.

AI HEADQUARTERS

Go behind HQ to dumpster. Open, search, and pick up the package for Simpson. Return to entrance. Push buzzer. When guard opens door, talk to him, then give package to him. Enter.

INSIDE AI HQ

Get note on desk and read (2112). Open copying machine; get and read memo. Enter security office. Take three VCR tapes, put in VCR, and play. The third tape contains Simpson's voice ID. Exit and go to Simpson's office.

SIMPSON'S OFFICE

Open painting. Open smoke detector and get AA battery. Get remote control from desk and insert battery. Push button on desk to open wall panel, exposing VCR. Insert the third tape and play it to open safe behind painting. Get tape from safe and play in VCR. Exit HQ and go west, then south to the used RV lot. Continue east to American Storage.

AMERICAN STORAGE

Enter and give van keys to attendant. When he returns with the box, remove the magnetic scan card from the box. Exit and return to RV lot. Use scan card on door and enter RV.

INSIDE RV

At computer you can access database and enter any names you know (Turner, Simpson, Withers, etc.) or engage autodrive to travel to either the cemetery, AI Weapons Plant, or City. Exit RV.

SHERIFF TUCKER

Pick up journal lying on ground and read it. Go to hospital and rescue the sheriff. He will give you a Level 4 badge for the AI Weapons Plant. Return to RV and select Weapons Plant.

GETTING INTO AI WEAPONS PLANT

Go east to Forest Road, then north to clearing. Pick up the branch and return to road. After truck passes by, drop the branch on the road. The truck will return and hit the branch, and the driver will exit the truck to check for damage. Enter the truck and you will be taken to the loading dock inside the fence at the weapons plant.

INSIDE WEAPONS PLANT

Open loading bay door and enter. Pick up the wood saw. Open fuse box and turn on power. Exit.

SCAFFOLDING

You can now use the scaffolding to go up. Use Level 4 badge on door to left to enter the electronic storage room. Access elevator by entering 2112 on touch pad and go down to sub-basement.

SECURED LAB

Cut trip wire with wire cutters and enter the secured lab. In this torture chamber, pick up the ledger on operating table and read ledger. Return to RV. Enter names from ledger in computer. Select "cemetery."

CEMETERY

Go to the church, then through the kitchen to the bedroom. Get crucifix from wall. Search floor for trapdoor. Open trapdoor and get the Tome of Banishment. Read it. Go to park and cut limb off dogwood tree with saw. Cut limb with saw to get a dogwood disk. Ride RV to suburbs.

THE SUBURBS

HOUSES

In Houston's house (332), get the gym bag, open it, and remove the items (you will need the shovel later). Enter Sterling's house (334) and open the cupboard in the garage to get the book on bombs. Read it.

EXPLORING

Walk to the library parking lot, open hatchback of car, and get crowbar and flashlight. Enter library and note computer and books in basement. Go to Carver's Bar and ask bartender about Sawbuck. Go to Stalker's.

STALKER'S

Enter by using mist or crowbar. Continue to dressing room and get Houston's note from the makeup stand. Read it. Go to Sixth Street and remove poster from wall, exposing entrance to gang hideout. Enter and talk to Rat. Get pills lying on floor.

HOUSTON

Go to Stalker's parking lot and open back of tour bus. Talk to Houston, then click cursor on him to remove his chip.

SAWBUCK

Return to bar. Sawbuck is holding a hostage at gunpoint. Back off. Exit bar. Have Vampire turn into mist. Enter bar. Move misted Vampire behind Sawbuck. Click on him. Follow him to basement, talk to him, then remove his chip.

STERLING

Return to RV. Sterling will be there. Talk to him, then remove his chip. Search the RV for explosive device. Disable bomb using wire cutters. Go to Elm Street and enter house. Get and read the Book of Magic. Go to the herbalist.

HERBALIST

Ask about "magic." Look at amulet that appears on counter. You will see Veronica in it. Talk to her and "agree" with her. Exit and follow Elmo, the cat, back to the RV. Drive to cemetery and follow cat to Veronica's house.

VERONICA

Enter house and immediately search Veronica to remove her chip. Go to the cemetery gates and use crucifix on green-headed monster (Stellerex).

THE MURDERER

Go to the church and talk to Father Dominic. (Just click the "talk" icon on him.) Ask about "demons" and "magic." Return to library in suburbs and use computer. Enter: Stellerex, Demons, Murderer. Return to cemetery.

PREPARING THE DISK

Look at grave stones until you identify Clemmen's grave. Use shovel on grave. Open casket to remove finger. Go to church kitchen and dip finger in blood on counter. Use bloodied finger on dogwood disk. Go to the mausoleum.

THE MAUSOLEUM

Enter. Go south, east, then north through the illusionary wall to confront Stellerex. He will give you the Level 6 badge. Return to the Weapons Plant.

WEAPONS PLANT

Ride scaffolding up and use Level 6 badge to enter Level 6 area. Put red pills (depressants) in cup on desk. Exit and reenter. Search drugged guard to get Level 7 badge. Use badge to unlock next door.

LEVEL 7

Use green pills (stimulants) on unconscious programmer. Talk to programmer. Enter corridor to right. Enter EMP lab. Get EMP device from pedestal. Use device on pedestal to recharge it. Exit and enter left corridor.

SIMPSON'S OFFICE

Use Level 7 badge to enter office. Open bust on desk to reveal door behind bookcase. Enter mainframe antechamber. Use EMP device on sign on wall. Return to EMP lab and recharge EMP device. Return to guard station.

MAINFRAME

Enter crawl space at lower-left corner of screen to reach secret mainframe access tube. Talk to Simpson. Sit in chair to access the virtual reality room. Use EMP device on Virus/Stellerex. Use Control Panel.

ORBS & STUFF

Object	See this Section for Location	Also See Section(s)
Paper machine	Alley	Location only
Superglue	Police Station	Location only
Ashtray	Police Station	Location only
Good fuse	Sheriff's Office	Messenger Service
J.P.'s jacket	Messenger Service	Location only
Van keys	Messenger Service	American Storage
Wire cutters	Rick's Electronics	Secured Lab, Sterling
VCR	Inside AI HQ, Simpson's Office	Locations only
Safe	Simpson's Office	Location only
Magnetic scan card	American Storage	Location only
Computer	Inside RV, Secured Lab, Exploring, The Murderer	Locations only
Level 4 badge	Sheriff Tucker	Scaffolding
Truck	Getting Into AI Weapons Plant	Location only
Wood saw	Inside Weapons Plant	Cemetery
Trip wire	Secured Lab	Location only
Crucifix	Cemetery	Veronica
Tome of Banishment	Cemetery	Location only
Dogwood disk	Cemetery	Preparing the Disk
Gym bag	Houses	Location only
Shovel	Houses	Preparing the Disk
Book on bombs	Houses	Location only
Crowbar	Exploring	Stalker's
Flashlight	Exploring	Location only
Entrance to gang hideout	Stalker's	Location only
Pills	Stalker's	Weapons Plant, Level 7
Explosive device	Sterling	Location only
Bomb	Sterling	Location only
Amulet	Herbalist	Location only
Cat	Herbalist	Location only

41

Object	See this Section for Location	Also See Section(s)
Stellerex	Veronica	Location only
Finger	Preparing the Disk	Location only
Level 6 badge	The Mausoleum	Weapons Plant
Level 7 badge	Weapons Plant	Level 7
EMP device	Level 7	Simpson's Office, Mainframe
Bust	Simpson's Office	Location only

DARK SUN: WAKE OF THE RAVAGER

BY
**CLANCY SHAFFER
& FRED PHILIPP**

TYPE
Fantasy Role-Playing

SYSTEM
IBM PC (Required: 386/33, 4MB RAM, VGA monitor, single-speed CD-ROM drive, CD driver MSCDEX 2.2. Recommended: 486/50, uncompressed hard drive. Supports: Aria, Sound Canvas, Soundscape, Wave Blaster, Soundman Wave, SW 32/GW 32, Sound Blaster family except AWE32, Gravis Native Mode, and 100% compatibles.)

COMPANY
Strategic Simulations Inc.

43

U NFOLDING ON THE SAME WORLD AS THE FIRST DARK SUN, WAKE OF THE RAVAGER FINDS ATHAS IN DECIDEDLY WORSE SHAPE. HORDES OF MUTATED CREATURES ROAM A LAND STRIPPED OF VEGETATION AND TRANSFORMED INTO DEADLY DESERTS. THE EVIL MAGIC OF THE LORD WARRIOR IS TO BLAME, AND YOU MUST TRACK DOWN FOUR ITEMS THAT ARE VITAL TO HIS DEFEAT. A WIDE RANGE OF MINIQUESTS KEEP YOU BUSY WHEN YOU'RE NOT FIGHTING ONE OF THE MORE THAN 200 TYPES OF MONSTERS. FORTUNATELY, YOU HAVE HUNDREDS OF MAGIC SPELLS, INCLUDING A NEW TYPE CALLED PSIONICS, AND A BAND OF WARRIORS AND SPELLCASTERS TO BACK YOU UP. SSI ALSO STREAMLINED THE ORIGINAL DARK SUN GAME ENGINE SO THAT IT NOW HAS ONLY FOUR MAJOR ICONS. THE AUTOMAPPING FEATURES SIMPLIFIES EXPLORATION. EACH AREA IS DISPLAYED FROM AN AERIAL VIEW WHERE YOUR PARTY IS DEPICTED WITH THE LEAD CHARACTER; ONLY IN COMBAT IS THE REST OF THE GROUP DISPLAYED, AND THAT'S WHEN you need them most! You get digitized voices and more music in the CD version, but the graphics are excellent in either version. Recommended for all AD&D fans, Wake of the Ravager is a fast-paced RPG with plenty of action.

THE SOLUTION

GENERAL

Use characters from Dark Sun: Shattered Land if you saved them.

TYR

Arsian is found in the back room of Stitch's bar, a large building in the central-east part of town. Tell him you want to join the Veiled Alliance and agree to find out what the Templars are up to.

FANINA AND ACAR

First visit Fanina the Thief, found in the inn in the southeast area of the city, which is bisected by roads running north-south and east-west. It is the only inn on the south side of the street going east. Before Fanina will help, you must agree to pay off a debt of 10,000 gold with Acar the Merchant.

If you're using a character from the first game, you will already have the money. If you're starting with a new character, you must sell items in Shadow Square or perform an additional chore for Acar. Acar is in a large mansion in the northwest part of town. After finding him in the northeast part of the building, tell him you wish to pay the debt. Apaku, from Dark Sun I, is in Shadow Square and will also assign you a quest to earn 10,000 gold if you need it. (Shadow Square is a large area in the west side of town where people are selling things from open stalls.)

THE TEMPLAR'S OFFICE

After you return to Fanina, she will describe a pattern of knocks to use on the Templar's office door to get in: two knocks, then one knock. She also gives you a key to their storeroom on the northeast side of their building. First go to the storeroom and use the key to unlock the door. Enter the room and listen to a conversation.

Get the loot in the chest. Leave and go to the door to the west, then knock on it to get in. Use the phrase "knock twice, then knock once." Speak to the Templar inside. You must enter the room east of the room you are in and get the journal out of the cabinet. To get in the room, tell the Templar that the Draxans are going to kill all the Templars. When asked for proof, say it's in the room to the east. He will drop a key for you to use. Open the door, enter the room, and slay the aurumvorax. Take the treasure and journal from the cabinet to the south. Then use the north cabinet as a portal to the north.

On the other side of the portal, polish off Kalambuta and pick up the note. Take it to Arsian in the tavern. He will lead you to the entrance to the Veiled Alliance headquarters. Follow him closely and he will tell you how to enter the headquarters.

THE VEILED ALLIANCE

Enter the Skeleton Building in the southwest part of town. Slay the giant skeletons and get their heads to sell to Natoku. Press the panel on the left of the cabinet to open it. (You must have heard Arsian tell you what to do.) Use the portal to reach the Veiled Alliance. Talk to Matthias the Leader and Romila.

There is a rest room just south of the entrance and a Healer named Saven just south of it. Get the Cup of Life from him. Just east of this room is Aleka's room. Speak with her, then go back to Romila, who will ask you to kill the Draxans in the Pyramid. Return to Aleka, who will tell you about Tasarla. When you find her in the big square, tell her you want to buy a jaguar cage (this is the password), and she will send you to the Merchant Kovar, who is due east. Enter the house and show the papers from Tasarla. The servant will allow you to enter the study. Look at the books, take one, and get the medallion behind it. Now go to the Pyramid in the northeast section of the town, stand in front of the statue, and insert the small medallion.

INTO THE PYRAMID

Downstairs, slay the great feyrs and get their teeth to sell to Notaku. They will continue to appear until you plug the four large holes around the outside wall in the Pyramid. Notice the grate just to your north when you enter the Pyramid. Proceed west past a large hole in the wall, then go west to the next grate and have your leader open it and take the cork from it. Go back and put the cork in the hole. You will find more corks and three more holes as you continue west, north, east, and south.

Return to the fire you passed to rest and heal. (As you are moving east, you can find treasure or monsters in the grills to the north.) As you return to the east from the resting place, you will find a statue with a lever on the other side. Shoot the lever with an arrow and go toward the Pyramid's interior.

Ascend the steep stairs as quickly as possible, for more enemies gather as time passes. Slay them, then go to the west side of the Pyramid. You will run into Neteki again. Neteki prevents you from climbing the stairs to the garden.

On the west side, open and enter the grate. You will emerge in a room. Do not go to the south part of the room because the man there is sick and very contagious. Instead, go through another grill to the northeast room and then go through a cabinet to the garden. Kill Neteki as soon as possible, and the garden will slay most of your foes. Then go back to the Pyramid's entrance. Go to Notaku and sell the great feyrs' teeth.

THE ALLIANCE IS ATTACKED

Return to the Veiled Alliance headquarters. You must try to save Matthias and Romila and as many others as possible. Send someone to stay with Matthias and defeat his attackers. After dispatching all of the attackers in the main building, go north into Matthias' bedroom. There is a secret door in the north wall. Finish off the balance of the Draxans, and you'll be told the War Lord got away with the Urn of Utatci.

Go through the books to learn the locations of three of the four items you need to oppose the Lord Warrior and his Urn: the Cup of Life from Saven the Healer, Promere's Hammer from the Mines, the Lyre of the Wind, and the Fire Ruby.

Get the torn tapestry off the wall. From the chest in this room, get the dye and fan. Go to Notaku and sell any unnecessary items. He tells you he wants drake skins.

THE MINES

Talk to Boric in the northwest part of town about getting a job at the Mines. Take the key and leave town to the west. Follow the path to the northwest corner and use the key on the mine door. Talk to Melody, the foreman. He thinks you are the crew sent to clear out the mines.

Go north into a room (there is a fire ring here) and talk to the dying miner. Go north into a room with four fans in it; do not move them. Go north again into a room with one fan; again, do not move it. Go east to a room with a hole in the ceiling and one fan. Turn this fan west.

Go west to a room and turn the fan south, then go south into the next room where there are four fans. Turn only the two north fans to the west. (You have been in these rooms before, but the fans must be turned in this order.)

Go west into a room and wipe out the umber hulks, then try to clear the rubble from the west end of the hall, which you can't do. Call for help. A dwarf named Winchester shows up and clears the rubble, then gives you a whistle. Proceed to the west into a room. You will find a wheel. Take it to repair a machine. There are two fans in this room; turn them to the west.

MORE FANS

Go to the next room to the west and turn the only fan north. Go north into the next room, which has one fan, and turn the fan west. Go west into the next room and turn the one fan there north. Go north, where you will find one fan and mine gas. Turn the fan to the west, then go to the west side of this room and rescue Blick, the elevator operator.

Blick gives you a piece of paper. Have all four members study it until it is engraved into their memories. Go south once, then west three times to the elevator. Use the southern item that looks like a plate, and the elevator will appear and take you down one level. Talk to the half-giant miners for information, then go north and use the north cart to reach Rattlenook Farm. Talk to the mushroom, then set the switch to down and go to Hourglass. To get the carts operating, click on the whistle beside each platform and use it, then switch a lever (up or down in most cases).

Hourglass is a small junction. Set the switch to down, use the whistle, and get on the platform. You will then arrive at Spiderweb South. Walk north to Spiderweb, then north to the mine cart. Set the switch down, use the whistle and platform, and go to Hadro's Half Acre.

Go west here to a switch north of the car. Set the switch to up and use the cart to go to Redrock. When you arrive, note the conditions, then take the car back to Hadro's Half Acre. Speak with the foreman, then take the west car to Lockout Tunnel. Set the switch to down. When you reach Lockout Tunnel, set the switch down and go to Old Digs. You can rest here. Note the wall on the north side near the west wall. Save the game.

Return to Lockout Tunnel and go to Hadro's Half Acre, Set the switch to up and walk east, looking for four or five characters with white hats. Talk to them, then kill them and the monsters that appear. If the monsters escape from this level, restore your saved game and try again; they must be killed now or they will kill everyone. You might want to check several levels to see if there are any miners left.

Return to the Old Digs. You will encounter two or three illithid or mind flayers. Slay them.

THE UNDERDARK LEVEL

Before entering this level, save the game and heal, then use protective spells. You will encounter other mind flayers in the tunnel. After slaying them, you will see Granger in the northeast corner. The mind devourers have taken him over but he will go along with you. (Eventually you will have to kill him.) Go north from this area, which is the kitchen, and wipe out the mind flayers.

Go west out of the dining room, then move south. Kill the mind flayers and search them until you find a key, which opens the safe in this room's northwest corner. Get the key and scroll, then leave the room by a passage to the north. This leads to a junction area.

Ignore Granger and go east toward the lab area. In the southeast corner, kill any slaves that interfere. Go west and kill any mind slayers in the lab area. Take the key from the interpreter and open the nearby safe. (To open the safe, keep the key in your possession and click on the safe; the program gives you several options, one of which is use the key.) The safe is in another nearby room to the northeast. Inside the safe is the second part of the key. Return to the junction room and go west. Kill the guards that attack as you enter the room. Save the game, then exit through the southeast door between the columns.

A gamemaster behind a wall is creating monsters that attack as you enter. Move to the wall at once. Get the grapple from the floor and use it climb over the wall. You can pass it from one character to another until the entire group is over the wall.

Slay the gamemaster and his guards, as well as any of the mind or intellect devourers. Get the key from the gamemaster's body. Go north, then east to the junction room. Before proceeding further, cast all the protective spells you have. Then go north to your goal. There are guards and intellect devourers in the first room. Slay them and go north through the glowing door.

BEYOND THE GLOWING DOOR

After you use the three-part key on the door, a large crowd of half giants, mind flayers, and intellect devourers will attack. Cast the Stone Wall spell (which may take several tries), bisecting the room from northwest to southeast. Then add a Thorn Wall and a Wall of Swords crisscrossing the other two. Use several elementals to guard the two openings, then proceed to slay the monsters that enter. You cannot break the ceramic brain until all are slain.

Get the key from the only body left in the room. Use it to open the room to the east, which contains a rest area. Very carefully click the key on the top of the door near the north side. (This may require several attempts.) After resting, open the chest and get the key and other items. Just north of this door is another door. Enter it and go west through a hallway. Save, then use protective spells and enter the large room.

PROMERE'S HAMMER

After slaying the stone beasts — and before your protective spells expire — go to the northeast section, slay the two stone golems, and take Promere's Hammer. Get the armor from the chest. Go to the southeast section of this area and use the Hammer to break up the rubble. Now return to your original entrance to the Underdark area, using the Hammer to exit.

THE OLD DIGS

Get on the car to Lockout Tunnel, to Hadro's Half Acre, to Spiderweb North, to Hourglass, to the Elevator, and then through the mines to the entrance. Go to the office and collect your reward from Melody (just south of the exit), who has already given you a brain scan. He is just south of the exit. Return to the Veiled Alliance headquarters.

THE RINGING MOUNTAINS

From the Veiled Alliance headquarters, follow the path back to the city. Go south of the path until you see a cave. Release the chained girl and slay the giants. She will be invaluable on the quest for the Lyre of the Winds.

Talk to Matthias, then go to the northeastern room containing a tapestry of a mountain. Examine the tapestry and note there is a place for a coal. Take an ember from the fire in the south part of the room and use it on the tapestry. Walk through it, and you will find yourself in the Ringing Mountains, location of the Fire Ruby. Be sure you have a grappling hook — four hooks would be better.

Go south until attacked by Draxans, then go east. To the northeast are two fire drakes, but they won't bother you if ignored. To the west, slay the fire elemental attacking Verini. Talk to Prosser, then proceed to the Verini guards in the southeast. Do not attack them, for they will shortly be attacked by Draxans. Help them in the fight. They will ask you to clean a Draxan camp to the west. Do so, and they will invite you into the Verini Temple. Don't disturb the meeting.

After the meeting, talk with the visiting merchant. Then talk with Novetmus. You will discover that the Temple is run by Novetmus, Galanix, and Sorvel (who has just died). After the meeting, talk with Fori the storyteller just north of the Temple. He asks you to investigate Sorvel's death. Carry this news to Novetmus, who will agree and give you access to all the Temple except the seal room and Galanix's quarters.

SORVEL'S MURDER

South and east of the meeting area is a rest circle. When ready to investigate, go to the north wing. In the center on this wing are three rooms more elaborate than the rest; go to the easternmost room and read a book on the floor that tells about statutes. Leave the north wing and go to the south wing.

Examine the eyes on the beast statue and a scroll emerges from its mouth. It shows that Sorvel was afraid for his life. Take it to Novetmus, who is gray in color and normally found just outside the seal room. He will hold a meeting and announce that Sorvel was murdered.

After the meeting, go to Prosser's room (very near the northeast corner of the south wing). Talk to him until you learn that Sorvel kept notes, then insist that he give the book to you. Read the book, noting that his journal was re-bound in a different cover.

Go to the room in the southeast part of the Temple. You will find the key and book. Note that one page is missing. Take the key to Eloven, who is green and can be located in the northeast corner of the north wing. Speak with him to learn that he made a locket for Sorvel and that you have the key.

THE FIRE RUBY

Go to the crypts between the north wing and the Temple. You will find that the tombs have been looted. You learn that the looter, Ulben, has been caught. Go to his cell, also in the north wing, and use the guard to frighten him. He will tell you where the Fire Ruby is hidden.

To find the Fire Ruby, go near the resting place in the south. Look for a stone in the north side, near lava. Go to Novetmus. In an animated sequence, you discover that Galinix killed him as well as Sorvel. At that instant, however, the seal blows, Galinix is killed, and you must go below to get the Fire Ruby.

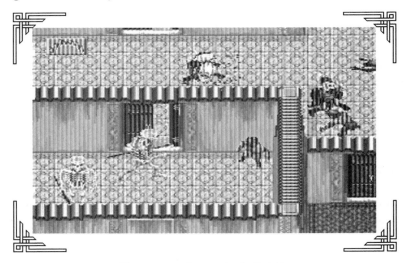

It's one maze after another in Dark Sun.

●●●●●●●●●●

IN THE VOLCANO

You only have a short time to get the Fire Ruby and seal the volcano before it blows up. Inside, go south. When the path splits to the east and west, go east — but do not engage the fire drakes. Kill any Draxans you meet, then go east.

On your way, a part of the ceiling falls into the lava, and there are Verini children on the rock that is sinking. To save the children, go to the west side and push the column into the rock. Do not escort them home. Go east until you are stopped, then go north and kill the Draxans who ambush you. Continue north and speak with the dying man, then get his grappling hook.

Go west to the large stone bridge with the two holes in it. Use grappling hooks to cross (if there are no holes in it, cross it by going along the upper rim of the bridge.) One hook is sufficient, but three or four make it easier. Go west to the maze of stones in the lava.

THE LAVA STONES

Save your game and go to the southeast after entering from the north. You can jump to the first stone in the north. Note that when you walk across the center of a stone, another stone either disappears or appears.

Walk on the edge of the stones that you don't want to disappear. After awhile, you will observe that you need two stones in the southeast section. By walking around, you will discover which stones to step on. As soon as you have discovered the pattern, go back to your saved game and cross quickly.

Slay the attacking Draxans and go southeast. As the path circles around, you will run into more Draxans. The Templar calls up some golems and leaves his men and golems to fight you. Slay them, then look to the north for two stones that allow you to cross the lava. Follow the path around toward the east to a gap. Click on it to jump over.

The Templar calls up skeletons to engage you and throws the Fire Ruby onto a column that starts to sink into the lava. Grab the Fire Ruby and leave as quickly as possible the way you came in. If the rock sinks, the Ruby is thrown on the shore by the magma. Go south, west, and north to the steps to exit.

When you get to the Temple, use the Fire Ruby on the seal to prevent the volcano from blowing up. After finishing with the Verini, go to the room just north and west of the Temple and use the Ruby on the tapestry. Then use the tapestry to return to the Veiled Alliance headquarters.

THE LYRE

Before leaving on the Lyre quest, be sure you have the torn tapestry and dye from the northeast room of Alliance headquarters. Then go to the south gate, enter the eastern room, and talk to the caravan master. Leave with the next caravan.

Check your map for the encampment around the oasis to the north. Go there and speak with Magnola, the girl you saved outside the Mines. She is in a blue tent to the southeast. Magnola sends you to the Sultan (in the tent with the guards in front). He sends you into his treasure room. Magnola asks you to go on a trip to trick one of the Janns, who is a traitor.

Go south to a tent and talk to the merchant Zorani. Slay him, remove your armor, and put on the jacket. The traitor will now deliver a note to you. Take the note to Magnola, who arranges for you to see the Sultan again.

Take the Tapestry to the weaver, who will agree to repair it. You will need thread from the Draxan jacket as well as the dye from Alliance headquarters. It will take two days. After the first rest period, go back and give her the dye and use the jacket to get the thread. When you return, it is completed. Take it to the Weaver with 10,000 and get credit points. Now return to Tyr by going to the western edge of the path and answering "yes."

Put the Tapestry in its frame, then use the feather duster nearby and go through the tapestry to the Land of Clouds. In the town of giants, proceed north to a house containing a resting fire.

LAND OF CLOUDS

You arrive at a tree stump, which you may reenter to return to the Veiled Alliance. Go north to the house and rest if necessary. Speak with Kiril, a giant, to learn they are being attacked by swarms of insects, wolf-headed giants, and air drakes. Before helping, search an abandoned house and get the canvas (white object).

Go south to the house and get the pole leaning against the wall (this is the home of Velden the Smith). Go to the north and enter the cave opening. You will pass a passage to the north, but go east and get the piece of wood shaped like a rudder.

Go back into the tunnel and take the north passage. You will arrive at an area of wolf-headed giants. Do not attack them. Talk to them to learn that the wolf-headed giants you're seeking are on an island to the northeast. Go there via the boat on the north shore. Use the pole for a mast, the wood for the rudder, and the canvas for the sail.

THE ISLAND

Sail to the nearby island. A wolf-headed giant takes you to their leader. Slay him and all the others on the island. Enter the tunnel in the island's northwest corner, which will take you to the air drakes.

Just to the south of where you enter is a house with a giantess inside. Ignore her. Use the resting circle if necessary, then leave the house and go around to the northeast side, You will find a path to the air drakes. Use all your protective spells and the best Haste spell you have, then head up the path. You will be deluged with spells, but continue and kill all the drakes there.

GETTING THE LYRE

In the northwest corner is a platform. Stand on it to be transported to another island. Use the platform in the northeast corner. Go back to the first platform, which transports you back to the beginning, but don't use it now. The path south to the air drake's nest is open, so go south and kill them, then talk to the woman inside. Go to the west side, click on the black sticks, and use them. When you hit the correct one, the nest will collapse.

The woman will give you a Cloak of Invisibility. Be sure to click on the inside of the drake's nest to get the Lyre. Get some drake hides and enter the cave west of the nest. You will be back in the village. Go to Velden's. He will make a set of armor for you. Give it to the weakest characters. Wear the armor from the Promere's Hammer chest.

Go to the tree stump just east of the house you are in and walk into it to get back to the Alliance headquarters. Talk to Romila, who has located the Lord Warrior's headquarters.

LORD WARRIOR'S HEADQUARTERS

You must have all four items to proceed further: the Cup of Life, Promere's Hammer, the Lyre of the Wind, and the Fire Ruby. Look for the Warrior's Tomb in Tyr. It's in the far north-central part of town. Enter the building that has two golems beside the tapestry. Take the tapestry off the north wall to reveal a door into the Lord Warrior's tomb.

Use the four elemental items to open the tomb. As you enter, you will meet a Templar. Ask him about the tomb. As you progress further, you will meet Kovar and must convince him that he should defend the Tyr. Give Kovar some equipment, then proceed to the level below by using the portal in the southwest section.

Go north until you meet Juma. Talk with him, slay him, and get the key beside him. Just to the north, look in the opening in the wall and find a hole leading to a lower level. Go this level, then look to the right to find a lightning rod in an alcove. Take it. Return to the top level and enter the large iron door by using the key from Juma. Draxans and Templars will attack when you enter. After slaying them, you must open each coffin and kill the skeleton warrior inside.

There is a large hole in the north wall east of the main door. Go to the north wall just west of the main door and dig another hole. Climb down the hole and find the bodies of the team you replaced in the mine. Move the bodies and kill the critters under them. You can rest here before facing the Lord Warrior. Save the game.

Now go back to the room above and use the lightning rod to open the main doors. Once inside, you are attacked by skeletons and giant skeletons. The Lord Warrior leaves. After killing the Skeletons, you can go back to the rest area if necessary.

But first, go to the west part of the room and read a book and scroll that will help you. Take the magic staff from the sarcophagus to the west of you. Activate the four items by using the staff and the four items along the eastern wall. These items are a sarcophagus, bellows, a rock, and a font. When touched with the staff, each turns into a rune. When you have all four runes, use them to activate the archway in the center of the room. Place them in the archway to go to the Temple of the Cosmos.

TEMPLE OF THE COSMOS

Slay the shambling mounds and continue until you meet Airindia, who asks for your help in destroying the Lord Warrior and tells you of the Lord Warrior's plans to awaken the Kaisharga. You must retrieve her scepter in order to open the gates of the Temple of the Cosmos, which is north of you. Go to the gate and kill the elemental on guard. If you have a cleric attuned to this gate, you can generate your own elemental to aid you. After killing the elemental and skeleton warriors, you will have the cosmic scepter. Use it on one of the gates to open it. Once you're inside, the Lord Warrior sends in skeleton warriors to attack you while he finishes calling the Kaisharga. Kill him as well as the Lord Warrior, which concludes the quest.

53

ORBS & STUFF

Object	See this Section for Location	Also See Section(s)
Cup of Life	The Veiled Alliance	The Alliance is Attacked, Lord Warrior's Headquarters
Medallion	The Veiled Alliance	Location only
Dye	The Alliance is Attacked	Getting the Lyre
Fan	The Alliance is Attacked	Location only
Torn tapestry	The Alliance is Attacked	Getting the Lyre
Promere's Hammer	Promere's Hammer	The Alliance is Attacked, Lord Warrior's Headquarters
Lyre of the Wind	Getting the Lyre	The Alliance is Attacked, The Lyre, Lord Warrior's Headquarters
Fire Ruby	The Lava Stones	The Alliance is Attacked, The Ringing Mountains, The Fire Ruby, Lord Warrior's Headquarters
Wheel	The Mines	Location only
Whistle	The Mines	More Fans
Cloak of Invisibility	Getting The Lyre	Location only

DEATH GATE

BY
PAUL SHAFFER

TYPE
*Animated
Adventure*

SYSTEM
*IBM PC
(Required:
386/33+, 4MB
RAM,
Microsoft-
compatible
mouse, VGA,
CD-ROM
drive.
Supports:
VESA, Sound
Blaster,
AWE32, Adlib,
Roland, MT-
32, and RAP-
10, General
MIDI.)*

COMPANY
*Legend
Entertainment
Inc.*

55

IKE LEGEND OF XANTH, DEATH GATE IS BASED ON A SERIES OF SCI-ENCE FICTION NOVELS. LEGEND, RATHER THAN ATTEMPT TO TURN ONE OF THE NOVELS INTO A GAME, CREATED A FRESH STORY SET IN THE DEATH GATE UNIVERSE. IT IS A UNIVERSE BROKEN INTO FIVE SEC-TIONS: THE REALMS OF AIR, WATER, EARTH, FIRE, AND THE NEXUS AT THE CENTER. THIS RESULTED FROM THE WORK OF THE EVIL SARTAN MAGICIANS, WHO IMPRISONED THE PATRYN RACE IN A LABYRINTH IN THE NEXUS. AS HAPLO, YOU SET OUT TO RETRIEVE THE FOUR PIECES OF THE WORLD SEAL AND RESCUE THE PATRYNS. THIS REQUIRES TRAVELING BETWEEN THE REALMS IN A SPECIAL SHIP WHOSE NAVIGATION DEVICE REQUIRES A DIFFER-ENT "NAMING RUNE" FOR EACH REALM. BEFORE LEAVING THE NEXUS, YOU MUST ACQUIRE THE NAMING RUNE FOR THE NEXT REALM, AND OTHER GOALS MUST BE ACCOMPLISHED IN ORDER TO OBTAIN OTHER RUNES. FINDING AND LEARNING TO USE MAGICAL RUNES IS ANOTHER PART OF THE QUEST, AS THEY ARE NECESSARY FOR SOLVING SOME OF THE WIDE VARIETY OF WELL-DESIGNED PUZZLES. THE PLOT, THOUGH LINEAR at the start, opens and becomes less rigid as you travel through the realms. Plenty of sound effects and digitized voices round out a thoroughly enjoyable adventure, and the SVGA graphics of the characters and backgrounds truly transport you to another world.

THE SOLUTION

GENERAL

Most information in conversations is helpful. Don't be rude or sarcastic in your replies or questions.

GETTING STARTED

Talk to Xar. Ask all (learning Identify and Rune Transfer spells), and he gives you the marker. Take glowlamp on right. Go west twice. Use magic on marker. Rune Transfer to steering stone. Use steering stone.

ARIANUS: WORLD OF AIR

DREVLIN: GETTING LIMBECK'S PARCHMENT

Go northeast twice. Talk to dwarf (don't say you're a god). Take shirt, elbow pipe, and marmalade. Take piece of bread. Go east. Talk to Limbeck. Ask all. Take cork. Put white shirt in ink jug (turns black). Put marmalade on bread slice (three times). Give bread slice to Limbeck, who drops parchment. Take parchment. Read it. Go north, then northwest.

GETTING ON ALIENS' SHIP

Take elbow pipe from box. Talk to dwarf (don't say you're a god). Ask for pipe in his hand (getting pipe). Go north. Use magic on sensor. Go north, then up. Take wine jug. Look at figurines. Down. Down. Talk to Duke. Ask about King Stephen (getting signet ring and location of castle). Return to your ship. Use steering wheel.

RESCUING CAPTIVES

Go to castle. Go northwest, north. Give ring to guard. Go west. Take shear. Open shutter. Lift bar with shear. Open shutter (getting Create Reality Pocket spell). Enter window. Take candle holder. Take book from bookshelf on Tower of Brotherhood. Read it.

Use magic on tapestry. Create Reality Pocket. Go west (enter tapestry). Talk to wizard. Give wine jug to wizard. Talk again. Ask about spells and Shroud of Darkness (last). You'll get the Swap and Create Shroud of Darkness spells.

Return to your ship. Use steering wheel. Return to Drevlin. Go to Limbeck. Give candle holder to him (getting pipe piece). Go north, north. Cast heat on sensor again. Go north, up. Use magic on black shirt. Cast Shroud of Darkness spell. Put black shirt on figurines. Go down, west. Open box. Take zinger. Activate zinger. When taken to the king, ask for information. (You're taken to Skirvash.)

JOINING THE BROTHERHOOD

Go north. Look at doll. Agree to get doll. Go west (getting doll). Use magic on street rat. Swap. Take net. Go northwest. Take prybar. Talk to street rat. Agree to his bargain. Return to ship's hold. Break lock on chest with prybar. Open strongbox. Take jewel sack and T-pipe.

Return to street. Enter tavern. Give jewel sack to bartender (he gives you coins). When Hugh starts to talk to you, agree to join Brotherhood. Agree to contract. Return to street rat. Give coins to street rat. Wait for him to return (getting picklock and coded paper). Return to street. Go southeast (to house). Examine house. Save.

FULFILLING THE CONTRACT

Put picklock in lock. Note the sounds that the picklock makes when you move it: push = clack, jiggle = tick, turn = thunk. Move the picklock in that order to open lock.

Enter house. Examine clock. Take poetry book. Read it. Examine clock again, turning the dial so the small end points at the following in this order: Mistmorne, Winetime, Toiltime (panel opens). Take journal. Read journal. Use magic on portrait. Cast Create Reality Pocket spell. Enter portrait. Tell man to take a break. Say you're a messenger. Say she wants the amulet. Wouldn't lie to an intelligent man. The three answers are: Bouncing Beans, Five, How much? (gets you amulet). Return to tavern. Give amulet to Hugh (takes you to tower, where you are given salve).

IN THE BROTHERHOOD

Push table. Open shutter. Examine floating continent. Southeast. Put picklock in lock of northeast doors. The key uses the same combination of sounds you heard when you picked the lock before. Shake = clack, pull = tick, tilt = thunk. Go northeast.

Look at doll (getting Motion spell). Look at statue. Use magic on statue. Cast Motion spell. Take necklace. Go southwest. Examine paper from street rat. The key to the door is the first word, with each letter representing a color. Push bloodstone hand on door, then umber, then yew (B-U-Y). Put necklace on pedestal. Take handbook. Take Book of Pryan. Take crystal globe (men appear). Take necklace again (dispatches Hugh). Read handbook and Book of Pryan. Go south (returns you to Drevlin).

THE KINSEY WINESY MACHINE

Talk to dwarf. Fix broken pipe with any pipe (gives close-up). Pipes fit in this manner:

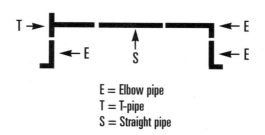

E = Elbow pipe
T = T-pipe
S = Straight pipe

Put cork in fixed pipe. Turn valve. Talk to old dwarf. Show parchment to him (getting lump of ore). Go southeast, east. Open compartment. Put iron ore in compartment. East. Look at coffins and statue. Put crystal globe on statue. Take Air seal piece, the first piece of the World Seal. Return to ship. Use steering stone. Go east, east. Give Air seal piece to Xar.

PRYAN: WORLD OF EARTH

Return to ship. Use magic on Book of Pryan. Rune Transfer onto steering stone. Use steering stone.

THE CITADEL

Go north. Take pink plant. Go west, west. Take shell and nut. Return to ship. Use steering wheel. Go to Tree City.

TREE CITY

Go northeast, northeast. Take clothesline. Go west. Agree to work. Give doll to elf child (asks you to follow). Go east, east. Give clothesline to elf prince. Agree to keep Zifnab a secret. Go southeast. Give poetry book to elf prince. When ember falls out of fire, take ember with your shell. When princess appears, talk to her. Wait for Zifnab to appear, then wait for him to leave (getting Transportation spell).

GETTING THE MAW'S STAFF

Use magic on white disc (on ground). Cast Transportation spell. Ask Zifnab about all. Take black disc. Tie clothesline to branch. Down. Take yellow and blue flowers. Go south, east. Throw black disk into Maw. Go southeast. Give blue flowers to elf prince. Use magic on white disc. Cast Transportation spell. Push corpse. Take arrow. Take toadstool. Throw marmalade at spider. Put shell with ember on hive. Crush yellow flowers. Cut pod with shears (getting staff). Transport back out. Give staff to elf prince (joins the party). Talk to princess (ask for favor) and ask her to join the party.

OPENING CITADEL DOOR

Return to ship. Go to Citadel. Go north, west, west. Put yellow petals in nut. Give nut to animal. Get nut meat. Go east, north, north. Talk to princess. Ask for favor. Ask her to play tune from book. Cut vine with shear. Ask female dwarf about golden hammer. Ask her to ask elders for hammer.

Wait for her to return. Introduce girl to companions (princess coughs). Ask for herbs. Ask dwarf girl to return to elders and try again (she leaves). Give toadstool, herbs, nut meat, and pink plant to princess (cures cough). North. Talk to princess. Ask her to play flute again. Go north, north, north.

Talk to elf prince. Ask him to climb tree and get crystal (getting crystal). Examine crystal. South four times. Pull branch. Put crystal fragment in stump. Go south. Wait (dwarf girl returns, and you get the stone from Zifnab when the Citadel door opens). Take Fire seal piece, the second piece of the World Seal. Return to ship. Use steering stone. Go east, east. Give Fire seal piece to Xar.

ABARRACH: WORLD OF FIRE

Return to ship. Use magic on crystal fragment. Rune Transfer to steering stone. Use steering stone.

TELESTIA

Go northeast, northeast. Talk to dead worker. Ask for bucket (getting bucket). Go north. Take rocks. Go south, east, north. Talk to dead butler. Ask about all. Go up. Take tea set. Take children's book. Read it.

OPENING CAVE DOOR

Close children's book on "Get that Snake" page. Talk to dead nanny. Ask her to accompany you: Say that you know where her book is and she joins party. Go down.

Give tea set to butler. Talk to him and ask what he's waiting for. Go south, west, north. Give book to nanny. Go south. Talk to dead worker. Ask him to follow (he joins party). Go north (worker grabs snake), north. Turn stones to all point down. Click on the stones in this order: top left, top right, bottom left, bottom right, top middle, center left, center right, bottom middle, top middle, center left, center right, bottom middle, center middle.

The door opens. Go north. Talk to dead dwarf.

ENTERING STUDY

Go south, south, east, east. Put rocks in bucket. Put bucket with rocks on hook. Go up. Turn time dial to 4 o'clock. Turn crank (wait for bell to ring; it's now 4 a.m.). Turn time dial full circle to 4 o'clock. Turn crank. Wait (bell should ring; it's now 4 p.m.). Pull release lever. Go down. Go west, north, east. Take book. Read it (adds Kleitus' Palace to map and teaches you the Possession and Ward spells). Return to ship. Use steering wheel. Go to Kleitus' Palace.

KLEITUS' PALACE

Go northeast, northeast. Be nice. Say you're alone. Say you're a Patryn. Turn down food (you're poisoned and incarcerated, but you get steak and you learn the Hunger spell). Use magic on dog. Cast Hunger spell. Give steak to dog. Use magic on dog. Cast Possession spell.

As dog, take the key ring. Give key ring to Haplo. Touch Haplo. Take key ring.

Unlock manacles with key ring. Unlock Edmund's manacles with key ring. Take vise. Talk to Edmund. Ask about all. Possess dog again. Go north, up. Take second bottle from the left (the bottle that doesn't filter out any lines). Go down, south. Give bottle to Haplo. Touch Haplo. Drink clear liquid. Give clear bottle to Edmund. Talk to Edmund. Ask him to join you (he joins party). Go north, west, southwest (you are taken to cave).

The adventurers huddle before the next quest in Death Gate.

●●●●●●●●●

SECRET CAVE

Go northeast, east. Talk to gamblers (getting rune bones). Talk to Balthazar (don't tell him you're a Patryn). Ask all. Possess dog. Enter hidden tunnel. Touch Haplo. Talk to Balthazar. Tell him about hidden cave (you learn Unravel Illusion spell).

Go east. Take spell book. Read spell book (getting Resurrection spell). Take robe (you learn Self-Immolation spell). Go west. Ask Balthazar about all. Return to ship. Return to Telestia.

GETTING TO COLOSSUS

Return to dead dwarf. Wear robe. Talk to dwarf. Ask him to come with you (he joins party). Go to clock tower. Go up. Tighten vise. Use vise on headpiece of clock statue. Loosen vice. Take headpiece. Return to ship.

Return to Kleitus' Palace. Go northeast, east (Edmund arrives), north. Take cloth. Show cloth to dog. Go north. Follow dog's directions through catacombs. Use magic on rune in column. Unravel Illusion. Put headpiece in hole (gets pendant from Edmund). Take Stone seal piece, the third part of the World Seal. Return to ship. Use steering stone. Return and give Stone seal piece to Xar.

CHELOSTRA: WORLD OF WATER

Return to ship. Use magic on pendant. Rune Transfer to steering stone. Use steering stone.

REMOVING WARD, ESCAPING DRAGON

Go northeast, north, west. Examine spell on city gate. Cast spell on rune bone (choose the rune bone that, when added to Ward spell on city gate, will change spell into Possession). Rune Transfer to spell on gate. Use magic on dog. Cast Possession spell. Go to Sartan City (getting Nullification spell).

GETTING OFF CHELOSTRA

Tell Samah the truth. Push globe. Use magic on rug. Create Reality Pocket (globe falls into rug). Take rug. Go east, east. Put water in clear bottle. Use magic on bottle. Cast Null Water spell. Drink bottle. Go north. Take scales. Go south, west. Put scales on rock pile. Take glowing stone.

Return to ship. Put rug on ship wall. Use magic on rug. Cast Create Reality Pocket spell. Enter rug. Push globe. Go through portal. Use magic on pendant. Rune Transfer onto globe. Use globe (returns you to Labyrinth).

THE LABYRINTH

TRACKING XAR

Go east, east. Take history book. Read it, noting location of runes for each wizard. Go northwest, north. Use magic on choke vines. Cast Cold spell. Go north, northeast, southwest, south. Use magic on choke vines. Cast Heat spell (kills tigermen). Throw zinger at choke vines. Use magic on vines. Cast Cold spell.

Take zinger. Go north, northeast. Take skull. Go east. Take bone. Look at cave painting. Put robe on zinger. Put skull on zinger. Go west, northwest. Activate zinger. Apply salve to tracker. Take cord. Talk to headman. Explain about shape-shifter. Talk to tracker. Ask for help tracking (tracker joins party). Go north. Put cord on bone (making bow). Shoot arrow at chaodin. Go north. Drink Null Water. Go north. Talk to dragon. Crush stone. Talk to Zifnab (takes you to Vortex).

THE VORTEX

THE STEPS

Talk to Zifnab. Go north. Use magic on arch. Cast Identify spell. Use magic on Haplo (self). Cast Reverse Self-Immolation spell (using undo and add commands to Self-Make spell). Search ashy remains (getting duplicates of everything you carry). Go north. Put shear on shear (making shears). Go north. Cut tentacle with shears (three times). Go north.

ENDGAME

Xar gives you seal pieces. Put Water seal piece in water spire. Use magic on Xar. Resurrection. Put Stone seal piece in earth spire. Talk to Xar (says The Heart). Put Air seal piece in air spire. Move focus. (The Heart is the Sartan called Orseph; if you examined the history book, you will find the location of the rune under Orseph name. Move focus to this rune.) Exit. Put Nexus seal piece in focus.

ORBS & STUFF ▬▬▬▬▬▬▬▬▬

Object	See this Section for Location	Also See Section(s)
Glowlamp	Getting Started	Location only
Shirt	Drevlin: Getting Limbeck's Parchment	Location only
Elbow pipe	Drevlin: Getting Limbeck's Parchment	Getting on Alien's Ship
Marmalade	Drevlin: Getting Limbeck's Parchment	Getting the Maw's Staff
Bread	Drevlin: Getting Limbeck's Parchment	Location only
Cork	Drevlin: Getting Limbeck's Parchment	The Kinsey Winesy Machine
Parchment	Drevlin: Getting Limbeck's Parchment	The Kinsey Winesy Machine
Pipe piece	Drevlin: Getting Limbeck's Parchment	Location only
Elbow pipe 2	Getting on Aliens' Ship	Location only
Pipe	Getting on Aliens' Ship	The Kinsey Winesy Machine
Wine jug	Getting on Aliens' Ship	Rescuing Captives
Signet ring	Getting on Aliens' Ship	Rescuing Captives
Shear	Rescuing Captives	Getting the Maw's Staff, Opening Citadel Door, The Steps
Candle holder	Rescuing Captives	Location only
Brotherhood book	Rescuing Captives	Location only
Zinger	Rescuing Captives	Tracking Xar
Skirvash	Rescuing Captives	Location only
Jewel sack	Joining the Brotherhood	Location only
T-pipe	Joining the Brotherhood	Location only
Doll	Joining the Brotherhood	In the Brotherhood, Tree City
Prybar	Joining the Brotherhood	Location only
Picklock	Joining the Brotherhood	Fulfilling the Contract, In the Brotherhood
Coded paper	Joining the Brotherhood	Location only
Coins	Joining the Brotherhood	Location only
Poetry book	Fulfilling the Contract	Tree City
Journal	Fulfilling the Contract	Location only
Amulet	Fulfilling the Contract	Location only

Object	See this Section for Location	Also See Section(s)
Salve	Fulfilling the Contract	Tracking Xar
Necklace	In the Brotherhood	Location only
Handbook	In the Brotherhood	Location only
Book of Pryan	In the Brotherhood	Pryan: World of Earth
Crystal globe	In the Brotherhood	The Kinsey Winesy Machine
Lump of ore	The Kinsey Winesy Machine	Location only
Air seal piece	The Kinsey Winesy Machine	Endgame
Pink plant	The Citadel	Opening Citadel Door
Shell	The Citadel	Tree City, Getting the Maw's Staff
Nut	The Citadel	Opening Citadel Door
Clothesline	Tree City	Getting the Maw's Staff
Ember	Tree City	Getting the Maw's Staff
Black disc	Getting the Maw's Staff	Location only
Yellow flowers	Getting the Maw's Staff	Opening Citadel Door
Blue flowers	Getting the Maw's Staff	Location only
Arrow	Getting the Maw's Staff	Tracking Xar
Toadstools	Getting the Maw's Staff	Opening Citadel Door
Staff	Getting the Maw's Staff	Location only
Nut meat	Opening Citadel Door	Location only
Herbs	Opening Citadel Door	Location only
Crystal fragment	Opening Citadel Door	Location only
Crystal	Opening Citadel Door	Location only
Stone	Opening Citadel Door	Location only
Bucket	Telestia	Entering Study
Rocks	Telestia	Entering Study
Tea set	Telestia	Opening Cave Door
Children's book	Telestia	Opening Cave Door
Steak	Kleitus' Palace	Location only
Clear bottle	Kleitus' Palace	Getting Off Chelostra
Key ring	Kleitus' Palace	Location only

Object	See this Section for Location	Also See Section(s)
Vise	Kleitus' Palace	Getting to Colossus
Rune bones	Secret Cave	Location only
Spell book	Secret Cave	Location only
Robe	Secret Cave	Getting to Colossus, Tracking Xar
Headpiece	Getting to Colossus	Location only
Cloth	Getting to Colossus	Location only
Stone seal piece	Getting to Colossus	Endgame
Pendant	Getting to Colossus	Chelostra: World of Water, Getting Off Chelostra
Rug	Getting Off Chelostra	Location only
Scales	Getting Off Chelostra	Location only
History book	Tracking Xar	Endgame
Skull	Tracking Xar	Location only
Bone	Tracking Xar	Location only
Cord	Tracking Xar	Location only
Duplicate shear	The Steps	Location only
Nexus seal piece	Endgame	Location only

DISCWORLD

BY
**STACEY PORTNOY
& JERRY VAN HORN**

TYPE
*Animated
Adventure*

SYSTEM
*IBM CD-ROM
(Required:
386/33 MHz,
4MB RAM,
256-color
VGA.
Recommended:
mouse.
Supports:
Sound Blaster,
Ad Lib,
General MIDI)*

COMPANY
Psygnosis Inc.

ASED ON BRITISH AUTHOR TERRY PRATCHETT'S BEST-SELLING BOOKS, DISCWORLD EMULATES THE STYLE OF LUCASARTS' ADVENTURES. YOU PLAY THE ROLE OF RINCEWIND, AN INEPT WIZARD FROM UNSEEN UNIVERSITY, WHOSE GOAL IS TO RID THE TOWN ANKH-MORPORK OF A MENACING DRAGON. YOU AND YOUR FAITHFUL COMPANION, THE LUGGAGE, WILL MEET MANY COLORFUL CHARACTERS AND TRAVEL THROUGH TIME. THE GAME IS DIVIDED INTO FOUR ACTS, WITH A MAJOR GOAL TO ACCOM-PLISH IN EACH. THE PUZZLES PROGRESS FROM SOMEWHAT EASY TO VERY COMPLEX AND DIFFICULT. DO NOT EXPECT TO FINISH THIS IN A FEW DAYS. ERIC IDLE FROM MONTY PYTHON PUTS IN AN EXCELLENT APPEARANCE AS THE VOICE OF RINCEWIND. THE INTERFACE IS VERY SIMPLE TO LEARN AND USE. THE LUGGAGE IS THE MAIN SOURCE OF YOUR INVENTORY. WHEN IT'S OPENED, YOU CAN RESIZE IT, AND THE GAME REMEMBERS THE SELECT-ED SIZE. A UNIQUE FEATURE IS THAT MANY OF THE INVENTORY ITEMS ARE ANIMATED WHILE INSIDE THE LUG-GAGE: AN IMP MAKES FACES AT YOU, AND A RABBIT SCAMPERS IN AND OUT OF A HAT. WITH EXCELLENT graphics, music, sound, and voices, punctuated with nonstop laughs, Discworld is a game not to be missed by adventure fans of any age. At last, Psygnosis has made a name for itself in the adventure genre. In fact, this is clearly one of the best adventure games of the year.

THE SOLUTION

GENERAL

When talking to the various characters, there is no penalty for using any of the icons; there are no wrong choices. Look at and interact with everything and everyone possible, or you will miss out on a good portion of the humor.

ACT 1: GETTING STARTED

ASSIGNMENT

Open wardrobe. Get pouch. Open door and go through it. Walk down the stairs. Go past the statue on second floor to the Archchancellor's room. He will ask you to get a book from the library.

Go down to the main floor. Enter the library. Look at librarian. Talk to librarian: greet, question, ask about book. Enter library stacks. Look at banana on head of Sleazy Guy. Talk to Sleazy Guy: sarcasm (learn about L-Space), ask about banana. Leave library.

DRAGON LAIR BOOK

Go to the closet. Get broom. Return to your bedroom. Use broom on luggage. Inside luggage is a banana. Return to the library. Give banana to librarian (getting book). Ask librarian about L-Space. Go see the Archchancellor. Give the book to him. The book now contains the names of the items needed for the formula to make the Dragon Lair Detector. Go to the kitchen. Talk to the cook: question. Get another banana.

DINING ROOM: STAFF

Talk to lecturer: greet, question, ask about librarian and luggage. Stand in front of Windle Poons. Take broom out of luggage. When he reaches over to get some food, use the broom on his staff to exchange them. Exit dining room. Leave university building through main door.

UNIVERSITY GROUNDS

Walk toward path to the right. Get bag of fertilizer. Continue walking right. Talk to apprentice wizard: question. Note bag of prunes next to wizard. Get frog. Open university door. Go through it to the area map, then to the palace.

The eyes have it in Discworld.

●●●●●●●●●

PALACE

Talk to guards: question. Enter palace. Talk to peasant, witch, and thief. Look at the patrician. Open door with star on it (fool's dressing room). Get mirror. Leave palace.

ALLEY: DRAGON BREATH

Go to alley (below southeast corner of Square). Place mirror in Rincewind's inventory. Walk forward a few steps until you step on a tile that ejects you up to the roof.

Go to the tower (rear of screen). Look at dragon (moves you up to tip of flagpole). Place mirror on the tip. Adjust mirror by using it, getting dragon's attention. Dragon breath will be on the mirror. Leave the tower (takes you back to landing spot on roof). Climb down roof. Walk toward crossplank. Get ladder. Enter window to return to the ground.

SQUARE

Go to the Square. Read notices. Talk to old-timers: greet. Open door to the Psychiatrickery office. Enter and talk to Troll. Exit the office. Get tomato in stall. Go to alley behind Dibbler. Wait for the Dunnyman to arrive and then talk to him: question. Leave the alley and walk past the stall to the right and talk to the urchin (getting bloomers from old-timers). This will give you the pickpocket skill (which will appear in Rincewind's inventory).

Throw tomato at tax collector in the stocks at the far right of the Square. Reach in for another tomato. Get worm on ground. Go back into Psychiatrickery office. The middle seat should be empty. Get butterfly net. Leave the Square.

STREET: HAIR ROLLER

Go to the street (northeast of Square). Click on north end. Go into toy shop. Talk to toy maker. Get string on counter. Take donkey from sales bin. Exit store. Continue walking on street.

Go to the corner. Monk will ramble. Walk toward the fishmonger. Get picture of octopus. Continue walking on street. Enter barber shop (door to the left of beggar). Talk to woman. Look at hair roller in her hair. Talk to woman again (now wants straight hair). Talk to barber. When thinking about maid, use pickpocket skill on barber's pocket (getting hair roller). Leave.

ALLEY: IMP

Go to livery stable (south of street by edge of map). Get corn from sack in front of cart. Note that the bumper bar cannot be read because the bag of corn is blocking it. Exit the stable and go to alley on the map. Walk around the ejecting tile by going on the right side of the alley. If you land on the ejecting tile, just keep walking past.

Enter alchemist's shop. Talk to alchemist. Look at box next to alchemist. Use cable release to see that an Imp is inside the camera. Make popcorn by dropping the corn into the flask of oil. Double-click on the Imp. Exit the shop. Combine the worm with the string. Use the worm on the hole (getting Imp). Leave the alley.

UNSEEN UNIVERSITY: FRYING PAN

Go to Unseen University. Walk to right of university entrance. Place butterfly net in Rincewind's inventory. Use ladder to climb up wall and enter window. Use net to catch a pancake (causes cook to leave). Try to catch it on the way up. Climb back down. Enter university. Go to the kitchen. Get frying pan.

MEET A DRAGON

Visit the Archchancellor. Give him the staff, dragon breath, hair roller, Imp, and frying pan. After speaking to him, you swipe the Dragon Lair Detector (which places you on the area map). The Dragon Lair will not appear on the map at the present time (nor will any other location). The closer you get to the lair, the more green rays the Detector emanates and the faster it pulses.

Head toward the southwest part of the map near the wall. Enter the Dragon Lair. The dragon talks to you. You will pick up some treasure automatically. You learn that the dragon has been brought here against his will by the Secret Brotherhood. The dragon tells you to seek out the thief of the Dragon Lair Book and then find the six golden artifacts needed to set him free.

ACT 2: INTO THE PAST

Note: Until you enter the Secret Brotherhood, many items and locations listed in the Orbs & Stuff table will be unavailable to you in Act 2.

BARN

Reenter Dragon Lair, now seen on the map as the barn. Get the screwdriver.

BROKEN DRUM

Go to Broken Drum (just south of the Palace). Talk to bouncer. Enter bar. Talk to barman. Get empty tankard. Get matches. Look at green bottle behind barman. Talk to barman again. Get empty glass. Talk to braggart. Get tankard of beer. Talk to Scared Guy (learn about stolen gate pass).

INN

Go to the inn (west of the university). Enter room of inn. Close door to inn. Note picture of safe behind door. Get sheet from bed. Go into the bathroom. Get bubble bath.

OPENING L-SPACE

Go to the library at Unseen University. Give banana to librarian. Librarian will return, saying that the Dragon Lair book has been stolen. Go into the stacks to see the Sleazy Guy. Give him all four pieces of treasure (getting the golden banana). Give golden banana to librarian. He will then open up the passage to L-Space. Go into L-Space.

THEFT OF BOOK

Shortly after you arrive in the library, a thief will appear and steal the book. Push a book (not the levitation book) next to the bookshelf to reveal a secret passage (you only need to do this once). Enter bookshelf to take you to the area map in the past.

THIEF'S HIDEOUT

You will see a small figure with a light running around. He will eventually go to his hideout on the southwest part of the map (hideout now appears on the map).

MONK'S ROBE

Go to the park. Place the frog in the drunk's (which is you) mouth. Use butterfly net on the butterfly. Go to the street. Walk to the corner. Get the pot. Talk to the Troll: question. Place the butterfly in the lamp (causing rain to come down on the monk in the present).

On area map, go to the hole (where university is in the present) to return to the present. Return to the street corner. The monk is without a robe. Go to the alley by the fishmonger. Get the robe off the clothes line. Go to the toy shop. Get the hogfather doll from the sales bin.

BROTHER PENCILHEAD

Enter L-Space. The Dragon Lair Book is located on the shelves to the right of the L-Space opening. (If you take the book and try to return to the present, you will see a scene with Mr. Death and three other gods, and then place the book back in the past.)

Go to the hideout. Turn the end of the drainpipe by the door so that the opening points toward the door. Hide behind the fence. Wait for the thief to arrive. Use the glass on the drainpipe next to you to eavesdrop on what the thief says to the keeper of the door (you learn password). Put on the monk's robe and knock on the door. After giving the correct password, you will sit in on a meeting of the six members of the Brotherhood. They summon a dragon.

LEAVING THE CITY

GATE PASS

Go to the inn (in the past). Use sheet on Rincewind so he will appear to be a ghost. Try to take the jewelry box (learn combination). You look at the hammer in the safe and put it back because you do not know what to do with it. Return to the present. If you witness card players in an animated sequence, wait until the thief takes the book.

Go to the Broken Drum. Talk to Scared Guy, who now fills in more details of his story. Return to the inn in the past. Try to take the jewelry box again. This time you use the hammer to smash open the jewelry box and get the gate pass. Go back to the present.

CITY GATE

Go to the city gate. Talk to guard on left: greet, sarcasm. Look at crate. Open crate (getting a keg of gunpowder and fireworks). Use fireworks on the matches to create a firecracker. Give guard your gate pass. Note that tall guard is a Dwarf. Walk through the gates.

WOODS

Go to the woods (just east of the city). Walk along until you come to a wishing well. Use the screwdriver on the crank to unloosen it. Get the crank.

MOUNTAIN PASS

Go to the center of the mountains. Your luggage will attack a cockatrice. Get the feather and egg that the cockatrice leaves behind.

DARK WOOD

Go east of the mountain to the Dark Wood. Walk along the woods until you come to a house. Enter Nanny Ogg's (the witch) house. Use pot on the cauldron, filling it with custard.

EDGE OF THE WORLD

Go to the Edge of the World, located in about the center rear of the screen. Shake the coconut tree. A coconut falls into the water. Use the butterfly net to get the coconut out of the water. Use the screwdriver on the coconut to open it up (getting coconut milk).

FIGHTING IN THE DRUM

Enter L-Space. Go to the drum (note that it is not broken in the past). Talk to Little Guy. Look at picture behind Little Guy. While Little Guy is looking at the picture, turn his glass upside down. A fight will start, and you will be booted out. Outside the bar entrance, use the ladder on the shingle. You will climb up, getting a drumstick.

APPRENTICE WIZARD

Return to the present. Go to the closet. Use matches on shape to your left. Get box of starch. Go to kitchen. Get corn flour. Go to dining room. Use drumstick on gong. The apprentice wizard comes in to eat. Exit the university. Get the prunes. Get the garbage can outside the kitchen window.

DUNNYMAN'S GOLD TOOTH

VISIT A SHRINK

Go to the Psychiatrickery office in the Square. The seat closest to the receptionist is now open. (If not, leave and reenter, because each time you do this, the girl and Troll switch seats). Wait for the receptionist to say "Next." If she does not call next within a few seconds, talk to the Troll. After leaving the office, you will find that you have added two inkblots to your inventory.

A SWEET TOOTH

In the Square, talk to the Dibbler: angry, greet (getting donut). Go to the alley behind the Dibbler. Talk to Dunnyman. Give donut to Dunnyman. He will run off to see the barber/dentist.

PLAY MATCHMAKER

Go to the barber's office in the street. The Dunnyman will be in the chair. Talk to the barber (agreeing to arrange a meeting with the milkmaid). Return to the Psychiatrickerist's office. Talk to the girl, who will give you a note.

GET THE TOOTH

Return to the barber. Give the note to the barber. He will run off to see her. Use the apparatus to extract the Dunnyman's tooth.

CHIMNEY SWEEP'S GOLD BRUSH

Go to the alley on the map. Place the hogfather doll in Rincewind's inventory. Walk to the ejecting tile (will take a few seconds to work). Drop the doll in the chimney, which causes the alchemist's shop to fill up with smoke.

GET THE BRUSH

Go to the alchemists shop. Place keg of gunpowder (from crates at the city gate's entrance) in the fireplace. Use the string on the keg to make a fuse that goes through the sink to the outside drainpipe. Exit the shop. Use the matches to light the fuse hanging out of the drainpipe. You will automatically get the brush.

FOOL'S GOLD BELL

Go to the palace. Show the inkblot picture to the guard. Enter the palace. Talk to the peasant, who allows you to enter the Shades. Look at the custard book that the witch is holding. Try to take the book. She explains that the custard is a love potion. Talk to the patrician.

GET THE BELL

Dump the can of garbage on the fool, causing Chucky to get dirty. Enter the dressing room. Pour the bubble bath into the bathtub. Get the cap off the hat stand. Look at the cap (has a gold bell).

FISHMONGER'S GOLD BELT

Go to the street to see the fishmonger. Use string on the octopus. Go to the alley behind the fish shop. Drop octopus and pot of custard into the toilet. Read the graffiti on the door to the toilet. Exit the alley.

GETTING THE BELT

Put some prunes in the caviar. The fishmonger runs off to the toilet. The octopus grabs him. Return to the toilet. Get the belt.

MASON'S GOLD TROWEL

Go to the Shades. Talk to the mason: greet, question. Look at trowel. Go to Square. Talk to the lovable street starfish. He does a secret handshake with the toy maker. In order for the starfish to teach it to you, you have to prove you are a man.

CATHOUSE

Go through L-Space. Go to street, then to alley beside the fishmonger. Look at graffiti on door of toilet (learn about Sally's special). Go to Shades.

Walk along until you come to the House of Negotiable Affection. Talk to the ladies. Sally is on the right. Discuss the special with her. Give Sally the ingredients: cornflour (from kitchen), egg (from cockatrice on mountain pass), and coconut milk (from the end of the world). You find out the special is custard. While Sally is bathing, you sneak in and get her bloomers. Return to the present.

GET THE TROWEL

Go to the Square. Give the starfish Sally's bloomers — your proof of being a man. Starfish teaches you the handshake skill (it is in Rincewind's inventory), and you practice on the old-timers (getting a bra). Go to the Shades and see the mason. Do the secret handshake with the mason. You will get the trowel.

THIEF'S GOLD KEY

Go to thief's hovel (in the Shades before the cathouse and toward the right). Use bra on ladder (muffles the ladder). Use ladder on hovel. Enter hovel. Try to take key from thief (he turns over). Tickle thief with feather (he turns back over). Take the key. Don't forget your ladder.

RETURN GOLDEN ITEMS

Go to the barn. Give the dragon the following: brush, skeleton key, belt, tooth, trowel, and cap. This frees the dragon, who promises to wreak revenge on both the members of the Brotherhood and you.

SWITCHING BOOKS

Go to the Square. Talk to Amazon warrior. Talk to the witch: greet, question, sarcasm. While the witch is puckering up to kiss you, quickly take the custard book from the stall. Get the carpet.

Wander around map of the present, and you will see the six Secret Brotherhood members individually being blown away to smithereens. Enter L-Space. Take Dragon Lair Book. Switch the covers of the Dragon Lair Book and custard book. Place the Dragon Lair Book (actually the custard book) back on the shelves. Wait for the thief to take the book.

ACT 3: WHAT IS A HERO?

CASTING OFFICE

Talk to the guards to learn that the odds of slaying a dragon are a million to one. You start off knowing three of the possible eight elements. Go to the barber shop. Get the scissors and appointment book.

Go to the Psychiatrickerist's office, which is now a casting office for a film. Talk to the Troll if he is in the middle seat. He mentions that a hero's mustache needs to be black. Leave the office and go back in. The girl should be in the middle seat. Talk to her. Give her the appointment book, and she will autograph it for you. While there, you will be called in to see the casting director. Leave the office.

A MILLION TO ONE

In the Square, talk to the Dibbler. Today he is selling leeches. Take the paper bag and remove the leeches. Talk to the Amazon warrior: question. She will mention a mustache and a sword that goes "ting." Talk to the old-timers: question. They tell you about the posing pouch.

Go to the Shades. Go to the cathouse. Talk to the Lady of Negotiable Affection (dressed in red) to learn about camel-flage. Go to the dining room at Unseen University. Talk to the Lecturer in Recent Runes: greet, question. He mentions the magic talisman. Return to the guards at the city gate. Talk to the guard on the left. On the dress-up doll of Rincewind, click on the talisman, mustache, birthmark, spell book, camel-flage, and magic sword. The odds will total to a million, so these are the items Rincewind needs to find to slay a dragon.

SPELL BOOK

Go to Unseen University. Go to the library and enter the stacks. Walk to the spot where the Sleazy Guy was. Look at the shelves in front of you and just a bit to the left to find a magic book. Walk to that spot. When you take the book, you will learn a spell. Go to the Archchancellor's office and get the hat off the desk. Look at the hat to see that it is filled with handkerchiefs and white rabbits. Go to the kitchen. Get the spatula off the rack.

CAMEL-FLAGE

Go to the Shades. Walk to the spot where the mason was. Look at the mural on the wall. Use the spatula to scrape the mural off the wall (getting a soot). Go to the thief's hovel. Use the muffled ladder to enter. Look at the bag of thief's tools. Open up the bag. Get the knife. Leave the hovel and get the ladder.

A MAGICAL SWORD

Go to the palace. Give the leeches to the guard on the left, who allows you to enter. Walk past the patrician and smoke device to reach the dungeon. Go past the cells. The fool and Chucky are tied up to a rack. If you talk to the fool, he will squirt water on you.

Talk to the torture master. Take a bone from the skeleton in the lower-right corner. Look at the bone (noting that there is very little meat on it). Use the crank (from the wishing well) on Chucky's rack. A sword that is out of tune pops out. The torture master will tell you that you need to see a Dwarf.

DWARVEN SMITH

Go to the city gates. Talk to Carrot (the tall guard who is a Dwarf): ask about the sword. He tells you that the Dwarves are in the mine and can tune a sword. Leave the city. Enter the mine in the mountain. Go past the first Dwarf you see. Give the second Dwarf the sword. Ask him if he can tune it. The Dwarf is more than willing, but Rincewind opens his big mouth and now has to get some elderberry wine first.

BOGEYMAN

Go to the Broken Drum. Talk to the barman. He cannot get you the wine because the cellar is filled with foxes. Go to the inn. Enter the room. Look at the door to see that there is something behind it. Try to close the door. You will speak to the Bogeyman: greet, sarcasm, question.

Use the screwdriver on the door to remove the hinges. Talk to the bogeyman again: anger. You take him to the bar to scare off the foxes and then return to the inn. Return to the Broken Drum. If you do not have an empty tankard, talk to the barman to get one. Go down to the cellar through the trapdoor. Talk to the Bogeyman. Fill the tankard with wine from the elderberry barrel (top row above mouse).

TUNED SWORD

Save the game. (Just for fun, if you go back to see the Dwarf and the tankard of wine is in the luggage, the luggage will drink it and get drunk. Restore the game unless you want to go back to the cellar to get some more wine.) Place the tankard of wine in Rincewind's inventory. Visit the Dwarf. Give him the tankard of wine, then give him the sword. He will tune it. It now goes "ting."

78

MUSTACHE

Go to the palace. Give the empty paper bag (from the bag of leeches) to the guard on the right, who allows you to enter. Go into the fool's dressing room. Take the brush from the right side of the bathtub.

If the pot is empty, go to the wishing well to fill it. Put the crank back on the well and use the crank to raise the bucket. Go to the inn. Enter the room. Go into the bathroom. Use the pot of water on the soap to make the water soapy.

IMPSTAMATIC

Go to the alchemists shop. Talk to the alchemist: sarcasm. He goes to the livery stables for some corn (to clear the bumper bar on the donkey cart). While he is gone, take the box, which is an Impstamatic. Look at it to see that an Imp is missing.

A CLEAN BUMPER

Go to the livery stables. Look at the bumper bar. Look at the bumper sticker (opens up Lady Rankin's dragon sanctuary). Look at number plate (it is covered with mud). Use the brush with the pot of soapy water. Then use the brush on the bumper bar to clean it. The bumper bar can now be read. It says "sore-ass."

ASSASSIN

Go to the alley on the area map. Place the knife in Rincewind's inventory. Eject up to the roof. Use the knife on the ladder between rooftops. Go through the window to get back down. The assassin, who is practicing on the rooftops, falls. Speak to him. You can now tell him the number of the donkey cart, which is sore-ass.

DONKEY'S TAIL

If you go to the livery stables, you will see that the donkey is gone. Go to the Square, where the donkey is in the stocks. Use the scissors to cut off a piece of the donkey's tail, which takes on the shape of a mustache.

BIRTHMARK

A LONG NET

Take an egg from the stall. The egg drops and breaks. Pick up the snake from the ground. Use the starch on the snake to straighten him. Then use the fertilizer on the snake.

Go to the dining room at Unseen University. Switch the snake staff with the staff of Windle Poons (getting a broom handle). Use the broom handle on the butterfly net to extend its reach.

SAILOR

Go to the toy shop. Take the bone (from palace dungeon) and rub some glue on it. Pick up stuffed dinosaur from sales bin. Go to the inn. Walk past the tree. Look at tattoo on the sailor. If you talk to the sailor, the dog does too. To shut him up, give the dog the bone. Talk to the sailor. He tells you he misses Polly. Talk to the innkeeper. Talk to the sailor, who gives you a whistle to find Polly.

POLLY

Go to the Edge of the World. Blow the whistle. Look at the parrot. Throw a firecracker at the parrot. Polly falls into the water. Use the butterfly net on Polly. In the process of retrieving Polly, you lose the whistle.

WHISTLE

Return Polly to the sailor. He is happy to have Polly back, but saddened that the whistle is missing. Return to the Edge of the World. Take the lamp, so the fork is exposed. Place the hat on the fork. Climb down the chain of handkerchiefs. Look at the glint (under the elephant farthest to the right), which is the whistle. Return the whistle to the sailor, who says to visit the barber shop if you want a tattoo.

TATTOO ARTIST

Go to the wishing well in the woods. Talk to the barber, who is waiting to hear from the milk-maid. Give him the appointment book that she autographed.

Go to the barber shop. Talk to the barber. Rincewind chickens out because of the potential pain. The barber offers him the alternate solution of getting a temporary transfer from his son: the lovable street starfish.

STARFISH

Go to the Square. Go to the alley behind the Dibbler. Use the knife to cut the rubber belt off the custard machine. Talk to the starfish. He holds up the transfer but will not give it to you.

GETTING THE BIRTHMARK

Go to the alley on the area map. Place the rubber belt in Rincewind's inventory. Eject up to the roof. Go to the tower. Tie the rubber belt to the tip of the flagpole. Rincewind will start to bungee jump right over starfish's head. He grabs the transfer, which will serve as the hero's birthmark. Climb back down.

MAGIC TALISMAN

IMP BAIT

Go to the Square. Talk to the old-timers: ask about Talisman. They tell you about the "Eye of Offler." Go to the broken drum. Look at green bottle behind barman. Order a drink. After finishing the drink, take the worm out of the glass. Tie some string around the worm. Look at pictures by braggart and barman. Note that they are all award-winning photos.

IMP FOR A CAMERA

Go to the palace dungeon. Walk to the hole by the cells. Use the worm on the hole to lure the rat out. Take the rat. Look at the rat then double-click on it to discover that it is really an Imp. Place the Imp in the Impstamatic.

LADY RAMKIN

Go to Lady Rankin's dragon sanctuary. Read the notice. Open gate and enter. Knock on the door. Talk to Lady Rankin (opens up path to left of house). Knock on door again. Before Lady Rankin comes to the door, go to the path that leads to the back of the house. (If she is by or in the cage, try again. This is a matter of timing.) Take the rosette off the cage. Take the leash hanging on the nail, then pull out the nail.

NANNY OGG

Go to the thief's hideout. Knock on the door. Brother Doorkeeper gives you a custard tart. Leave the city. Go to Nanny Ogg's house in the Dark Wood. Look at the potion in the purple bottle.

Talk to Nanny Ogg: greet, ask about potion. When she puckers up, use the custard tart on yourself so you can kiss her. She will now let you take the truth potion. Take the purple bottle.

AWARD-WINNING SHEEP

Pull the wool in front of Nanny Ogg to see that it leads to a sheep outside. Put the rosette on the sheep. Use the Impstamatic to take a picture of the sheep. Frame the picture by using the octopus picture with the sheep picture. Take the mallet from in the wood pile.

BRAGGART TELLS TRUTH

Go to the Broken Drum. Use nail (along with mallet) on beam next to braggart. Hang the sheep picture on the beam. Talk to the braggart to get two tankards of beer. Pour the truth serum into the beer. Give the beer to the braggart. After looking at all the award-winning pictures, he will eventually drink the laced beer and reveal the location of the Temple of Offler.

EYE OF OFFLER

Go to the gorge in the mountain. Talk to the monk on the bridge. You will fall into the river and climb out. Roll out the carpet onto the bridge to make the monk slip and fall. Enter the temple. Take the bandana off the hat stand (getting a blindfold). Tie the leash to the luggage. Put the blindfold on yourself. The luggage will lead you through the traps to the altar. Fill up your money pouch with sand. Switch the sand-filled pouch with the Eye of Offler (getting the talisman).

SQUARE GATHERING

After acquiring the six necessary items to become a hero (spellbook, camel-flage, sword, mustache, birthmark, and talisman), you will arrive at the Square. You will put on all the items of the hero. The dragon shows up. Rincewind recites a magic spell, but it fails.

82

ENDGAME

In the Square, take the key off of Lady Rankin. Talk to the strange man next to her. Go to the dragon sanctuary. Open up the door to the dragon cage with the key. Enter the cage. Walk over the molten pile (this may take a few tries). Take Mambo (M16).

Go to the city gates. Get fireworks out of crate. Light the firecracker with a match. Feed Mambo four firecrackers, or as many needed until he is smoking. Back at the Square, the M16 will keep missing the dragon. Throw the custard tart at the dragon. He falls in love with Mambo and they fly off together.

ORBS & STUFF

Object	See this Section for Location	Also See Section(s)
Pouch	Assignment	Eye of Offler
Broom	Dragon Lair Book	Dining Room: Staff, A Long Net
Banana	Dragon Lair Book	Opening L-Space
Staff	Dining Room: Staff	Meet a Dragon
Bag of fertilizer	University Grounds	A Long Net
Frog	University Grounds	Monk's Robe
Mirror	Palace	Alley: Dragon Breath
Dragon breath	Alley: Dragon Breath	Meet a Dragon
Pickpocket skill	Square	Street: Hair Roller
Worm	Square	Alley: Imp
Butterfly net	Square	Unseen University: Frying Pan, Monk's Robe, Edge of the World, A Long Net, Polly
String	Street: Hair Roller	Alley: Imp, Get the Brush, Fishmonger's Gold Belt, Imp Bait
Paper mache donkey	Street: Hair Roller	Location only
Picture of octopus	Street: Hair Roller	Award-Winning Sheep
Hair roller	Street: Hair Roller	Meet a Dragon
Frying pan	Unseen University: Frying Pan	Meet a Dragon
Treasure	Meet a Dragon	Opening L-Space
Screwdriver	Barn	Woods, Edge of the World, Bogeyman
Empty tankard	Broken Drum	Bogeyman, Tuned Sword
Matches	Broken Drum	City Gate, Apprentice Wizard, Get The Brush, Endgame
Empty glass	Broken Drum	Brother Pencilhead
Tankard of beer	Broken Drum	Braggart Tells Truth
Sheet	Inn	Gate Pass

84

Object	See this Section for Location	Also See Section(s)
Bubble bath	Inn	Get The Bell
Dragon summoning book	Brother Pencilhead	Theft of Book, Switching Books
Monk's robe	Monk's Robe	Brother Pencilhead
Hogfather doll	Monk's Robe	Chimney Sweep's Gold Brush
Pot	Monk's Robe	Dark Wood, Fishmonger's Gold Belt, Mustache
Gunpowder	City Gate	Get the Brush
Fireworks	City Gate	Endgame
Firecracker	City Gate	Polly, Endgame
Crank	Woods	A Magical Sword
Cockatrice feather	Mountain Pass	Thief's Gold Key
Cockatrice egg	Mountain Pass	Cathouse
Coconut	Edge Of The World	Cathouse
Drumstick	Fighting In The Drum	Apprentice Wizard
Box of starch	Apprentice Wizard	A Long Net
Corn flour	Apprentice Wizard	Cathouse
Prunes	Apprentice Wizard	Getting the Belt
Garbage can	Apprentice Wizard	Get the Bell
Inkblots (2)	Visit A Shrink	Fool's Gold Bell
Milk maid note	Play Matchmaker	Get the Tooth
Gold tooth	Get the Tooth	Return Golden Items
Gold brush	Get the Brush	Return Golden Items
Cap with gold bell	Get the Bell	Return Golden Items
Octopus	Fishmonger's Gold Belt	Award-Winning Sheep
Gold belt buckle	Getting the Belt	Return Golden Items
Sally's bloomers	Cathouse	Get the Trowel
Handshake skill	Get the Trowel	Location only
Bra	Get the Trowel	Thief's Gold Key
Golden trowel	Get the Trowel	Return Golden Items
Golden skeleton key	Thief's Gold Key	Return Golden Items

Object	See this Section for Location	Also See Section(s)
Carpet	Switching Books	Eye of Offler
Scissors	Casting Office	Donkey's Tail
Appointment book	Casting Office	Tattoo Artist
Paper bag	A Million to One	Mustache
Leeches	A Million to One	A Magical Sword
Magic book	Spell Book	Square Gathering
Magic hat	Spell Book	Whistle
Spatula	Spell Book	Camel-Flage
Soot	Camel-Flage	Square Gathering
Knife	Camel-Flage	Assassin, Starfish
Bone	A Magical Sword	Sailor
Sword	A Magical Sword	Dwarven Smith, Square Gathering
Brush	Mustache	A Clean Bumper
Impstamatic	Impstamatic	Imp for a Camera, Award-Winning Sheep
Mustache	Donkey's Tail	Square Gathering
Stuffed dinosaur	Sailor	Location only
Whistle	Sailor	Polly, Whistle
Parrot	Polly	Whistle
Rubber belt	Starfish	Getting the Birthmark
Worm	Imp Bait	Imp for a Camera
Transfer	Getting the Birthmark	Square Gathering
Rosette	Lady Ramkin	Award-Winning Sheep
Leash	Lady Ramkin	Eye of Offler
Nail	Lady Ramkin	Braggart Tells Truth
Custard tart	Nanny Ogg	Endgame
Truth potion	Nanny Ogg	Braggart Tells Truth
Mallet	Award-Winning Sheep	Braggart Tells Truth
Sheep picture	Award-Winning Sheep	Braggart Tells Truth
Eye of Offler	Eye of Offler	Square Gathering

DRAGON LORE

BY
PAUL SHAFFER

IN THIS FRENCH-DESIGNED QUEST, YOU PLAY THE PART OF WERNER VON WALLENROD, A YOUNG FARMER IN AN ANCIENT LAND SO VAST, THE GRAPHICS CONSUME A PAIR OF CDS. YOUR QUEST IS TO BECOME A DRAGON KNIGHT, WHICH REQUIRES THE VOTES OF THE OTHER MEMBERS OF THIS PRESTIGIOUS GROUP, WHOSE NUMBER IS RESTRICTED TO A DOZEN. YOU CAN SWAY THEIR DECISIONS BY RELYING MORE HEAVILY ON WISDOM OR COMBAT WHEN SOLVING PUZZLES AND DEALING WITH VARIOUS SITUATIONS AND PEOPLE. OR JUST FIND OUT WHO'S VOTING AGAINST YOU AND WHACK HIM! DYNAMIC BAR GRAPHS SHOW YOUR CURRENT RATING IN AREAS SUCH AS VIOLENCE AND WISDOM SO THAT YOU CAN CHECK YOUR PROGRESS. THE INTERFACE IS ALL POINT-AND-QUEST, AND THE HIGHLY STYLIZED GRAPHICS, OFTEN LUSH AND DETAILED, MAKE YOU WONDER WHY THE DESIGNERS WENT TO SO MUCH TROUBLE WHEN YOU CAN'T EVEN PICK UP MANY OF THESE ELABORATELY CRAFTED ITEMS. PUZZLES ARE PREDOMINANTLY OBJECT-ORIENTED AND GROW PROGRESSIVELY MORE DIFFICULT. COMBAT PLAYS AN IMPORTANT ROLE. THE QUEST IS NOT RIGIDLY LINEAR, SO YOU MAY PROCEED DOWN

TYPE
Animated Adventure

SYSTEM
IBM PC (Required: 486DX/33+, 4MB RAM, 8MB free hard disk space, 2MB free EMS, SVGA card with 1MB RAM, 100% Microsoft-compatible mouse, double-speed CD-ROM drive, DOS 5.0. Supports: Sound Blaster and compatibles, EMM386, MEMmaker, QEMM.)

COMPANY
Mindscape

ALTERNATE PATHS TO ONE OF SEVERAL CONCLUSIONS. ULTIMATELY, THOUGH, IT IS YOUR RATING BY THE OTHER DRAGON KNIGHTS THAT DETERMINES WHICH ENDING YOU'LL WITNESS. WHILE PUZZLES ARE ACCESSIBLE ENOUGH FOR NOVICES, DRAGON LORE OFFERS AN ATTRACTIVE AND INTRIGUING QUEST FOR EVEN THE MOST HARDENED ADVENTURER.

THE SOLUTION

GENERAL

The key to combat is to take a couple swings as the enemy gets close, then move on past them, turn, and whack again. Repeat until they're dead.

GETTING STARTED

Talk to uncle. Take sword from cart. Go behind house and get war hammer. Go through the fence and follow the right path. Go to pasture and take bone. Go to corral and use bone on creature (chases bone). Enter corral and get bowl.

Return home. Use bowl on uncle. Enter house. Take sulfur from table and rope from timber. Take staff, shield, leather armor, and flint. Wear armor and shield. Exit house and go down left path. Enter pen and use rope on cow. Return to pasture (cow walks away). Use rope on tree by cow (secures cow). Return home and talk to uncle (getting ring and whistle). Talk to uncle again (tells you to go to castle).

THE DUNGEON

Go past the cow pen and kill creature blocking the path. Continue on path to the stone circle. Walk to left skull outside circle and enter passage underneath. Take key on ground. Enter passage under right skull. Save.

Use key on gate. Kill skeleton with sword. Go down hall and push small square panel on wall (releases ball). Go to broken ball and examine closer. Take key. Go to end of hall and use key on gate. Enter gate and go through trap door on floor. Below level, use signet ring on next door. Enter. Try to take ruby on coffin (dragon talks to you). Talk to dragon (getting Open Door spell).

GETTING PAST THE CAVE

Return to surface. Continue on path. Talk to Chen-li. Follow path to cave. Enter cave. Use war hammer on left wall in cave (reveals spell book). Take book. Examine spell book (noting runes for Open Door spell). Put spell book in your hand. Go to closed door at end of tunnel. Select proper runes for Open Door spell and cast it (right mouse button) on locked door (opens).

SPIDER WEB

Follow path and go left at crossroads. Enter tavern. Talk to keepers until they give you ladle. Exit tavern and go straight into dragonfly cave. Kill dragonfly. Cross cave to full nectar pod in alcove. Use ladle on pod (filling it).

Return to tavern and use ladle on keepers (getting morning star, Fireball spell, and rope). Exit tavern and go to web that's blocking path. Use Fireball spell on spell book. Cast Fireball on web.

CROSSING RIVER

Continue on path. Talk to baron. Save. Kill guard. Examine guard (right mouse button) and take oar from his inventory. Use oar on barge. Move onto barge (crosses river).

MAN-EATING PLANT

Talk to Thane. Continue on path. At plant creature, pick up skull on right side of screen. Use skull on your rope (makes grappling hook). Use makeshift hook on tree to left of plant (swings across).

THE SWAMP

Talk to Tanathia. Cross bridge and pass through village. Talk to blue woman. Cross other bridge (arrive at fountain). Follow path to right (goes to swamp). Take apple. Give apple to creature. Pull lever (takes you to tree house). Talk to woman until she gives you a key. Pull lever on shack's balcony (to return to shore). Return to fountain.

PICKING FLOWERS

Continue on next path to right (garden). Pick blue flowers (you pass out and return to fountain). Talk to Altoos. Take remaining path to tree house. Enter tree house and talk to woman (gives you cog).

Go up stairs. Examine drawer in dresser and get piece of cloth. Return to fountain. Use cloth on fountain. Use cloth on self (acts as a mask). Return to garden and take blue and yellow flowers. Return to sprite village.

THE SPRITES

Use blue flowers on self (shrinks you). Kill scorpion. Enter mushroom. Climb stairs. Talk to sprite (getting Dispel Illusion spell). Use spell on spell book. Exit mushroom and seek only other mushroom you can enter. Climb stairs. Enter room and examine cupboard by bed. Take potion. Exit mushroom. Use potion on self (grow). Talk to blue lady. Return to garden.

This is no Love Boat.

● ● ● ● ● ● ● ● ●

HOUSE WITH GEARS

Continue on path through garden to house with gears. Use cog on wall where there's an empty peg. Face wall with outline of door. Cast Dispel Illusion on wall. Enter door. Go to torch room (see map) and take torch. You can use the key in the locked door, but don't take the gold chest in the room beyond.

Go to red room and take bucket. Go to water room and fill bucket with water on ceiling. Return to outside and put filled bucket on lever above gears (opens gate). Enter passage and take silver chest. Go to skeleton room and use chest on skeleton (getting Fujitomo's ring). Use torch on exit to north.

HURO'S GEM

Talk to Huro. Follow path to under bridge. Enter water and get swallowed by fish. Take diamond. Use yellow bush or your weapon on side of fish (spits you back out).

Continue on path on other side of water. Walk over edge of cliff. Enter waterfall. Give diamond to duckbill dragon. Get dragon's gem. Return to Huro and use gem on him (getting his vote).

GETTING PAST ROCK PILE

Return to base of cliff beside waterfall and cross lake by jumping across stepping stones. Continue on path to raised spiral platform. Climb circular path to top of mound. Enter circle of pillars (dragon arrives). Use signet ring on girl. Fight girl until she gives you her vote and pickaxe. At base of mound, face pile of boulders at end of path. Use pickaxe on boulders (clears them). Continue on path.

GETTING VASE

Talk to baron (gives you his axe). Use axe on tree and cross makeshift bridge. Talk to thieves. Continue on path between cliffs. Talk to Silvan and Alexander. Return to thieves and kill them. Search their inventory and take bag. Examine bag and take unbroken vase. Give vase to either Silvan or Alexander.

ENTERING CASTLE

Before entering castle, drop the cloth from your face, grappling hook, morning star, broken vase, and hammer. Use bag for extra storage. Follow path to castle. Go through foyer to bridge. Talk to dragon. Use your ring on dragon. Continue into castle.

GROUND FLOOR

Fight skeleton guard until he leaves you alone (or you kill him). Enter library. Examine dragon podium (getting list of ingredients for freeing soul). Go to chapel. Take holy water sprinkler from altar. Go to rear room of chapel. Take Bible from podium and candles from cabinet. Return to chapel and use candles on candelabra (getting piece of seal).

Go to bottle room. Break bottle with sword. Examine bottle and get stone eye. Take dragon effigy above bed. Go to bedroom. Move iron post at fireplace. Go to chess room and take key from lowered chandelier. Use key on chest in corner (getting second seal piece). Use second seal piece on first. Go down stairs and take sword at bottom. Return to ground floor and go to crest room. Use sword on crest that has only one sword. Get last seal piece. Use last seal piece on seal. Go back down stairs and use whole seal on door. Enter.

FIRST FLOOR DOWN

Go to key room and climb ladder. Get broken key. Go to bunk with skeleton. Touch skeleton. Get stone eye from his skull. Go to banquet hall and get crowbar. Go to kitchen and get ladle. Go to second bunk room and move blanket on bunk, getting third stone eye. Go to forge and enter rear room, taking sack of coal.

Return to forge and use coal on forge. Use flint on sulfur (making flame). Use flame on coals in forge. Move bellows to increase fire. Use broken key on fire. Use broken key on anvil. Take hacksaw from floor and hammer from table. Use hammer on key. Use ladle on water trough. Use full ladle on reforged key (cooling it and taking it). Exit room to common area and use reforged key on double doors. Go through doors and down to next level.

SECOND FLOOR DOWN

Go to armory. Get fourth stone eye from weapons case on wall. Use one stone eye for each eye socket on the two skulls on the wall (removes protective shield from the four display cases). Take crossbow, shield, straight sword, and key. Return to common area on this floor. Take skeleton from middle cell. Use skeleton, Bible, dragon effigy, and holy water in that order on skeleton in first cell. Touch skeleton (disappears). Get key on floor.

Go to treasury and get map of castle. Go to torture room and get pliers. Go to pool room. Climb stairs and enter pool. Get crank. Exit pool by the way you entered and return to common area. Save.

TO THE DRAGON'S LAIR

There are three ways to reach the dragon's lair. (1) Use the crank on the dragon fountain in the corner (draining the pool). Then return to pool and enter it. Go through door and follow cliff path to lair. (2) You can use the crowbar on the door in the pool room, which will flood this level but gives you access to the cliffside path. (3) You can use the key from the skeleton to open the door at the bottom of the stairway into the foreroom of the lair. Choose any of the paths, but go to the lair.

GETTING THE EGG

Talk to dragon (getting magic powder and sleeping powder). Return to ground floor. Go to castle foyer. Look up. Use sleeping powder on dragon. Take molten sphere. Return to castle stairway. Use magic powder on glass barrier (removing it). Go up.

Go to south hallway (you can see the dragon nest through the window). Use hacksaw on mesh. Enter nest. Step out onto balcony. Use molten sphere on nest (drops it). Use pliers on molten sphere (cracks it open). Touch sphere (getting hatched dragon egg). Return to dragon's lair.

SECRET CHAMBER

Talk to dragon twice (give dragon any item except spell book or ring to be taken to the secret chamber). Take Teleport spell from wall and use it on your spell book. Examine case on floor and take vial of Diakanov's blood. Cast Teleport spell. Teleport to Level 1.

FIRST LEVEL UP

Go to bedroom and take metal ball from dresser. Go to room with stairs leading up and take second ball from planter in corner. Go to toy room and take third ball on floor. Go to second bedroom and take fourth ball from shelf. Go to scroll room and examine two scrolls on table (giving you hints on the falcon statue).

Go to falcon room. Take twig from fireplace. Use flint on sulfur (making flame). Use flame on twig. Use flaming twig on falcon (holes appear in floor). Put four balls in holes in floor beneath falcon. Touch falcon (case opens). Take talon. Go to stairs and go up. Use key from armory on door.

SECOND LEVEL UP

Go to room with bowls. Examine bowl with hole in bottom. Use talon on hole (getting key). Go up stairs. Use key on door.

THIRD LEVEL UP

Enter wizard's room. Talk to wizard. Put crossbow, shield, and straight sword from armory on floor. Talk to wizard. Cross room to stairs and go up. Climb ladder. Take ruby. Teleport to stone circle (actually takes you to crypt under the circle). Use ruby on coffin. Open coffin. Take dragon armor and dragon shield. Wear them. Teleport back to wizard room. Talk to wizard.

ENDGAME

Give vial of blood to wizard, who gives you the chalice. Use vial on circle (Diakanov appears). Examine chalice. Take amulet from chalice. Use amulet on Diakanov (getting dragon effigy and crystal ball). Pick up sword, shield, and crossbow. Teleport to dragon's lair. Enter dragon foreroom and take lance and saddle. Return to lair and use saddle on dragon. Use sword on dragon effigy (breaking it). Click on dragon for endgame.

ORBS & STUFF

Object	See this Section for Location	Also See Section(s)
Sword	Getting Started	Location only
War hammer	Getting Started	Location only
Bone	Getting Started	Location only
Bowl	Getting Started	Location only
Sulfur	Getting Started	First Floor Down, First Level Up
Rope	Getting Started	Location only
Staff	Getting Started	Location only
Leather armor	Getting Started	Location only
Flint	Getting Started	First Floor Down, First Level Up
Ring	Getting Started	The Dungeon, Getting Past Rock Pile
Whistle	Getting Started	Location only
Key	The Dungeon	Location only
Open Door spell	The Dungeon	Getting Past the Cave
Spell book	Getting Past the Cave	Location only
Ladle	Spider Web	Location only
Morning star	Spider Web	Location only
Fireball spell	Spider Web	Location only
Rope	Spider Web	Location only
Oar	Crossing River	Location only
Skull	Man-Eating Plant	Location only
Apple	The Swamp	Location only
Key	The Swamp	Location only
Blue flowers	Picking Flowers	Location only
Cog	Picking Flowers	House with Gears
Piece of cloth	Picking Flowers	Location only
Blue and yellow flowers	Picking Flowers	Location only
Dispel Illusion spell	The Sprites	House with Gears

Object	See this Section for Location	Also See Section(s)
Potion	The Sprites	Location only
Key	House with Gears	Location only
Bucket	House with Gears	Location only
Silver chest	House with Gears	Location only
Fujimoto's ring	House with Gears	Location only
Diamond	Huro's Gem	Location only
Dragon's gem	Huro's Gem	Location only
Pickaxe	Getting Past Rock Pile	Location only
Baron's axe	Getting Vase	Location only
Theives' bag	Getting Vase	Location only
Vase	Getting Vase	Location only
Bible	Ground Floor	Second Floor Down
Candles	Ground Floor	Location only
Piece of seal	Ground Floor	Location only
First stone eye	Ground Floor	Second Floor Down
Dragon effigy	Ground Floor	Second Floor Down, Endgame
Key	Ground Floor	Location only
Second piece of seal	Ground Floor	Location only
Sword	Ground Floor	Location only
Last seal piece	Ground Floor	Location only
Broken key	First Floor Down	Location only
Second stone eye	First Floor Down	Second Floor Down
Crowbar	First Floor Down	To the Dragon's Lair
Third stone eye	First Floor Down	Second Floor Down
Hacksaw	First Floor Down	Getting the Egg
Fourth stone eye	Second Floor Down	Location only
Crossbow	Second Floor Down	Third Level Up, Endgame
Shield	Second Floor Down	Third Level Up, Endgame
Straight sword	Second Floor Down	Third Level Up, Endgame
Skeleton	Second Floor Down	Location only
Key	Second Floor Down	To the Dragon's Lair

Object	See this Section for Location	Also See Section(s)
Map of castle	Second Floor Down	Location only
Pliers	Second Floor Down	Getting the Egg
Crank	Second Floor Down	To the Dragon's Lair
Magic powder	Getting the Egg	Location only
Sleeping powder	Getting the Egg	Location only
Molten sphere	Getting the Egg	Location only
Teleport spell	Secret Chamber	Location only
Vial of blood	Secret Chamber	Endgame
Metal ball	First Level Up	Location only
Second ball	First Level Up	Location only
Third ball	First Level Up	Location only
Fourth ball	First Level Up	Location only
Twig	First Level Up	Location only
Talon	First Level Up	Second Level Up
Ruby	Third Level Up	Location only
Dragon armor	Third Level Up	Location only
Dragon shield	Third Level Up	Location only
Chalice	Endgame	Location only
Amulet	Endgame	Location only
Crystal ball	Endgame	Location only
Lance	Endgame	Location only
Saddle	Endgame	Location only

97

DREAMWEB

BY
FRED PHILIPP &
CLANCY SHAFFER

TYPE
*Animated
Adventure*

SYSTEM
*IBM PC
(Required:
386/25+, 3MB
EMS, VGA,
Microsoft
mouse compat-
ible. MSCDEX
and double-
speed CD-ROM
drive required
for CD ver-
sion. Supports:
Roland, Adlib,
Sound Blaster,
and compati-
bles.)*

COMPANY
*Empire
Software*

HE WEB, A EUPHEMISM FOR DREAMWEB, IS THE PLACE YOU TRAVEL TO IN YOUR DREAMS. DEEP BELOW (OR BESIDE, OR SOMEWHERE IN THE GENERAL NEIGHBORHOOD OF) YOUR SUBCONSCIOUS, IT IS THE SETTING FOR THIS CYBERPUNK THRILLER, WHICH PITS THE FORCES OF EVIL AGAINST THE KEEPERS OF THE WEB. AND IN DREAMWEB, YOU ARE ONE OF THESE KEEPERS. CHARGED WITH THE GOAL OF RESTORING BALANCE TO THE WEB BY WIPING OUT THOSE PESKY FORCES OF EVIL GUYS WHO JUST SEIZED THE NODES OF POWER, YOU TRAVEL FIRST CLASS TO DISTANT LOCATIONS BY CLICKING ON A "TRAVEL SCREEN" WHERE NEW DESTINATIONS APPEAR AFTER YOU SPEAK WITH THE RIGHT PEOPLE. YOU'LL SPEND A LOT OF TIME TALKING WITH PEOPLE AND LOOKING FOR CLUES, AS IN A SHERLOCK HOMES ADVEN- TURE. ONE QUEST-FRIENDLY FEATURE, A MAGNIFYING GLASS, IS VITAL FOR EXAMINING SOME OF THE TINY BUT IMPORTANT OBJECTS. COMBAT CONSISTS OF SIMPLY USING THE CORRECT WEAPON AT THE RIGHT TIME, ALTHOUGH IT DOESN'T HURT TO BE QUICK ON THE DRAW. THE EGA-QUALITY GRAPHICS ARE SIMPLE, DEPICTING

YOUR CHARACTER IN AN AERIAL VIEW AS HE MOVES FROM ROOM TO ROOM, AND THE SOUND EFFECTS ARE LESS EFFECTIVE THAN HOPED FOR. THE CONCLUSION IS DREARY, AND THE TIME SPENT CONVERSING WITH DREAMWEB'S CAST WOULD PROBABLY BE BETTER SPENT TALKING WITH REAL PEOPLE.

THE SOLUTION

EDEN'S APARTMENT

Pick up wallet from desk. Go to kitchen, open microwave, get key. Use controls to open elevator, enter, and use controls to descend to garage. Pick up the screwdriver and wrench. Exit building to bring up travel screen. Select Ryan's apartment.

RYAN'S APARTMENT

Enter building and walk to door on left. Use keypad next to door and enter 5106. Go to bedroom and get knife off of the bed and red network cartridge marked "Important" from floor. Open network interface by window and insert cartridge.

THE NETWORK

Look at network monitor to access it. When initialized, type the following sequence (you must use the Enter key after each entry: list, logon ryan, blackdragon, list cartridge, read private mail. (This will provide you with Eden's and Louis' door numbers.) Exit apartment, use elevator, and go to travel screen to go to Louis' apartment.

LOUIS' APARTMENT

At this point, you will be unavoidably mugged. Enter building and enter 5238 on keypad to open door. Talk to Louis. Open cupboard near monitor, get red pool hall card, and examine it. Look in shower and get pair of running shoes. Use each shoe to put them on. Exit building and go to travel screen. Select Sparky's Bar.

SPARKY'S BAR

Pick up empty beer bottle on ground, enter bar. Sit on stool in front of Sparky. Talk to Sparky. From your inventory, open your wallet and remove your credit card. Use the card on the card reader on the bar. Look at card to see current balance. Talk to the man sitting next to you. Exit bar and travel to the pool hall.

THE POOL HALL

Use elevator and talk to man behind bar. Go left as far as you can and enter 5222 on keypad next to door. In the office, use your credit card on card reader on desk. Take the gun from the desk. Exit building and travel to the hotel.

THE HOTEL

Talk to receptionist and use card on card reader. Take tiny key from desk in front of receptionist. Go to elevator and use pad on wall. Enter elevator and use your key on control. Exit elevator and go left to fire box. Open box and get axe.

PENTHOUSE

Return to elevator. Use knife on control box. Examine the exposed wire and cut it with knife. Look at elevator handle and use it. Climb to top of lift. Save game.

COMBAT

Do all of the following quickly. Use axe on penthouse door. In combat, open your inventory and use axe. After guard misfires ("click" is displayed), use your gun. Enter room to left. Walk to bed, then look at gun in inventory, then use gun to shoot man on bed. This will take you to the Dreamweb.

DREAMWEB

Talk to the monk. Go down and right to first door at bottom of room. Use the door to exit. Go to plinth in next room and use the key from the microwave. You will find yourself in an alley. Exit alley and travel to Ryan's apartment.

RYAN'S APARTMENT

Access the network monitor. After logging on, enter the following sequence: list newsnet, readtvspecial, exit. Exit building and travel to the TV studio.

TV STUDIO

Walk to right, then down to sign on ground. Go left to barrier and use gun to shoot guard. Examine controls behind window by barrier, then use controls. Walk left and into TV studio. Remove brochure from counter to find passcard under brochure.

THE GENERAL

Go left to storeroom and use passcard to enter. Look at fuse box, then use screwdriver to remove fuse. Exit room and go all the way right. Climb ladder up. Go to winch control, examine it, and open it. Remove the blown fuse and insert the new fuse. Use the winch control. You will return to the Dreamweb.

DREAMWEB AGAIN

Speak to the keeper of the Web, the monk. He will inform you that Sartain is now the leader. Go to bottom of location and get the crystal. Go down and left to first door. Open door and use key on plinth. You will find yourself outside Sparky's. Travel to Eden's apartment.

EDEN'S APARTMENT

Enter 2865 on keypad by door to enter building. Use elevator to go up to apartment. Eden will be in the bathroom. Go to bedroom and look at organizer on bed. Keep hitting the "N" key until Sartain Industries address appears. Exit building and travel to Sartain Industries.

SARTAIN INDUSTRIES

Enter 7833 to get inside. Use your gun on computer. Go left and enter elevator. Use controls. Once in combat, open your inventory, examine the crystal, then use the crystal. Walk down hall and examine the briefcase. Open it and take the papers from inside. Examining the papers will give you the location of Underwood and the Chapel.

ESCAPE

Go to the right and up the stairs to the roof. Go left onto the helipad. Use the gun to explode the helicopter. Dream 3 kicks in here. Go down to door on right, use door. Use key on plinth to exit Dreamweb. You will find yourself in a parking lot.

PARKING LOT

Locate van with tarpaulin in it and get wire cutters. Exit to north and travel to Chapel's house.

Dreamweb — or should that be Nightmare Web?

CHAPEL'S HOUSE

Use the wall on the left to climb over it. Walk south to the wreckage. Look around to find a picture of Chapel that will give you information about the Church. You will also find a cartridge. Examining the cartridge will give you the names Beckett/Septimus.

BECKETT/SEPTIMUS

Exit Chapel's house and travel back to your apartment. Insert cartridge and access monitor. Log on as Beckett. Password is Septimus. Read contents of cartridge, especially brief. Exit apartment and travel to Underwood's boathouse.

UNDERWOOD'S BOATHOUSE

Look at pipe in water and use it with empty beer bottle. Pick up railing. Walk right to boathouse. Look at metal plate at top left. Use metal plate to reveal an electrical junction box. Use railing with metal plate to open box. Pour water into the box using the water-filled beer bottle.

UNDERWOOD

Climb up to balcony on right by using hole in balcony. Use hole in window to enter boathouse. Talk to Underwood. Shoot Underwood with gun. This will take you back to Dreamweb. Talk to keeper. Go south, south, west. Open door on left. Use key on plinth to return you to the beach. Travel to the ruined church.

THE RUINED CHURCH

Use the wire cutters on the chain on the gate. Enter church. Pick up the hand near remains. Walk to altar and remove cloth and candlesticks. Examine altar and use it. Look at hole in altar and use hand on hole. Move altar forward to further expose hole. Climb down into hole to arrive at the tomb.

THE TOMB

Open tomb by pulling back lid. Inside you will find two crystals, a dagger, and a rock. Take all. In jar by tomb is another crystal. Take it. Place all three crystals in the stone design on the floor to open exit from tomb.

THE STATUE

In the first section of the corridor, your way southwest is blocked by a grate. At the top of the corridor is a statue. Use the statue. Rotate the symbols to match the symbol on your Dreamweb key (this can be found in the manual). The symbol looks like a circle with T-like extensions at 12, 1, 6, and 11 o'clock. The grate will now be open.

THE TROLLEY

Enter grate and go up to the trolley. Check all areas for rocks. There are eight of them. Put rocks in trolley. Use trolley to push it off the screen to the south. Go south to a door, which is now broken open. Walk down, west, then up stairs. You will find a priest changing from human form into a monster. You will see his remains, then there will be a hole where the priest was.

Enter the hole, which goes to the outside.

SUBWAY

Get down onto tracks by using ramp at top of screen. Walk forward until you see a hole in left tunnel wall. Enter this to find the Madman's Lair. The Madman will appear and try to kill you. Quickly exit room back to tracks to lure Madman underneath a passing subway.

ABRUPT END

You will be whisked back into the Dreamweb. The keeper will speak to you. You will wake up in the real world to the sound of sirens. You will then be shot by waiting police.

ORBS & STUFF

Object	See this Section for Location	Also See Section(s)
Wallet	Eden's Apartment	Sparky's Bar
Key	Eden's Apartment	Location only
Screwdriver	Eden's Apartment	The General
Wrench	Eden's Apartment	Location only
Knife	Ryan's Apartment	Penthouse
Red network cartridge	Ryan's Apartment	Location only
Red pool hall card	Louis' Apartment	Location only
Running shoes	Louis' Apartment	Location only
Beer bottle	Sparky's Bar	Underwood's Boathouse
Gun	The Pool Hall	Combat
Tiny key	The Hotel	Location only
Axe	The Hotel	Combat
Fuse	The General	Location only
Crystal	Dreamweb Again	Sartain Industries
Wire cutters	Parking Lot	Location only
Beckett cartridge	Chapel's House	Beckett/Septimus
Hand	The Ruined Church	Location only
Three crystals	The Tomb	Location only
Dagger	The Tomb	Location only
Rock	The Tomb	Location only

ECSTATICA

BY
PAUL SHAFFER
& MARK PEARSON

TYPE
Animated Adventure

SYSTEM
IBM PC (Required: 486SX/25+ CD-ROM drive, 4MB RAM, 10MB free hard disk space, 256-color VGA monitor, mouse. Supports: Sound Blaster, AWE32, Gravis Ultrasound/ Max, Roland LAPC-1 and SCCI, General MIDI.)

COMPANY
Psygnosis Inc.

IN ECSTATICA, YOU PLAY A MALE OR FEMALE EXPLORER TRAVELING THROUGH A RANGE OF MYSTERIOUS MOUNTAINS. THE FIRST VILLAGE YOU STUMBLE ACROSS TURNS OUT TO BE CURSED, AND YOU ARE STUCK IN THIS MEDIEVAL TOWN UNTIL THE CURSE IS LIFTED. SOME COMBAT IS INVOLVED IN YOUR QUEST TO END THE CURSE, WHICH SPAWNED A HORDE OF BIZARRE, TWISTED CREATURES. THE OBJECT-ORIENTED PUZZLES DON'T REQUIRE COLLECTING A LOT OF OBJECTS, ALTHOUGH YOU WILL HAVE TO BACKTRACK OCCASIONALLY BECAUSE YOUR INVENTORY IS LIMITED TO TWO ITEMS. THE GRAPHICS AND ANIMATIONS HAVE A MORE NATURAL APPEARANCE THAN IN MANY 3-D GAMES, THANKS TO THE USE OF ELLIPSOIDS RATHER THAN POLYGONS. THE MOVEMENT OF CREATURES, FOR EXAMPLE, SEEMS MORE REALISTIC THAN IN THE ALONE IN THE DARK SERIES. ECSTATICA'S PLOT WILL DELIGHT ADVENTURERS WEARY OF OVERLY LINEAR QUESTS, FOR THERE ARE VARIOUS AVENUES ALONG WHICH YOU MAY COMPLETE THIS QUEST. EXPECT THE UNEXPECTED, AND DON'T BE DISCOURAGED WHEN YOU'RE TURNED INTO A FROG OR FERRET — THESE ARE BUT A FEW OF ECSTATICA'S SURPRISING EVENTS THAT LEAD TO A THOROUGHLY ENJOYABLE CONCLUSION.

THE SOLUTION

GENERAL

If you approach the sorcerer before being knighted, he will turn you into a frog. But you can do a lot of exploring in frog form; you can also fight, but you cannot pick up objects. As a frog, you can enter the catacombs via a path along the cliffs (if you try to enter as a human, you'll get skewered). To return to human form, enter the house by the lake (where the magic broom is located). The fat girl there will kiss you and turn you back into a human.

COMBAT

Punch, dodge, punch, dodge. Repeat until your enemy is dead. Werewolves appear to be undefeatable, but they will avoid you once they're hurt. If a creature proves too powerful for you, run away! If creatures get in too close in combat, you won't have a chance, so restore a saved game.

FINDING A WEAPON

Go to shack to the west, just beyond the chapel in the southeast part of the town. Get knife from table. You must kill the table in the process. Go to the girl's house. Kill the bear on the ground floor. Go up. Read diary. Get teddy bear. Go up. Examine Spell Book (sprout + stick figure + flower = animal).

GIRL IN THE BARN

While holding the teddy bear, go to the barn. The girl will take you to the chapel. Follow her down to the dungeons. Wait for her to open the door for you. Descend and slay skeletons. Go down one more flight (your character will become frightened and run back up).

MAKING A SPELL

Go to the shop north of the tavern. Help kill the small dragon that's attacking the man. Take the mace that was dropped, leaving your knife behind in the process. Walk close to the man (you'll pick him up and take him to rear room of tavern).

Take sprout from shelf (expect a werewolf attack). Take sprout to upper room of girl's house and put sprout in mixing bowl (this happens automatically as you near it). Go to the chapel and get the stick figure that is beneath the hanging priest. Add stick figure to mixture in upper room of girl's house. Go to path that leads to the monastery. Take flower in path. Add flower to mixing bowl, which turns you into a weasel-type creature.

GETTING KNIGHTED

Return to the chapel catacombs. Enter the small opening where the girl previously went. To get past the trolls, use attack mode and run past them. After getting through the tunnel, you will return to normal size. Climb stairs at end of the tunnel. Walk to the old man, who will drop his sword. Get sword. Go to lake. Stand on stone by lake's edge (you'll throw the sword and be knighted by the Lady of the Lake).

SORCERER'S TOWER

Go to the castle. (If you go through the gate entrance, tiptoe through or you'll be crushed.) Don't kill the sorcerer's assistant or the sorcerer. Follow the sorcerer to his study and listen to his tale. When he's done, go through the study to the tower. Go up the tower stairs and examine the Spell Book there (relic + Magic Book = stone circle).

GETTING THE RELIC

Go to the chapel and get the Holy Book. Go to the monastery entrance. Enter monastery (listening to monk's tale). Go to library and walk to each section of the shelf the reading monk is standing at (you'll find three different books, and the monk will explain each one to you). Go to the chapel and take relic (fight or avoid the angry monks). Return to library and escape through hole in floor. Follow passage back to stairs and exit into town.

GETTING THE MAGIC BOOK

Return to the sorcerer's tower. Go downstairs. Run past the statue and then attack from behind (he'll go stiff when he's dead). Go north (fight invisible warriors). Go north. Go around stairway via the path that goes past the dragon (avoiding his fire). Where the stairs meet again, tiptoe along a diagonal path across the intersection or you'll be pierced by spears.

At the base of the stairs, enter the chamber in the middle of the room (run past the spikes). Open both caskets by walking next to them (you must slay the skeleton in one and enter the second after it opens — it will wrap you in armor). Use the "Up" key to reopen the coffin and get out. Go under the stairs you just came down to find another stairway down. Descend.

In the pool room, you will find another flight of stairs going down even further, so descend again. Cross the room (fighting the mirror image of yourself) and walk up to the skeleton king. When he's done talking, go back up to the casket level.

Walk to the grate on the east side of chamber (from a perspective with the stairs to the south). The grate will rise. Drop items before entering this passage. Go east (you'll be caught and imprisoned). In cell, move left and right arms (attack keys) until you free your arms from the shackles. Walk to cell door (guard will enter). Keep swinging until he drops. Exit room to cell entrance, killing the second guard the same way. Back in the main chamber, retrieve all items. Cross the casket chamber and enter the western passage. Get Magic Book from stand (you should now have both relic and book). Try to go south through doorway (the dragon stops you).

Novel 3D graphics give Ecstatica a unique look and feel.

●●●●●●●●●

ENDGAME

Go to the stone circle above ground and stand in the middle of the circle (you get hit by lightning). Return to the Magic Book room in the tower and go south through doorway (the dragon is gone). Go down the long stairs.

At the bottom of the stairs, follow the floating ball to the table and sit in chair. Wait for conversation to end (demon asks you for relic). Save. Just for fun, go ahead and drop the relic at this point. Restore. Get up from table and run away (demon changes into dragon). Use relic on dragon in attack mode (shoots fireballs) until dragon dies.

ORBS & STUFF

Object	See this Section for Location	Also See Section(s)
Knife	Finding a Weapon	Location only
Teddy bear	Finding a Weapon	Girl in the Barn
Mace	Making a Spell	Location only
Sprout	Making a Spell	Finding a Weapon
Stick figure	Making a Spell	Finding a Weapon
Flower	Making a Spell	Finding a Weapon
Sword	Getting Knighted	Location only
Spell Books	Finding a Weapon, Sorcerer's Tower	Locations only
Holy Book	Getting the Relic	Location only
Relic	Getting the Relic	Getting the Magic Book, Endgame
Dragon	Getting the Magic Book	Endgame
Caskets	Getting the Magic Book	Location only
Magic Book	Getting the Magic Book	Sorcerer's Tower, Endgame

HELL: A CYBERPUNK THRILLER

BY
CLANCY SHAFFER

TYPE
Animated Adventure

SYSTEM
IBM PC (Required: 386SX/33, CD-ROM drive, VGA with 1MB, 20MB free hard disk space. Recommended: 486SX/33+, double-speed CD-ROM drive. Supports: VESA, Roland, Adlib, Sound Blaster, Sound Master II, Pro Audio.)

COMPANY
Take 2 Interactive Software

A HUNDRED YEARS IN THE FUTURE, THE HAND OF GOD PARTY HAS TAKEN OVER THE U.S.A. THESE RELIGIOUS ZEALOTS SAY THEY'VE GOT A HOT LINE TO GOD BUT ARE ACTUALLY AGENTS OF THE DEVIL, FOR WHOM THE GATES OF HELL HAVE BEEN OPENED AND WHOSE DEMONS NOW TREAD THE STREETS OF WASHINGTON WITH CLOVEN FEET. YES, HELL IS CLEARLY A ONE-OF-A-KIND STORY. YOU, AS EITHER RACHEL OR GIDEON, ARE WORKING FOR AN AGENCY GUARDING AGAINST THE ILLEGAL USE OF CYBERSPACE. SET UP TO BE ASSASSINATED BY THE DEMONS WHO HAVE SEIZED CONTROL OF THE GOVERNMENT, YOU PROCEED TO PENETRATE THEIR DEVILISH SCHEME. TO GET TO THE BOTTOM OF THIS SINISTER PLOT, YOU'LL ULTIMATELY TRAVEL TO HELL AND FIGHT THE DEMONS ON THEIR OWN GROUND. GRAPHICALLY, THIS IS A TOP-FLIGHT QUEST, AND DENNIS HOPPER AND GRACE JONES PLAY THE HEAVIES. AN INNOVATIVE FEATURE LETS YOU REPLAY EVERY PIECE OF DIGITIZED DIALOGUE FROM THE BEGINNING OF THE GAME SO THAT YOU CAN LOOK FOR CLUES YOU MISSED THE

FIRST TIME. SOME OF THE DOZENS OF PUZZLES ARE EXTREMELY DIFFICULT, AND SEVERAL QUALIFY AS DOWNRIGHT HELLACIOUS. THE SVGA BACKGROUNDS, SOUND EFFECTS, AND MUSIC TURN HELL INTO A HEAVENLY DELIGHT FOR ADVENTURE GAMERS, AND THE BIZARRE BLEND OF CYBERSPACE AND THE OCCULT MAKE HELL ONE OF THE YEAR'S TOP QUESTS.

THE SOLUTION

DANTE

Converse with Dante to learn about Captain Frank Jersey, Aldous Xenon, and Nick Cannon. Take the key he offers. Click on the Washington, D.C. map. In the northwest section, find Georgetown. Click on Georgetown, then click on Captain Frank Jersey's kitchen. Any location you are able to go to will flash when the cursor is on it.

CAPTAIN JERSEY

Get the scrub list on the table and examine it. Jersey tells you about Mr. Beautiful, who is at the Interface at Foggy Bottom, as well as Swivel O'Leary and Jean St. Mouchoir, who has an office in Sin Central (a.k.a. the Transgressor Complex in Federal Triangle).

THE INTERFACE

Talk to Karl, who is behind the door. Note the writing on the door. The password is Sesame. Karl will open up the manhole, which is the entrance to the bar. Recruit Cynna Stone, an explosives expert. To recruit Sophia Bene, a crack forger, promise to help her daughter Chastity. Also recruit Scub Stevens, an expert rigger.

Talk to Kween Chaos about seeing Mr. Beautiful to get the password Condemn. In discussion, a demon hunter named Dean Sterling was brought up as a possible contact (you cannot see him yet). You'll learn you need to contact Jean St. Mouchoir (at Sin Central), Nick Cannon (at the Voice of God radio station), Dr. Clean (at McPherson Square), and Pap Pap and Anna Mae (at the Comix Shop).

Talk to Mindrunner for a clue that Swivel O'Leary is speaking in Latin. Later you will need to translate and combine the Latin clue you learn here with other Latin phrases. Professor Coronary will help you translate.

MR. BEAUTIFUL

Go through the door on the west side to Mr. Beautiful's hangout. Talk to the demon Abonides. Say Condemn to call up Mr. Beautiful. Agree to do a job for him in Hell. Save.

ARMS STORAGE

After a long ride through tunnels and shafts, speak with Pike and Tantlinger. Then search for and take all weapons, including the nerve gas, Hell Blade, and the Buddy Weapon. Save. Go to a door on the east or right side of the screen, enter, and talk to General Mangini. Click on Sanguinarius, who will attack you. It may take up to three tries to shoot him and knock him into a hole. The General is released, and you find yourself back with Mr. Beautiful. Talk to him. Go through the east door back into the bar. Right-click on Sophia's plate to use her forgery skill to obtain a fourth-level pass. Use the D.C. map to reach Aldous Xenon in Chinatown/Gallery Place.

ALDOUS XENON

Xenon will agree to help only if you agree to plant a homing device on the Imperator Limousine. This requires going to the Pentagon garage and giving the fourth-level pass to a guard, then entering the garage. When you find a mechanic working on a limousine, talk to her. Look for her lunchbox. Use it to discover her name: Jo Boyle.

Return to the garage office and ask the dispatcher to page Jo Boyle. Leave at once, return to the garage, and plant the device on the limousine. At the same time, take the mechanic's creeper.

Return to Aldous Xenon, who will send you to see Senator Burr at the British embassy in Dupont Circle in the north part of the map. Talk to Vivid, Charles, and Derek in the waiting room. Enter the door to the left. The Senator will give you an assignment to find the rest of a team she sent to scrub the Imperator.

COMIX SHOP

Go to Pap Pap John's Comix Shop in Chinatown/Gallery Place. Talk to Pap Pap and Anna Mae, who will tell you of the problem they are having with their computer. Use the next-to-last letter of each word on her computer screen to get the password Imperator, which gets rid of the Locust virus.

115

GANG ALLEY

Go to the Gang Alley in McPherson Square and visit with both the Deadly 7 and the Cleans. Talk to Christopher Modesta, leader of the Cleans. Then talk to Chastity Bene, Dolph Van Ittey (leader of the Deadly 7, who is standing up), and Blood McGrath. Enter the Deadly 7's building and talk with Electric Sex and others.

There is a separate room called the Rec Room. The door is to the south. Speak with Languo and Barbara. They want you to get them a still (make it from the copper tubing, two beakers, a tin cup, and kerosene, which you will find later).

Now go to the Clean's building and talk with Gracie Lovell, who outlines the problem she is having with Drip and Electric Sex. She also tells you about her problem with Temperance. Talk to Drip. Before visiting Temperance, go to Pap Pap's place and pick up a disk of Erotix Comics, then return to the Cleans and talk with Temperance. Give the disk to her, and she'll promise not to bug Drip and Electric Sex. Then speak with Phrackie (he is sitting down), who will jack some money out of Dick Covett's (one of the Deadly 7s) bank account, and you'll have $101,000. Talk to Gracie and tell her the good news that Temperance will ease off.

DOLPH'S COMPUTER

Go across the alley to Electric Sex and give her the key to Dante's place. She will tell you Dolph Van Ittey's password (Bloodnet), which you will need. Go to the Rec Room and then use the door behind Languo to get to Dolph's room. Use the computer and Dolph's password. Read all the files. Tell Christopher Modesta that Dolph is a spy for the Hand. Talk to Chastity and then to Dolph.

CYBERSHOP

See Dr. Clean at the Cybershop in McPherson Square. She wants to sell a picklock graft for $6,000. Buy it. Pick up the roll of copper tubing.

ST. MOUCHOIR'S OFFICE

Go to the Transgressions Entrance in the Federal Triangle. Use the picklock on the door. To enter the computer, pick up the pencil and rub it on the pad beside the computer to get the password God's Justice.

To open other sections of the computer, type Hell Pit when the computer displays llt, type Jeremy Verdi for remyrdi, type Foggy Bottom for ggyttom, and type Dean Sterling for anerling. (You can't open the rest of the computer until you get the last Latin phrase and have it translated by the professor, you'll then obtain the password Gesticulate.)

On the computer, read all about Demons, Dean Sterling, Citizens Freedom Front, Solene Solux, Gideon Eshanti, Rachel Braque, and Act/Deck. Then read about the Fringe Operation, the Government Operations File, Night of the Titans, Massimo Eddie, and the ARC. (You cant read the rest of the files until you get the passwords Triangle and Gesticulate. The professor will help translate the Latin phrases to help you get the passwords.)

You will wind up with new addresses: the Gnostics office in Capitol South, Psionic League Headquarters in Georgetown, Dean Sterling's office in Farragut North, Eschatology, Inc. in Watergate, and New Corporeal Biologics in Federal Center S.W. You also pick up more names: Randal Singh CFF, Townson Ellers (a former British ambassador), Brett Carew, and Eddy Commerce. Listen to all of St. Mouchoir's notes.

Go and talk to Dean Sterling. He asks you to check back in a few days, because he is seeking the address of Asmodeus, a major demon.

THE PENTAGON

Go to the Pentagon and General Mangini's office. To enter, talk to the receptionist. Click on Mangini's name, then on the moving stairs. Talk to Sanguinarius. You'll be sent to Hell again, this time to Mr. Beautiful's Hell Pit. Listen to the gangsters, then fill the mug from the table by using it on the acid vat. Pick up the steel lid. Use the Hell Blade on Krystal Getty and free her.

117

OSCAR DREXLER

Go to Nick Cannon at the Voice of God radio station and learn about the Phreakbeats at Judiciary Square. Go there, talk with them, and learn that they want to kill Oscar Drexler at Union Station. Go to Drexler. Talk to him and then go to Dante's apartment.

ASMODEUS

Return to Dean Sterling, who has now located Asmodeus in Union Station and wants you to plant an explosive device that will flatten Asmodeus and Hell's Steel Mill. Agree to go and apply for a job at Asmodeus' porn studio. Talk to Grinda (the girl on the desk), Rutterkind (a small demon), then Asmodeus. Agree to join Asmodeus at his headquarters in Hell. Go to his studio. Talk to Asmodeus. After he falls over, you'll be back in his storefront office with Dean Sterling. Asmodeus will be dead (he is an android). Take the Psychopomp.

DEEP THROAT

Return to Dante for aid. Dante tells you of a message he received from Deep Throat somewhere in the Pentagon. Use the Psychopomp and give it the address Garage. Deep Throat will tell you the truth about Hell.

DAT

Go to Mr. Beautiful's office in the Interface. Return to see that Beautiful's head has been blown off (he is also an android). The gangsters you first saw on your second trip to Hell want their buddies freed. One gangster will give you a DAT for help. Go to the jukebox and enter E3, E8, and D9. The pentagram will go down, disclosing the gangster hostages. Talk to the gangsters. Get the DAT and take the cue stick. Talk to Mr. Beautiful's head but do not recruit him. Take the DAT tape to Nick Cannon, who will translate it for you. You'll hear the message, "God is dead."

ESCHATOLOGY, INC.

Go to Eschatology, Inc. at Watergate. Talk to Christy Abraxis and Hercule Rue Des Couers, who will tell you about Resurrection Unlimited.

RESURRECTION UNLIMITED

You will find Dr. Zip Honey. Go right through this room into the hallway, where you'll find a lot of laser beams. Save the game. If a beam touches you, you'll be taken to Solene Solux. Examine the pattern of the beams as each time you restore there is a variation to the pattern. Use the mechanic's creeper to slide under the laser beam field; move quickly to avoid contact with randomly moving beams. (This will be easier if you adjust your mouse to a very slow speed and use the Turbo button on your computer to slow down the animation.) In the morgue, examine the cryogenic coffin containing Schonbrun. You will obtain the phrase, "Vocbulum est acquirer Ominus Venire ab Genitor."

If you fail to get past the beams, you can bypass this scene by simply not doing it. You can use the password Gesticulate to unlock the Night of Re-Entombment file after visiting Professor Coronary.

MAKING A STILL

Go to New Corporeal Biologics to find out about Hennelly, then talk to Ben Brewer. Get the Electro Magnet and a small and large beaker required for the still. Use Scubs jury-rigging skill to make the still by right-clicking on the copper tubing. Return to Gang Alley. Enter the Deadly 7's clubhouse. Talk to Laura Prophet. Agree to her offer to learn about the Solux Stakes. Go to the Rec Room. Give Languo the still, then talk to him.

COLLECTOR APARTMENT

Go to Gnostics office in Capitol South, talk to Professor Coronary, and learn about the Collector Apartment at L'Enfant Plaza. Use the Electro Magnet on the Blaze Parchment. Return to Gnostics office and give Coronary the parchment. Go through the main office to the computer room. Talk to Daniel. Get the list of readings off O'Connor's desk. Return to the main room. Coronary translates the Latin quotations and comes up with Gate, Slate, Late, and Date, and he gets the word Gesticulate.

NIGHT OF THE RE-ENTOMBMENT

Go to Transgressions Entrance in the Federal Triangle. Use the picklock to enter. Use the computer and type God's Justice. Open up the Government Operations subject. Open the Night of the Re-Entombment file by using the password Jeremy Verdi. Then use the second password: Gesticulate. A re-entombment memo will appear in your inventory. Read it and you will find out that you and Rachel are brainwashed commandos.

SENATOR BURR AND KATERINA

Return to the Resistance at the British embassy with this news. Go through the door on the right to the Resistance Headquarters computer room. Talk to Senator Burr and find out that the assassination attempt on Solux failed. You also tell her that Hell is a virtual environment. Talk to Katerina Goertz. She gives you information about some of the hostages. Use the Psychopomp on yourself and the address that Katerina gave you: Charon.

HELL'S DENTIST OFFICE

You will arrive at the river Styx in Hell. Tell Charon you wish to visit the dentist's office. Here you will encounter Malebolge and Alfred Czeschew. Talk to them. Use nerve gas on the dentist tanks of NO_2. Take the drill, NO_2 cartridge, and the gauze bucket. Click on it and Charon will arrive. Go to the Wall of Flame Pit.

THE WALL OF FLAME PIT

Talk to Prudence Alala. Place yourself next to the steam hole. Put the steel lid over the steam hole and stand on it, then release Alala. Return to Charon and go to Hell's Zoo.

HELL'S ZOO

Talk to Eddy Commerce and Machalus. Take jar of food, empty food jar, staff, floating beasts, gauze bucket of Styx water, and zoo keys. Place the food on Machalus, then use the keys from the wall to release Rachentieren. Return to Charon and go to the Rat Room.

RAT ROOM

Talk to Dingo Tucker. Use the NO_2 cartridge on the rat cage to free Tucker. Return to Charon and go to the Ice Fields.

ICE FIELDS

Conklin Danforth is here. Use the floating beasts on yourself to float across to Danforth and use the gauze bucket of Styx water to free him from the block of ice. Return to Charon and go to the Music Room.

MUSIC ROOM

Talk to Alice Trenton. Press the stones coded with the notes B, E, C, A, and G (the silent letters in the verse) to release Alice. Return to Charon and click on D.C. map to return to the British embassy.

OFFICE OF COMPUTERIZED RECORDS

Return to Dante to find out that Deep Throat wants to talk to you again. Use the Psychopomp on yourself and type garage. Talk to Deep Throat. Go to the Bureau of Records in the Federal Triangle. Speak with Mr. Calcutta and Miss Stinson to get a clue to Massimo Eddie's password in St. Mouchoir's computer. Go to Transgressions Entrance in the Federal Triangle. Use the picklock to enter. Use the computer and type God's Justice. Open up the Government Operations subject. Read the Massimo Eddie file there and use the password Triangle to unlock the credentials under Massimo Eddie. Use Sophia Bene's forgery skills on the credentials template. Return to the Bureau and give the credentials to Mr. Calcutta. This provides you with the location of Massimo Eddie. He warns you to be prepared for many security measures at Lee Mansion.

PSIONIC LEAGUE

Go to the Psionic League Headquarters in Georgetown. Talk to Katlin Connor and Batch Hachardo. Go through the door to the Psionic League think tank. Talk to Suzy Toast and Columbus Spatola about the Menials.

THE MENIALS

Go to the Menials' Headquarters in Capitol South and talk to Mick to learn the location of the Asylum. Take two bottles of beer from the refrigerator. Right-click to use Scub's dream powder to drug one of the bottles of beer. Place the drugged beer back in the refrigerator. Shortly thereafter, Mick will drink the drugged bottle and pass out. Get the collector unit. Return to the Psionic League think tank. Give the collector unit to Suzy, then talk to her. She makes the collector unit into a cyberfry.

THE ASYLUM

Go to the Asylum Waiting Area in Foggy Bottom. Talk to Phyllis Dancing-Till-Daybreak and Clap to learn the location of Splits Magnola, who is at Fitzgerald's Speakeasy at L'Enfant Plaza. Enter the Asylum Dormitory. Talk to Chet, Rita, Hump, and Cora. Use the collector unit with cyberfry on Chet.

FITZGERALD'S

Go to Fitzgerald's Speakeasy at L'Enfant Plaza. Talk to the two bar patrons by the entrance. Talk to bartender and then talk to Milwaukee Jack, who is sitting across from the bartender (not at the bar). If you did not get an extra bottle of beer from the Menials, take a bottle from the bar. Talk to Splits Magnola, who is sitting at the bar. He will ask you to create a diversion. Do this by throwing a bottle of beer at the video screen. Talk to Splits again. Recruit him and drop Sophia. Return to the Psionic think tank. Talk to Suzy, then talk to Columbus.

GUARD ROOM OF LEE'S MANSION

Go to Lee Mansion in Arlington. Have Splits Magnola uses his psionic skills to get the two guards to kill each other. Go through the guard room and into the Cyberpanther Room. Use the cue stick on the lamp so you can push the lamp off the table without getting to close to the cyberpanther. The lamp will shatter and electrify the metal panther. (You may also use explosives to drop the lamp into the water.) This leaves the door to Massimo Eddie's room unguarded. Enter the room. Talk to Massimo Eddie, who will give you two notes: a note with algorithms on it and a note with a color chart. Examine both notes. Look at the color chart on the wall. Return to the Resistance Headquarters Room and get the list of other people to be freed. Use the Psychopomp on yourself and type Charon.

ABYSS

Give Charon the address: Abyss. Talk to Jeremy Verdi and Gack. Use the Hell Blade on the beer mug filled with acid. Give the mug of acid to Gack to free Jeremy. Get the tar bucket. Return to Charon and go to the Belly of the Beast.

BELLY OF THE BEAST

Talk to Thelma Bay Chesapeake. Pick up the human femur and sharpen it with a stone, then use it on the belly of the beast to free Thelma.

JEREMY VERDI

Return to the Resistance Headquarters Room. Jeremy Verdi will be there. Talk to him. Give him Massimo's computer algorithm note and talk to him again. Verdi says he will start a computer program to kill Satan.

SOLUX STAKES

Go to the Racetracks Results Room in Judiciary Square. Talk to Cy Barnes (the man crouching) who tells you that the races are fixed. Go into the racetrack betting parlor. Talk to Carol Metz. Look at the betting machine. Only bet when it says "Solux Stakes Trifecta Races." Bet all your money. The key to winning is to look at the color chart you got from Massimo Eddie and pick out the set of primary, secondary, and tertiary colors. To win, pick the horse with silks (symbols) of two primary colors; to place, use secondary colors; and to show, use tertiary colors. If there is more than one possible match, pick the symbols with the worst odds. After winning, go back into the other room. Talk to the two men to receive congratulations.

THOMAS MEACULP

Go see Dante, who tells you he has had contact with Deep Throat. Use the Psychopomp on yourself and type Garage. Talk to Deep Throat, who tells you that his real name is Thomas Meaculp and he is at the Pentagon. To save Deep Throat, go to the Pentagon reception area. Have the receptionist direct you to Thomas Meaculp's office. Use his computer. Enter the following: Shudder is to fear as crying is to sorrow. Fan is to air conditioner as keyboard is to decking unit. Suicide is to death as embezzlement is to wealth. Charon is to perdition as freeways are to Los Angeles.

SAVING DEEP THROAT

You will learn that Deep Throat is in the jail at the Pentagon Building. Return to the receptionist and have her direct you to the Pentagon jail. When you arrive there, only Steel Jack and Deep Throat are present. Have Cynna Stone use her EMP grenade to kill Steel Jack. Then use her microexplosives to blow open the door to his cell. Go to the British embassy. Talk to Derek. You will meet Deep Throat at Resistance Headquarters shortly afterwards. Talk to

Jeremy about the plot to crash the Hell program. In talking to the senator, Deep Throat mentions the address of the Miraculum Sepulcrum as a way to send information.

FINAL HOSTAGES

Talk to Katerina to get the names of the rest of the hostages. If this does not occur, just revisit past locations and check back with Katerina until she does give you the names. Use the Psychopomp on yourself and type Charon to return to Hell. Go to Charon and give him the address Hell's Steel Mill.

HELL'S STEEL MILL

Talk to Brett Carew. To release Brett, put the staff into the gears in front of him. Have Charon take you to Hell's Desert.

HELL'S DESERT

Talk to Walker Dash. To release Walker, use the drill on the bucket around his head. Now move on to the high school.

HELL'S HIGH SCHOOL

Talk to Randal Singh and Maledictum. To free Randal, answer Maledictum's quiz with Des Moines, Iowa; Little Rock, Arkansas; Helena, Montana. (If this fails, answer Baton Rouge, Louisiana, instead of Helena.) Now you must defeat the Demon Lords Beelzebub, Mephisto, and Belial. Have Charon take you to Beelzebub's Throne Room.

BEELZEBUB

Use the tar from the tar bucket on the floor. Talk to Beelzebub. After winning the battle, get Beelzebub's wing from the floor. Then go to Mephisto's Throne Room.

MEPHISTO

If you have not previously dipped the Hell Blade in the mug of acid, go back to Mr. Beautiful's Hell Pit to refill the mug. Talk to Mephisto and a fight will start. Once you make contact with the Blade, the process of killing him begins. Then get his hand from the floor. Go to Belial's Throne Room.

BELIAL

Use the explosive charge on the flashing circle near the bridge, which makes it easy to kill Belial. Get the medal from the floor. Return to Resistance Headquarters to be sure that Jeremy has finished the computer program to kill Satan. Then have Charon take you to Cerberus. (You must have the wing, hand, and medal, or Cerberus will tear you to pieces.)

CERBERUS

With three parts from the Demon Lords, you may pass Cerberus and enter the gates to Satan's lair. After the demon leaves, take the paintbrush. Use the paintbrush on Satan's door to write "God is dead" on the skulls, then enter the gates to Satan's Throne Room.

SATAN

Townson Ellers and Satan are here. The difficult part of defeating Satan has already been completed by Jeremy. Go through the conversation with Satan, then kill him. Return to Resistance Headquarters. One of you must make a very difficult run to get data for the crash bug. Use the Psychopomp and type "spawner." After the run, get the Hell crash bug from Jeremy and go to the Pentagon delivery room.

PENTAGON DELIVERY ROOM

Jute is present. Pick up a pneumatic tube. Put Cynna Stone's gas bomb in the delivery tube and give it to Jute. Also give him the address of the Miraculum Sepulcrum: Pentagon. Return to reception area and go to the chapel.

CHAPEL

Pick up the taper that is on the floor. The list of readings contains the correct order to light the candles. Light the candles left to right in the following order: 6, 3, 1, 4, 7, 2, 5, 10, 8, 9. Do this by using the taper, then put the bony pointing finger against the candle and right-click with your mouse.

When Solene Solux enters, dispose of her. Enter the computer room there and use the Hell crash bug on the Hell mainframe.

ORBS & STUFF

Object	See this Section for Location	Also See Section(s)
Dante key	Dante	Dolph's Computer
Scrub list	Captain Jersey	Location only
Hell Blade	Arms Storage	The Pentagon, Abyss, Mephisto
Buddy Weapon	Arms Storage	Location only
Nerve gas	Arms Storage	Hell's Dentist Office
Lunchbox	Aldous Xenon	Location only
Homing device	Aldous Xenon	Location only
Mechanic's creeper	Aldous Xenon	Resurrection Unlimited
Disk of Erotix Comics	Gang Alley	Location only
Picklock graft	Cybershop	St. Mouchoir's Office, Night of the Re-Entombment, Office of Computerized Records
Copper tubing	Cybershop	Making a Still
Pencil	St. Mouchoir's Office	Location only
Mug	The Pentagon	Abyss
Steel lid	The Pentagon	The Wall of Flame Pit
Explosive device	Asmodeus	Location only
Psychopomp	Asmodeus	Deep Throat, Senator Burr and Katerina, Office of Computerized Records, Guard Room of Lee's Mansion, Thomas Meaculp, Final Hostages, Satan
Beautiful's head	DAT	Location only
DAT	DAT	Location only
Cue stick	DAT	Guard Room of Lee's Mansion
Electro Magnet	Making a Still	Collector Apartment
Small beaker	Making a Still	Gang Alley
Large beaker	Making a Still	Gang Alley

Object	See this Section for Location	Also See Section(s)
Blaze Parchment	Collector Apartment	Location only
List of readings	Collector Apartment	Chapel
Re-Entombment memo	Night of the Re-Entombment	Location only
Drill	Hell's Dentist Office	Hell's Desert
NO$_2$ cartridge	Hell's Dentist Office	Rat Room
Gauze bucket	Hell's Dentist Office	Location only
Jar of food	Hell's Zoo	Location only
Empty food jar	Hell's Zoo	Location only
Staff	Hell's Zoo	Hell's Steel Mill
Floating beasts	Hell's Zoo	Ice Fields
Bucket of Styx water	Hell's Zoo	Ice Fields
Zoo keys	Hell's Zoo	Location only
Two bottles of beer	The Menials	Fitzgerald's
Collector Unit (Cyberfry)	The Menials	The Asylum
Algorithm note	Guard Room of Lee's Mansion	Jeremy Verdi
Color chart note	Guard Room of Lee's Mansion	Solux Stakes
Tar bucket	Abyss	Beelzebub
Human femur	Belly of the Beast	Location only
Beelzebub's wing	Beelzebub	Cerberus
Mephisto's hand	Mephisto	Cerberus
Medal	Belial	Cerberus
Paintbrush	Cerberus	Location only
Pneumatic tube	Pentagon Delivery Room	Location only
Taper	Chapel	Location only
Hell crash bug	Satan	Chapel

JORUNE: ALIEN LOGIC

BY
**CLANCY SHAFFER
& FRED PHILIPP**

ALIEN LOGIC IS ONE OF THOSE RARE GAMES THAT TRULY EARNS THE ADJECTIVE "UNIQUE." BY BLENDING ELEMENTS OF ADVENTURE, ROLE-PLAYING, ACTION, AND SCIENCE-FICTION GAMING, IT REFUSES TO FIT INTO ANY OF THESE GENRES. THE STORY UNFOLDS ON THE WORLD OF JORUNE, WHERE NEARLY ALL THE ORIGINAL INHABITANTS, THE SHANTA, WERE WIPED OUT BY SETTLERS FROM EARTH 3,500 YEARS AGO. THE RED SHANTA STILL LURK IN HIDDEN PLACES, EMERGING TO KIDNAP THE OCCASIONAL HUMAN. YOU PLAY THE ROLE OF A HUMAN DETERMINED TO RESCUE YOUR KIDNAPPED FRIENDS AND EXACT REVENGE. YOUR CHARACTER MOVES THROUGH JUNGLE AND DESERT DEPICTED IN A PROFILE VIEW. AN AUTOMAP SIMPLIFIES KEEPING YOUR BEARINGS, AND YOU CAN TRAVEL QUICKLY BY CLICKING ON IT. COMBAT IS EXTENSIVE, AS IS THE USE OF ISHO, OR ENERGY TO CREATE SPELLS, WHICH THE SHANTA CALL DYSHA. OBJECT-ORIENTED PUZZLES ARE DOWNPLAYED IN FAVOR OF INTERACTING WITH VARIOUS CHARACTERS

TYPE
Science Fiction Hybrid

SYSTEM
*IBM PC
(Required:
386/33+, 4MB
RAM, 1MB
SVGA card,
DOS 5.0+,
10MB free hard
disk space,
CD-ROM
drive.
Recommended:
486, uncom-
pressed hard
drive.
Supports: key-
board, Gravis
native mode,
Sound Blaster
family, Pro
Audio family,
and 100% com-
patibles.)*

COMPANY
*Strategic
Simulations,
Inc.*

AND FULFILLING MINI-QUESTS FOR THEM, WHICH IS THE PRIMARY GOAL. DEVELOPING SUFFICIENT EXPERIENCE AND DYSHA TO DEFEAT SOME OF JORUNE'S FIERCEST FIENDS AND OPENING ENOUGH "WARPS" TO WIN RECOGNITION AS MASTER OF THE WARP SKIES SERVE AS SECONDARY GOALS. MUSIC AND SOUND EFFECTS ARE SPARSE IN ALIEN LOGIC, BUT THE SVGA GRAPHICS ARE SHARP AND COLORFUL. PUZZLE-HUNGRY ADVENTURERS MAY FIND THIS TREK LESS THAN SUBSTANTIAL, BUT WILL ENJOY IT IF SEEKING AN ORIGINAL GAMING EXPERIENCE WITH A LOT OF COMBAT.

THE SOLUTION

GENERAL

To discover hidden rooms and the like, use Tra-Sense by holding the Shift key and right-clicking anywhere in the display area. In the Weave World, capture the four small displays: Regenerate, Morph, Walk on Lava, and Fall. If you have a Reco Respirator, you can travel short distances underwater. Before visiting the Temple at coordinates 179,167 in the center Doben-Al, be sure you have Walk on Lava. Coordinates for locations of major people and places are provided at the end of this solution. You may click on the automap to reach many locations (new warps in particular).

ARDOTH

Before visiting the island of Delsha, you must be trained and acquire very heavy weapons. Also explore ancient cities and acquire ancient knowledge. Solrough advises you go Ardoth and talk to Sha-Intha, the Shanta that rescued you. You will meet and talk to others in this city by going along streets and stopping at each red dot, which are the only places accessible to you. The following shows approximate locations of key people and locations in Ardoth.

1. Daclish, who will give you the cork cutter.

2. Kearning Bay and Sarella, a girl who will take you to the Weave World. The first time she takes you for free; thereafter, it costs six gimlinks and you will need your own weave crystals (about 100 per trip). Here you learn all the dysha shields and defenses.

3. A merchant who will sell you limilates of healing, Isho invisibility, protection from Scragger, poison blood, and more.

4. A merchant who will sell you bio corks, cut or raw, which are used to create Reco Diggers, Reco Surgeons, and Reco Miners (you may also buy them complete).

5. Crystal Palace, where you can buy most crystals. Shop carefully, for prices vary.

6. Merchant who sells Bio-Tech.

7. Merchant who buys artifacts and sells warp crystals. Don't sell him artifacts, but do buy his Crundorra. After collecting a few artifacts, you can sell them for twice his price at a location given later and reached via warp or ferry (see the Dobre section).

8. Tavern.

9. Ferry.

10. Training in Beasts (free).

11. Reptile who will buy dead Beagre and Scraggers from you, a good source of revenue.

12. Healing place.

13. Asailia, a friend from long ago, who will force Daclish to give you the cutter.

EXPLORING ARDOTH

Go to Daclish, who will send you packing. Visit Asailia, who will listen to your story and send you back to Daclish. After he refuses, return to the girl, then revisit Daclish. He will give you a cork cutter that you can use to generate Diggers and other Recos.

Buy as many healing limilates as you can afford. Also buy a Scragger limilate, which makes you unpalatable to the Scragger. Go to the Kearning Bay, and Sarella will take you to the Weave World for free (this time). She will also supply the weave crystals. Go there and stay as long as possible to acquire as many different dyshas as possible. After this, you must acquire your own weave crystals by digging or buying from the merchant. It takes about 300 crystals to gain full knowledge.

RUINS

Go north of the city, enter each circle shown, and use the power orb to kill all Beagre. To distinguish between them and Scragger, use the Scragger limilate. These bodies may be sold to the Reptile at "11" in the city. Near coordinates 212,169 are the ruins of the dwelling of Ana Ci-Eshta. Save before entering and after each discovery.

Put power crystals in all outlets. Examine the two skeletons and get 17 gimlinks from one and more items from the other. When you encounter an evid, kill it with power orbs. They and other creatures of the ruins leave a power crystal behind after they die. If you have obtained a power regenerator from the Weave World, use this in front of a power source for healing.

Use power orbs at the green door to break it down. Enter and get the Sarceen, which will teach you reco knowledge. After all the power sources are filled, you will be able to descend on the last of three lifts. If you have not activated this lift, jump down and use the Shantic cle-eshta to open a warp into the Warp World from an island in north Kodre.

SOLROUGH

Before investigating the new warp, go back to Solrough Gomo at the Mountain and attempt to see him. You will be stopped by Herrid Go-Atego, so leave the area and go to the group north of Herrid. They will give you a pass to see Solrough. Tell Solrough about your problems.

Solrough has discovered the Crossroads of the Warp World (see coordinates below). You must follow each quest from the Crossroads in order to thwart an invasion of Mountain Crown. There are many cle-eshtas at the Crossroads.

But before setting out to accomplish these tasks, go to the new warp in north Kodre. There are several sites here containing limilates and weave, rate, and power crystals. The ruin at 158,116 has two wells. Go to the north well first and use a power crystal to turn on the power. Slay the Beagres. There is also a red locked door.

At the south well, you will find an artifact and a key. Take the key to the north well and open the locked door, then return to the south well. You will find three more artifacts, a key, and two crystals. Blast open the green door and an evid emerges. Slay it and get the power crystal.

On the third elevator, go to the bottom and get the loot. On the floor above is a Shanta guardian and a cle-eshta. You cannot defeat him, so leave and come back after you are able to use all four of your offensive slots. This is vital, for you must eventually slay the Shanta. The cle-eshta he guards is the only one that will transport you into the Doben-Al area to meet with the Caluntra Shantas.

CROSSROADS

You may meet a girl called Cassy at 214,88 and learn that all the warp crystals have been removed from the cle-eshtas. Go to the bottom of the wells and activate all power lifts. Kill the red crawly things for crystals.

Return to Solrough Gomo and tell him about the crystals. He wants you to speak to the commander of the invasion army to ascertain their strength.

You will discover five circles at 204,184. Enter the center circle and you will see a light-blue marker in the west center. Go there and you will again meet Cassy and learn about the warp crystals. Slightly to her left is the general of the army. Talk to him, leave as soon as possible, and go to 218,183. Use this cle-eshta to reach Solrough.

He will now want eight warp crystals. Go back to the camp and you will see eight mineral-bearing circles around it. Enter the first carefully and click to locate the dolomite holding the crystal; try to get there when the Clesh are elsewhere. You will have about 10 battles. Slay the fiends quickly, then jump on the first ledge and click on the dolomite. Get the crystal and leave. When you have all eight, go back to Solrough, who says that when you master 25 warps you will be considered the Master of the Warp Skies.

SETTING UP THE WARPS

Go back to the crossroads of the warps, reinstall the warp crystals and activate them to create the extra warps in the Warp World. There are four crystal holders here, two on the top level and two on the bottom. Holder "A" will be on the west side of level one and create a warp in Voligire. Holder "B" is on the east side and creates a warp at 217,246 on one of the Sillipus Islands. Holder "C" is on the west side of the bottom level and creates a warp at 281,141 in Lundere. Holder "D" is on the east side of the bottom level and creates a warp at 68,83 on an island off the extreme west coast of the land of Temauntro.

PREPARING FOR WAR

Return to the city and sell everything possible. Buy weave crystals and improve your fighting ability. You will find crystals almost anywhere, but the ice and desert areas are the best. You also need warp crystals for the empty cle-eshtas. Get about 300 weave crystals to reach the Weave World. You need about 12 rate crystals to increase your Isho replacement speed, and you should get two Shanta Grud Crundorras to fill the two offensive slots in your attack dysha.

Go to Shemas-Abey at 158,116 in the east Trinnu Jungle. At the north well, you will find a locked red door and some Beagre. Install power crystals. In the south well you will find artifacts. Go through the door, then left. On level three, you will find three artifacts, a key, and some crystals. Blast open the green door on the second level. Slay the evid and get the power crystal. Go through this door to the red door, grab the key, and open the door. Then move west where you will find a Shanta guardian. You cannot defeat him now, so return later. Copy any writings by Ana Ci-Eshta, which reveal the locations of more temples.

WELL, WELL; WELL

There is a temple at 208,210. Enter the well to the southwest, descend, and jump over the holes in the floor. Go east and power up the station; an Isho ride is nearby. Then get out and go to the other well. Jump into holes in the floor, go east, kill red crawlers, and get power crystals. Activate the power source. (If you can regenerate yourself, do so at each station.) Then use Isho ride, which takes you to a different section of the wells. To enter the next room, use the key you found on the red door earlier. In the room is a cle-eshta that opens a warp in the Temauntro area. Save the game, then use Grud Warp to get out of here.

Go to other well, save the game, jump in, and land on level two. Get the artifacts, jump down to the next level, and bypass the Shanta guard to reach the bottom floor. Activate the power source and the lift will start to run. Save, then use lift to reach the level with the Shanta guard and a green door on it. If you don't have the strength to slay him now, return later.

Just north of these wells, at 219,183, is a warp generator that creates a warp just north of Ardoth. You can also obtain a lot of limilates here.

BEHIND THE GREEN DOORS

At 224,168, go to the north well. On the first level, you will find an artifact. Go east through the door and activate the power cell. (Regenerate if you can.) This a place called Ma-Eshira. When you find the green door, blow it open and go through to a dead lift. Activate the power holder and the lift will work. Save the game.

Return to the first lift and go down three floors, where you'll find one eye and one evid to kill (if you use limilate Invisible, the evid cannot see you). Both will drop power crystals. Blast open the green door, go east, and get three rate crystals. Go east through another door to a functioning lift. Use power crystal and get artifact. Going west, you will find a Shantic sarceen of Holding. Go up the other lift to red door so that you'll know where to use the corresponding key later.

DOBRE

Once you've opened a warp in Dobre, go there. From the warp, walk east to a bay, then north along the bay. Click on the building at the top to meet Bronth. This scholar will pay more for your artifacts than the broker in town. (The warp station at 219,182 will not add additional warps.)

Go to the Lundere warp at 281,141. You have been informed of a Shantic site at 312,122. On the way there, you will pass a cle-eshta at 297,145, which adds a warp at 111,189 on an island south of Temauntro.

When you arrive at 312,122, enter the Isho ride. Go down three floors where you'll find three dead bodies. Use the Taro and locate a key on this floor. Go through the room until you slay three evids. One will drop a red key. Power up all stations, then go up three floors in the elevator to get lots of loot. Use the cle-eshta to add a new warp in Gilthaw at 359,46.

Go to the new warp and look around. At 371,36, you will find additional ruins. Enter and search. Save. If you jump in any hole, use Walk on Lava and Tra to find the exit from the first lava room. After checking everything, use the Grud to get out.

SAVAGE CRYSTAL

At 184,162 is a Shantic site in an oasis. One of the Caluntra Shantas will tell you they need to recover the savage crystal and replace it in the volcano. This powers the Isho rides, the only way to reach the underground rooms, which you must visit.

The savage crystal is in the Drail Jungle. First, go back to Solrough Goma for advice on how to handle the Caluntra Shantas, visit Sha-Intha for information about the savage crystal, then visit Benned Go Wago (in the tavern at Ardoth) to learn how to reach the Drail Jungles. At 187,161, talk to Callentha, then go to the oasis southwest of him.

DRAIL

After speaking with Benned Go Wago, you can warp to Drail in north Burdoth. At 134,223, just southeast of the warp, is a Trarch village. Speak to the king about seeing the savage crystal. If he won't grant permission, it's because you have not told him that you would taste better if you were spit-roasted. The wood is wet, so he will allow you to leave and return later when the wood is dried. When you return, the wood will still be wet, so tell him you don't mind waiting. This gives you a chance to buddy up to the king, who will see you as a friend rather than as food.

Keep revisiting the king and asking about Drail and the savage crystal, which he will refer to as a magic stick. Return to Sha-Intha for more suggestions. The king will also give you a key to access the magic stick. You will learn that the magic stick is a Crundorra of Inner Peace, which is at 223,168 in the Shantic site east of Ardoth.

UNDERGROUND

After you get the savage crystal, return to the oasis in Doben-Al and place it in the volcano to gain access to the Shantic sites nearby. Go to the Isho ride at 186,164. It takes you down four levels to a small room with a power source. Exit to the right, where you will find two evids. You must have Walk on Lava or Morph to cross the large lava pit. There is also an Isho ride that will take you up three floors, where you'll meet an evid. In the center of the room is a cle-eshta that transports you to the center of the Voligire Region.

At the Shantic site (184,159), scanning will reveal two Isho rides. Enter the left one to reach an underground Shantic site. Exit to the right to a lava pit and power source, which requires a power crystal. From here, there are two exits: a hole in the ceiling and a passage-way to the right. To exit via hole, you must have Morph. You can fly to the level above and get a power crystal, a rate crystal, a power source, and Grud. If you use Walk on Lava, you can exit to the right and find two red orbs, a power crystal, and a cle-eshta. Slay the orbs and take all.

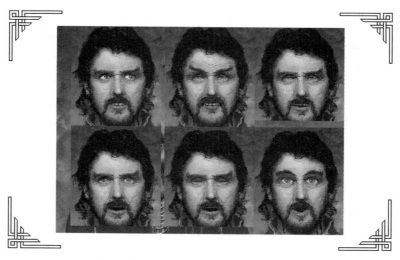

Saturday morning hangover, Alien Logic style.

● ● ● ● ● ● ● ● ● ●

You can enter the cle-eshta and be transported to a floating island in north Burdoth. Before doing this, use your Tra-Sense to discover a hidden passage. Save. There is a lava pit you'll find if you jump in. If you can warp out, or have Walk on Lava, you can leave the room. There is a power crystal, a power source that needs a crystal, and a regenerate. You can recharge one of your Isho abilities.

SKY REALMS

After you have 25 warps, a special warp will appear. You will be transported to a Shantic site at 143,32. Cassy will give you a key to enter the site (but you must retrieve her Crundorra from the general). Take the elevator down one level. You need Morph or Walk on Lava to pass the Lava Pit, beyond which you will find a warp that opens a passage to Delshia Island.

Go north from your arrival point to a cle-eshta at 12,164 that will transport you to the Sky Realms above the island. Scan the floating island to find an entrance into the Red Shanta hideout. Save.

Upon entering, you will find a sliding floor. Keep restoring until you get across without falling into the pit. You can escape the Shanta guard by jumping down the hole just in front of him. On the second floor, go to the left via a sliding floor. In this room, slay the evid. Search the walls for a power source. You will need Morph or Walk on Lava to reach the third floor by jumping down the hole in the floor to level three and going right.

You will find a power source and an elevator shaft. Take the elevator down, exit to the right to another shaft going down, and again exit to the right. Save, then go through a hole in the floor. Slay the three evids and get the key.

RED SHANTA

Use the key on the left door. Slay two evids and continue left to a power source. At the far end of the room is an Isho ride to the level below. Save. The ride will take you down one level, where two Shanta guards will immediately attack. If you don't think you can beat them, dash right into the next room. They will follow. As soon as you enter the room, use your "Tra powers" to uncover several secret exits. The third passage from the left will take you to the Red Shanta. As soon as you enter, the guards will stop.

Be prepared to kill three evids, then exit to the right. Behind the sliding floors is a green door. Blast it open and enter. In this room you will find the Red Shanta. Experience is the key to victory here, and you'll win the game by winning this battle.

135

ORBS & STUFF

Due to the unusual nature of this game, the coordinates for the most important people, places, and things are provided in a straightforward list rather than in the standard format.

Ana Ci-Eshta's dwelling: 212,179. (A warp here opens another warp in north Kodre Island.)

Ca-Gobby temple of Sha-Yesh in central Anasan: 208,210.

Ci-Ebba Dwelling of Do-Enesha: 200,173.

Cle-eshta: 173,177 in Trantter area opens a warp to the Dobre area at 241,113.

Cle-eshta: 174,174 adds a warp at 184,162.

Cle-eshta: 219,283 can be used to warp, but no new warps opened.

Cle-eshta: 297,145 adds a warp at 111,189 on island south of Temauntro.

Cle-eshta: 312,122 adds a warp at 359,46 in Gilthaw.

Cle-eshta: 377,93 does not add a warp in Voligire.

Cle-eshtas: 173,177-219, 183-204,189.

Cle-eshtas: 209,207 adds a warp in Dobre.

Crossroads of Warp World: 215,187 in east Trinnu Jungle. After they are replaced, warps will take you to: Voligire at 206,74; Sillipus Islands at 217,246; and Lundere at 281,141.

Double cle-eshtas of Ana Ci-Eshta: 173,176.

Ramian's House: 355,84 in Voligire.

Ruins Gama-El: 312,122, in north Kodre Island.

Ruins of Gama-El: 312,122.

Ruins of Iscin's lab: 146,142.

Ruins: 158,116 has cle-eshtas whose access is thwarted by a Shanta guard.

Shal-Shellan's dwelling in eastern Gilthaw: 371,36. (Look for secret room in the room that has a pool of lava.)

Sus-Cassen, a Ca-Desti outpost: 171,238. (Look out for evids.)

Tellemes in Ca-Tra dwelling: 281,116. (Bring a warp-out Crundorra.)

The Guarded Place: 92,96.

Underground complex near volcano in Doben-Al: 179,167.

Warp to Drail: cle-eshta at 205,161.

Warp to Drail: open by using a cle-eshta at 205,161.

Warp to the island of Eserran: 112,219 in western Drail opens warp.

Warp to the Sky Realms: beneath the Doben-Al in the lost temple of the Ca-Launtra.

KING'S QUEST VII

BY
TRACY HICKS

TYPE
*Animated
Adventure*

SYSTEM
*IBM PC
(Required:
386/33, 4MB
RAM, 5MB
hard drive,
SVGA,
Windows 3.1+,
CD-ROM
drive.
Recommended:
486/33, 8MB
RAM.
Supports: 100%
Windows-com-
patible sound
cards.)*

COMPANY
*Sierra On-Line
Inc.*

N SIERRA'S LATEST INSTALLMENT OF THE EVER-POPULAR KING'S QUEST SERIES, YOU PLAY THE PARTS OF BOTH QUEEN VALANICE AND PRINCESS ROSELLA ON THEIR QUEST TO SAVE THE MAGICAL FAERIE LAND OF ELDRITCH FROM BEING DESTROYED BY THE EVIL ENCHANTRESS MALICIA. FROM DESERT TO CAVE TO DARK AND TWISTED CEMETERY, YOU'LL GET AN EYEFUL OF THE NEW LOOK SIERRA HAS DEPLOYED FOR THE KING'S QUEST GAMES. AND YOU'LL BE THRILLED — IF YOU LIKE DISNEY. THE GAME PLAYS MUCH LIKE A TYPICAL SIERRA ADVENTURE, WITH A FEW MAJOR EXCEPTIONS. THE FIRST IS THAT YOU CANNOT DIE. ACTUALLY YOU CAN, BUT THE GAME BRINGS YOU BACK TO LIFE AT THE MOMENT BEFORE YOU DIED WITH NO ILL EFFECTS. AND IN A MOVE THAT'S SURE TO OFFEND HARDENED ADVENTURE GAMERS, SIERRA REMOVED THE SAVE GAME FEATURE. THE GAME IS SAVED AUTOMATICALLY WHEN YOU QUIT, BUT YOU CANNOT SAVE AT ANY OTHER POINT. HOWEVER, THE MOST VISIBLE CHANGE IS THE LACK OF THE CHARACTERISTIC SIERRA MENU BAR. ALL GAME MANIPULATIONS ARE NOW CARRIED OUT WITH ONE ALL-PURPOSE CURSOR. UNDER THE NEW INTERFACE, YOU BASICALLY CLICK ON THINGS AND SEE

What happens. In general, the new features work well, and the game overall should provide the novice adventure gamer with a decent taste of the genre.

THE SOLUTION

— CHAPTER 1: WHERE THE BLAZES AM I? —

CLOTH

Pick up the torn cloth hanging on the cactus. Go south into the desert. Walk back and forth until you see the Desert Spirit. Talk to him.

THE DESERT SPIRIT

Walk back to where you started the game. Go west one screen. Look into the pool, then pick up the stick and the salt crystals lying near it. Look at the base of the statue. Look again for a close-up. The pictures show how to make fresh water. Walk north. You will see a cactus with a purple prickly pear on it. Use the stick to retrieve the pear. Walk east from the pear bush and look at the pictures on the large rock; these show how to drain the pool back at the statue.

Enter the cave to the north. Pick up the basket and click it on eye icon next to the inventory. Click on the basket to open it, then rotate it until you see the corn kernel inside. Take the kernel and return the basket to your inventory. Take one of the four clay pots from the cave. Leave the cave.

Outside the cave you will see a gourd and some dripping water. Plant the kernel under the dripping water and a stalk of corn will magically appear. Take an ear of corn and walk east. Take a look into the Jackalope's hole. Read the sign above the small door, then knock on the door. Talk to the Kangaroo Rat. The Jackalope has stolen his glasses, so he won't trade with you yet.

Return to the pool. Place the corn into the statue's empty hand, then fill your pot with water from the pool. Pour the water into the statue's bowl. Click Rosella's comb on yourself, then click it on the statue's bowl. The salt water is now fresh water. Fill the pot with the fresh water, then head south into the desert.

When you find the Desert Spirit, give him the water. He will be grateful and lead you to the spot where he died, promising you a reward for having helped him. Take either the rope or a vial of powder. (If you've been here before and picked up the horn, only the powder will be available.) If you take the rope, you won't be able to take the horn that's lying nearby. If

138

you've chosen the powder, be sure to pick up the horn before you leave. Walk two screens north.

THE JACKALOPE AND THE KANGAROO RAT

Return to where you planted the corn stalk. The gourd has split, and inside is a seed. Take the seed and walk east. You can get the glasses from the Jackalope in either of two ways, depending on what you took from the Desert Spirit.

First Solution: If you have the horn, use it on yourself to clear the sand from it. Then use it on the Jackalope's hole. Pick up the glasses and the Jackalope's fur.

Second Solution: If you took the rope, return to the screen where you started the game. Use the rope on one of the cacti and it will be strung between the two. When the Jackalope comes zooming along, he'll hit the rope and be spun for the ride of his life. Pick up the glasses and get his fur from off the cactus. Now visit the Kangaroo Rat, knock on his door, and return his glasses. Then give him the seed and he will give you a pretty blue bead. Go south to the sandstone temple.

THE SCORPION AND THE TEMPLE

There are two ways to handle the oncoming scorpion, again depending on what you took from the Desert Spirit.

First Solution: If you took the powder, use it on the scorpion. He will shrink and be gone for good.

Second Solution: If you don't have the powder, click the torn cloth on the stick to make a flag. Use the flag on the scorpion, and he will attack it, getting his tail stuck in the wall. This is only temporary, so don't dawdle. Don't worry about losing the cloth, which you no longer need. Now look at the statue on the altar. When you get a close-up, you will see symbols covering the altar's face. Click on the upside-down raindrop in the center of the altar. This will cause a stream of sunlight to shine down through the statue's hands, and reveal three colored gems. Place the blue stone in the statue's left hand, the yellow one in the right hand, and the red one in the receptacle just to the right of the statue. This will reveal an oddly shaped piece of turquoise. Take it and leave the temple.

THE POOL AND THE PORTAL

Return to the pool, go to the statue and turn his head. Look at his choker. Move each blue bead so that they line up in the third hole from the left. Exit the close-up, then turn his bowl upside down by clicking on his wrist (the one holding the bowl). The pool will now drain, and you can enter it.

At the bottom is yet another statue. This one is holding a tray. Look at the tray. Click on the tray — and only on the tray! Place the blue bead you got from the Kangaroo Rat in the tray and take the piece of turquoise on the right, the one V-shaped one. Click your new turquoise piece on your old one to form one big piece. Return to the portal (the big stone head next to the prickly pear bush) and put the piece into the hole in the portal. Enter the portal and check out the big lizard that looks like he wants to make a meal of you as the chapter ends.

— CHAPTER 2: A TROLL IS AS A TROLL DOES —

POTION INGREDIENTS

Watch the cartoon and note that the Troll King's eyes are green. At the end of the animation, you will be in your chambers. Look at everything you can, especially the picture. Notice the color of the king's eyes, which are now purple. Open your door and leave.

You're now in the throne room. Notice the five exits. Upper left is to your chambers. Just to the left of your door is the entrance to the mud baths. Lower left leads to the blacksmith. Upper right leads to the kitchen. Lower right leads to a bridge over a lava river.

Watch the cartoon and note the ingredients — a gold bowl, emerald water, silver spoon, baked beetles, and a crystal dragon scale — needed to make a potion that restores Rosella to her human form. Pick up the toy rat that the troll child dropped. On the wall between your door and the throne is a spiked shield. Take it. Look at the throne. Look again. Look at the hole above the throne. (It's a little hard to see, but it's there.)

Enter the mud baths and click on the trolls. Leave, then watch the cartoon that follows. After the animation, talk to the trolls as much as you can stand. You now know a little bit about Malicia.

THE GOLD BOWL AND BAKED BEETLES

Enter the kitchen and watch the animation. When tossed out, go right back in, but this time, use the toy rat on the cook. Take the gold bowl from the shelf. Look at the bottom of it in you inventory to make sure that it's not brass. If it is, put it back and take the other one (which has 14K Gold stamped on its bottom).

The machine to the right of the shelf contains the baked beetles. Click on the machine to get them, then leave.

EMERALD WATER

Enter the blacksmith's area and talk to both trolls. Look at the pail and the fire. Enter the passageway at the back of the room. Take the lantern off the wall, then use the gold bowl on the green liquid. Now you've got emerald water.

While you are here, look in the northwestern part of the room. You'll notice a yellowish substance on the wall across from the crevice. Look at it twice. It's sulfur. Now, on your side of the crevice, there is a piece that juts out toward a small shaft of rock. Walk over toward it. On the way, you'll get hit by an updraft. Now walk to the piece that juts out. Click on the shaft of rock to jump to it, then click on the ledge below the sulfur. Take some sulfur, then jump back the way you came. Leave the room. When the blacksmith stokes up the flames, click the lantern on them to capture a spark, then go back to the throne room.

THE SILVER SPOON

Enter the mud baths and listen to the troll women to learn how to use the sulfur. Talk to them, then leave. Return to the blacksmith and use the sulfur on the fire. Get the tongs from the back wall and click them on the spoon mold. Click them on the pail, and you now have your silver spoon. Return the tongs to the wall and return to the throne room again.

CRYSTAL DRAGON SCALE

Go to the bridge over the lava. Start across the bridge. Talk to the troll as much as you can. Look at your shield in inventory. Remove the spike from the shield. In the northwestern corner of the room, you'll see a wagon. Look at it. It's missing a wheel, but you can fix that. Take your shield and use it to replace the missing wheel. Then take the spike and use it on the shield to hold it in place. Now ride the wagon. The troll is knocked off the bridge.

Continue across the bridge and go two screens east to the crystal dragon's lair. Walk to the bottom of the stairs, then talk to the mournful dragon. Use the lantern on her to give her back her spark. She'll give you a gigantic gem in return. Watch the ensuing cartoon, then return to the blacksmith's area. Give the gem to the jeweler, and he will give you his hammer and chisel.

Go back to the dragon. Stand at the bottom of the stairs and watch her tail. Have the hammer and chisel ready. As soon as she puts her tail on the ground, use the hammer and chisel on it. Do not attempt this while her tail is on the pile of gems or you'll be flattened when she lowers it. Now you have all the ingredients for Mathilde's spell, so return to the throne room and talk to her. Give her the ingredients, then watch. You're back to normal, but here comes Malicia.

After the fireworks, you find yourself locked in your chambers. Look around. Smoke is coming out of the picture's nose: There's a secret passage behind it. Take the brown stool and put it on the floor beneath the picture. Put the footstool on top of the nightstand, and finally, put the cushion on top of both of them. Climb up and watch the animation. At the end, you'll fall back into the throne room. Pick up the dragon toad that you dislodged when you fell. Walk back to your chamber door, then watch the cartoon. Show the toad to Mathilde, and she will give you a magical rope. Here comes Malicia again. Notice that she doesn't like bats, rats, and snakes? When she leaves, head for the lower-right exit. Malicia will appear again. Use the toy rat on her, and she'll run screaming. Use the rope on the makeshift elevator, then get in it and hold on — the elevator shaft is collapsing around you.

CHAPTER 3: THE SKY IS FALLING!

OFF TO FALDERAL

When you left Valanice back in Chapter 1, she was confronted by an overlarge, hungry lizard. Give the lizard the prickly pear and it will take off. Continue through the tunnel into a forest. Look at the marble statues, bridge, and flowers. Walk west and talk to the stag as much as you can. Look at the tree and the stake stuck into it.

Show Rosella's comb to the stag, then walk one screen west, then another north. You'll have to jump on the stepping stones to cross the muddy river bed. Use the basket on the spider, then click on the bird to free her. With the web gone, you can see a passageway north. Take it. You have reached the town of Falderal. The guard won't let you in, but it's no problem. Just use the little door to the right of the main gate and ignore the guard's frustrated threats. Show Rosella's comb to the Archduke.

Enter the China Shop (the yellow building to the north) and talk to the bull as much as possible. Look at the mask on the wall, then leave the shop. Read the note on the Town Hall door. Go east.

CHINA BIRD RESCUE

Read the note on the Faux Shop door. On the right side of the merchant's cart is a hastily covered cage. Uncover it, then open the cage door. Talk to the china bird, and she will come with you. Talk to the merchant. He wants a magical statuette in trade for the salve that will let you pass through the were-woods intact. Return to the China Shop and give the china bird to the bull. Fernando will give you a mask in return. Leave the shop.

MAGICAL STATUETTE

Wear the mask and knock on the Town Hall door. Inside, go through the door in the back of the room. You're now in a room of weird, twisted stairs. Go east, west, and down. Click on the door. You will get a face full of powder. Click on the door again to enter the room. Look at the third mirror from the door, and you will get pulled through into another room. Open the drawer on the side of the desk and take the statuette. Click Rosella's comb on the statuette, and it'll show you Rosella in a collapsing elevator shaft. Leave the room. Go northwest, then west, then south to leave. You'll automatically put the mask back on before returning to the wild party. Don't bother sticking around, just leave the Town Hall and go east.

WAKING UP THE ROCK SPIRIT

The moon will fall into the pool and scare away the mockingbird, as well as traumatize Chicken Petite. Talk to her, then try to get the moon. Click on the empty mockingbird's nest to get a wooden nickel. The Faux Shop is open now, but eat the salt crystals before entering.

Talk to the clerk as much as possible. Look at the books to his left. Even though you have what you need to pay for the book, you can't get it yet. Look at the rubber chickens on the left wall. Look at the mask sign. Give your mask to the clerk, and he'll give you a rubber chicken in exchange. Check out the chicken in your inventory and remove the feather from its rear.

Leave town. Go east. Don't cross the river bed. Go east two screens and you'll find the Rock Spirit. Use the feather on him twice. He tells you that you must get the River of Life flowing and replenish the cornucopia. You can't do anything about the cornucopia yet, but you can get the river going again.

THE RIVER OF LIFE

Go back to the river bed and cross it, then go back to the statues. Click on the flowers and the little bird you saved from the spider will offer to help you collect some nectar. Click the clay pot on the flowers and she will fill it with nectar. Pour the nectar into the pitcher of the closest statue. Now the river's flowing again. Attis will drink from the river and be restored to human form. Cross the bridge and go east. With the river flowing, this is the only way across now.

Go back to town and visit the Faux Shop. Now you can buy that book. While you're in there, show the clerk Rosella's comb. You've got to go back to the desert now. The passage back to there is south of the statues in the forest. Visit the Kangaroo Rat and trade him the book. He will give you a shepherd's crook in return — just what you need to drag the moon out of the pond in Falderal. Go back to Falderal and use the crook on the moon in the pool.

CHAPTER 4: WILL THE REAL
TROLL KING PLEASE STAND UP?

DR. CADAVER'S HOUSE

This chapter begins with you stuck in the crumbling elevator shaft. When the grave digger offers you the shovel, click on it and he will pull you out. Talk to him as much as possible. Go east and look at the graffiti on the wall. Note the pictures and their order: skull, bat, and spider. Don't worry about the dog's shadow — yet. Go south, but do not talk to the crying woman. Go south again. Take a good look at the deadfall, then go north, then east, and you'll be in front of an odd little house. Knock on the door and talk to Dr. Cadaver as much as possible, then leave and go east to a pumpkin-like treehouse.

Note: When and if you see the bogeyman, leave the screen as quickly as possible, or you will experience a painful death by Ooga Booga!

GETTING A SPINE

If you don't see a rope hanging down, exit to the west and reenter the screen. Do this until you see the rope (although it should be there the first time you exit and reenter). Click on the rope to go into the treehouse.

Inside, get the yellowish blob to your left. It's the spine. Get the foot-in-a-bag from the coffin. Click on the elevator to leave. If you hear the Ghoul Kids coming, jump out the window behind you. Go back to Dr. Cadaver's and give him the spine. Now that he has some backbone, he'll give you a box with a weird pet inside. Leave and go back to the treehouse.

SUPER RAT

Talk to the kids and show them the box with the weird pet. Put it in the elevator, and you will get the rat in exchange. Don't accept the Ghoul Kids' offer to go inside the treehouse. Go north and give the rat back to the grave digger. He will give you a horn and an offer of a free grave.

FINDING THE TROLL KING

Go southeast to the treehouse. When the brats leave, use your hammer and chisel on the coffin to free the kitty. She will tell you where the king is and give you an extra life as a gift for freeing her. Go two screens west and one south back to the deadfall.

Look at the tree next to the deadfall. If the twisted branch is pointed up, leave the screen and come back later: The bogeyman's home. When the branch is pointed down, it's safe to continue. Blow the horn that you got from the gravedigger. He'll show up and dig you a grave in front of the deadfall. Climb inside. At the bottom of the hole you will find a locked casket. Look at the lock. Click the symbols in this order: skull, bat, spider. Don't stay here long because the bogeyman may still show up. The casket will open, revealing the real Troll King. Malicia will arrive and lock both of you in the coffin.

ESCAPE

Show the dragon toad to the king. He needs the gem in his arm band to awaken the toad, so use your hammer and chisel to get it. The toad will dig a hole in the bottom of the coffin, and you and the king will escape. You end up in the Ooga Booga cemetery, and the bad guys will be looking for you.

Once you've turned the Troll King into a beetle, take the black cloak that appears and wear it. Hurry! As long as you are wearing the cloak, the bogeyman will not harm you when he shows up. Go north and visit Dr. Cadaver again. Talk to him as much as you can stand, and he will give you a defoliant spray. Talk to him some more after he gives you this, then leave. Go east and talk to the kids, then go north. Get the shovel that's leaning against the building. Go back to the treehouse, then go south. When the moss monster shows up, spray him with the defoliant. Talk to the hungry plant as much as possible, then give the foot-in-a-bag to the plant. Grab the flower that's growing next to it while it's eating, then walk east.

145

MALICIA'S HOUSE

Don't mess with the gargoyle. Listen to the king, then walk north to get behind the house. Click on the tangle of vines next to the house to reveal a small hole. Use the shovel to make the hole bigger.

It gets tricky here. If you hear the dog barking, don't enter the hole or Malicia will get you. Sometimes just waiting awhile will work. If not, step back to the last screen, then go back behind the house. If the dog is still barking, try waiting until the bogeyman shows up and leaves. If the dog is still barking, repeat the steps above until it shuts up. When you no longer hear the dog, click on the hole. You will peek up through a trap door in the floor of Malicia's house. When you hear her return, lower the door and you'll view a close-up of a knothole in the trap door. When the dog comes over, spray his nose with the defoliant. Malicia and the mutt will leave, and you'll be free to enter the house. Go to the dresser and click on the third drawer down. Keep clicking on the drawer until you find the device you're looking for. Click on the clothes to return them to the drawer, then pick up the stocking that fell out. It'll come in handy later. Go back through the trap door and very quickly put the cloak back on.

THE SECRET ENTRANCE IN FALDERAL

Now you're ready to go through the were-woods. Go north, then click the lump of silver on the stocking to make a sling. Go east. Keep going east. About halfway through the were-wood screen, a were-bear will jump out and threaten Rosella. Use the sling on him.

Now you're in the forest just outside of Falderal. Remember, you have to cross the bridge to go to town. The guard isn't going to let Rosella in either, but she can enter by using the small door just as Valanice did.

You will meet the Archduke when you get into town. After you're done with him, enter the Town Hall, and go through the door in the back. Go east, west, and down the stairs. Click on the door twice to enter. Look at the plaque on the cherub, then use the stocking to wipe it off. Look at the plaque again. On the post next to the boarded-up mirror is a bunch of golden grapes. Use your hammer and chisel to get one, then give it to the cherub. The fountain in the center of the room will begin to open, revealing a passageway. Zap the scarab with the wand, and the King will be restored to his usual form. He will open the passage. Enter the passage and follow the king. Take note of how he opens the steel-faced door.

— CHAPTER 5: NIGHTMARE IN ETHERIA —

SHOOT THE MOON

Use the rubber chicken on the branch of the tree outside the Town Hall. Now click the moon on the rubber chicken, and you will sling-shot the moon back into the sky.

GETTING PAST THE WERE-FOLK

Go east to the merchant and give him the statuette. He will give you the salve you need to get through the were-woods. Leave town and walk around to the bridge. Walk two screens to the west, and you will be at the entrance to the were-woods. Mix the Jackalope fur with the salve, then rub the salve on yourself. You will become a Jackalope and race madly through the woods, past the were-bear.

When you return to normal, the moss monster will appear, but Attis will arrive and blow it away. Walk west and talk to the plant until it repeats itself. Show Rosella's comb to it. Walk north through the gate into Ooga Booga Land.

OOGA BOOGA LAND

Walk west and knock on the door. Talk to Dr. Cadaver until he asks you to leave. Go to the treehouse. The elevator should be down. (If it's not, walk offscreen, then return.) Click on the elevator to enter the treehouse.

Look at the bone the mummy is holding. Click on it again to take it. Leave and walk north, then west. When the shadowy dog appears, give him the bone and talk to him. He will give you his collar. Talk to him again until he has nothing more to say.

BREAKING THE CURSE

Walk south and give the collar to the crying woman. Do not talk to her. Walk east to the treehouse. Pick up the firecracker. Walk back to the crypt where the woman was crying. Look at the door and the lock, then put the firecracker into the lock to blast open the door. Enter the crypt and click on the coffin lid to move it. Click inside the coffin to get the skull, then leave.

Stand in the middle of the path next to the crypt. When the headless horseman appears, click the skull on him. You have broken the curse, and he will give you a fife you can use to summon his horse, allowing you to travel up to the clouds of Etheria. When you arrive in Etheria, you will notice four rainbows. These lead to different places on the land below. The upper-left rainbow goes to the desert; the upper-right rainbow goes to Falderal; lower-left goes to Ooga Booga; and lower-right goes to the woods.

Go east and listen to the notes the dragonettes sing. Go north and you will see an object that looks like a harp with a ball on top. You have to play the notes the dragonettes sang to activate the doorway to the Three Fates. From left to right, pluck these strings in this order: 1, 5, 6, 4. These notes will always open the doorway. The harp will play a few more notes, and the ball will sparkle. Click on the ball, and you will be sucked into another dimension. Talk to the Three Fates until they send you back.

DREAMING

Take the rainbow to Ooga Booga. Go north and talk to the kids, then see Dr. Cadaver. Talk to him all you can. He will let you sleep in his coffin. Click on the coffin, and Valanice will fall asleep. When you wake up, you will automatically leave. Play the fife to summon the horse, and it will take you back to Etheria. Visit the Three Fates again.

RESTORING LADY CERES

Go south from the Three Fates, then east. Follow the path up the mountain and exit north. Click on the bent tree to climb it, then click on the purple fruit to take some. You now have ambrosia, sacred food of the gods. Return to the rainbows and take the one that leads to the forest. Cross the bridge, put the ambrosia in the cornucopia, and it will be magically replenished. Take a piece of fruit, cross the bridge again, and go west.

Talk to Attis. Give the fruit to the tree. You have now restored Lady Ceres. Talk to her as much as possible. You now know how to thaw Mab. Go back and talk to the Three Fates. They'll give you a dream catcher, along with some advice.

SUNLIGHT AND WAKING DREAMS

Go back up the mountain and click on the cave. When the nightmare comes out, use the dream catcher on it. Enter the cave and talk to the Dream Weaver. Show him the dream catcher and he will give you a magical tapestry. Go back to the rainbows and take the one that leads to Ooga Booga.

Go to Malicia's house and look in the window to find the crystal. Go behind the house. Entering works the same way as when Rosella was here. Listen for the dog. Try waiting, and if that doesn't work, try leaving and coming back. When you don't hear the dog, enter the hole. You will peek out the trap door.

When you hear Malicia, go back down. You will view a close-up of a hole. When the dog shows up, use the ambrosia on it. Click to go up through the trap door, and you will see Malicia and the dog. When they leave, enter the room and take a crystal from the lamp. Go back through the trap door, go north, then call the horse to go back up to Etheria.

Take the rainbow that goes to the desert. Walk north two screens, then east. Enter the temple. Use the crystal shaft on the beam of sunlight shining on the altar. Use the magic tapestry to go to Dreamland.

When the nightmare appears, use the dream catcher on it. Walk south, and you will fall into the water. You will swim east to an island. Enter the building and use the shaft of sunlight on the ice. You have thawed out Mab. She will give you a horse harness and send you to the bottom of the mountain, with the mission to harness the wind.

VISITING THE WINDS

Don't stand around too long or the floating creatures will knock you off of the mountain. Go back up the mountain. On the right side of the bent tree, you should see a green plant growing against the wall. Click on this plant to walk to it. When the white horse floats by, click the harness on him. (If you see the harness fall, you're not standing in the right place and have to try again. Don't worry, the harness is still in your inventory.) When you finally harness the horse, he will carry you up to the winds, and another animated sequence ensues.

CHAPTER 6: READY, SET, BOOM!

FIGHTING KINGS

We return now to Rosella, who is watching the two Troll Kings fight. You have to zap the imposter, but first you'll need to change the setting on the wand from T to F. Look at the wand while in the inventory. Rotate it so you can see the letter on the gem. It should say T for trolls. Turn it again so you can click on the handle. Look at the gem again, and it should say F for fairies.

Do you remember the color of the King's eyes in the picture? They were purple. The imposter has the green eyes. Zap him with the wand set to F to return him to his true form.

STOP THE VOLCANO!

After the fireworks with Malicia, you find yourself on a ledge inside the volcano. From this point on, you must hurry because this portion of the game is on a timer. After the cartoon, use the shovel on the volcano wall behind you and a little to your right. Go northwest through the tunnel. If you don't have the flower from the swamp in Ooga Booga, there will be one here that you can get.

Use the shovel on the boulder to make a handy step, then climb up and pick the flower. Next, click the left eye, the right eye, then the nose to open the metallic door. You're back in the control room. Plug the device you took from Malicia's drawer into the socket next to the unconscious king. Wait until it is pulsing a yellowish color, then remove it. Use the flower on the king. He will wake up and stop the volcano.

ENDGAME

Rosella and Valanice are happily reunited, but it's not over yet. Malicia will show up and zap Edgar, killing him. Use the device on Malicia, then on the little dog when he shows up. Quickly use the extra life on Edgar before his spirit leaves his body. You will finish the game even if you don't revive Edgar, but the ending will be sad.

ORBS & STUFF

Object	See this Section for Location	Also See Section(s)
Stick	The Desert Spirit	The Scorpion and the Temple
Salt crystals	The Desert Spirit	Waking Up the Rock Spirit
Purple prickly pear	The Desert Spirit	Off to Falderal
Basket	The Desert Spirit	Off to Falderal
Kernel	The Desert Spirit	Location only
Clay pot	The Desert Spirit	The River of Life
Ear of corn	The Desert Spirit	Location only
Rope	The Desert Spirit	The Jackalope and the Kangaroo Rat
Vial of powder	The Desert Spirit	The Scorpion and the Temple
Horn	The Desert Spirit	The Jackalope and the Kangaroo Rat
Gourd seed	The Jackalope and the Kangaroo Rat	Location only
Glasses	The Jackalope and the Kangaroo Rat	Location only
Jackalope's fur	The Jackalope and the Kangaroo Rat	Getting Past the Were-Folk
Blue bead	The Jackalope and the Kangaroo Rat	Location only
Oddly shaped turquoise	The Scorpion and the Temple	The Pool and the Portal
V-shaped turquoise	The Pool and the Portal	Location only
Toy rat	Potion Ingredients	The Gold Bowl and Baked Beetles, Crystal Dragon Scale
Spiked shield	Potion Ingredients	Crystal Dragon Scale
Gold bowl	The Gold Bowl and Baked Beetles	Emerald Water
Baked beetles	The Gold Bowl and Baked Beetles	Location only
Lantern	Emerald Water	Crystal Dragon Scale
Emerald water	Emerald Water	Location only
Sulfur	Emerald Water	The Silver Spoon
Gigantic gem	Crystal Dragon Scale	Location only

150

Object	See this Section for Location	Also See Section(s)
Hammer and chisel	Crystal Dragon Scale	Finding the Troll King, Escape, The Secret Entrance in Falderal
Dragon toad	Crystal Dragon Scale	Escape
Magical rope	Crystal Dragon Scale	Location only
China bird	China Bird Rescue	Location only
Mask	China Bird Rescue	Magical Statuette, Waking Up the Rock Spirit
Magical statuette	Magical Statuette	Getting Past the Were-Folk
Wooden nickel	Waking Up the Rock Spirit	Location only
Rubber chicken	Waking Up the Rock Spirit	Nightmare in Etheria
Feather	Waking Up the Rock Spirit	Location only
Book	The River of Life	Location only
Shepherd's crook	The River of Life	Location only
Spine	Getting a Spine	Location only
Foot-in-a-bag	Getting a Spine	Escape
Weird pet	Getting a Spine	Super Rat
Rat	Super Rat	Location only
Horn	Super Rat	Finding the Troll King
Kitty	Finding the Troll King	Location only
Extra life	Finding the Troll King	Endgame
Black cloak	Escape	Malicia's House
Defoliant spray	Escape	Malicia's House
Shovel	Escape	Stop the Volcano
Flower	Escape	Stop the Volcano
Lump of silver	The Secret Entrance in Falderal	Location only
Device	Malicia's House	Stop the Volcano!, Endgame
Stocking	Malicia's House	The Secret Entrance in Falderal
Golden grape	The Secret Entrance in Falderal	Location only
Salve	Getting Past the Were-Folk	Location only
Bone	Ooga Booga Land	Location only

Object	See this Section for Location	Also See Section(s)
Collar	Ooga Booga Land	Breaking the Curse
Firecracker	Breaking the Curse	Location only
Skull	Breaking the Curse	Location only
Fife	Breaking the Curse	Location only
Ambrosia	Restoring Lady Ceres	Location only
Piece of fruit	Restoring Lady Ceres	Location only
Dream catcher	Restoring Lady Ceres	Sunlight and Waking Dreams
Magical tapestry	Sunlight and Waking Dreams	Location only
Crystal	Sunlight and Waking Dreams	Location only
Horse harness	Sunlight and Waking Dreams	Visiting the Winds

KNIGHTS OF XENTAR

BY
**JERRY VAN HORN
& STACEY PORTNOY**

TYPE
Adult Role-playing

SYSTEM
*IBM PC
(Required:
386/33+,
640KB RAM,
VGA monitor,
MS CD-ROM
Extensions.
Supports:
Sound Blaster
and Sound
Blaster Pro,
Pro Audio,
Adlib.)*

COMPANY
Megatech

A S DESMOND, THE KNIGHT OF XENTAR, YOU FACE TWO CHALLENGES. THE MAIN QUEST IS TO RECOVER YOUR FALCON SWORD AND GENJI ARMOR FROM THIEVES. A MORE SUBTLE SIDE OF THE STORY IS DISCOVERING YOUR TRUE IDENTITY BECAUSE YOUR PARENTS ABANDONED YOU AT BIRTH. ALTHOUGH YOU GET NO RESPECT FROM THEM OR ANYONE ELSE IN THE GAME, A PAIR OF FRIENDS, ROLF AND LUNA, WILL ASSIST IN BOTH QUESTS. ALONG THE WAY, YOU WILL RESCUE

MANY FAIR MAIDENS, WHO REWARD YOU WITH ITEMS OR THEIR BODIES — EXPLICITLY SO IN THE NR-18 VERSION. EVEN THE NR-13 VERSION (BOTH ARE INCLUDED IN THE PACKAGE) CONTAINS ENOUGH NUDITY AND ROUGH LANGUAGE TO MAKE IT UNSUITABLE FOR CHILDREN. THE GAME CONSISTS OF SLAYING DEMONS AND FINDING TREASURES; THERE ARE FEW PUZZLES TO SOLVE. IN ADDITION TO THE JAPANESE ANIME-STYLE GRAPHICS, HUMOR IS ANOTHER HALLMARK OF XENTAR, SO LISTEN CLOSELY TO EVERYONE. IN THE CD-ROM VERSION, WHICH HAS FULL SPEECH SUPPORT, THE VOICES GIVE THE GAME THE FEEL OF A SATURDAY MORNING

CARTOON. A UNIQUE FEATURE OF XENTAR IS AN OBJECT CALLED THE MIRROR OF ILLUSION. AFTER COMPLETING THE GAME, YOU MAY USE IT TO VIEW NAKED PICTURES OF ALL OF THE LADIES YOU SAW IN THE GAME AT THE PHOTO SHOP. (OBVIOUSLY, THIS GAME IS FOR ADULTS ONLY.)

THE SOLUTION

GENERAL

Talk to everyone you meet to get vital clues. Save often. Carry lots of heal potions with you at all times. Search all jars for sovereigns, items, and an occasional gem. Save Vitamin Mix for Luna because she is the only one who has magic. Many battles are not actual fights, they're simply events that occur when you speak the people. When fighting with the "Knowledge" option, you will increase your knowledge even if you run away from the battle.

SQUALOR HOLLOW

Talk to Larrouse. Go to bar in the northern section of town and rescue Mona from the thieves. Talk to bartender and get 50 sovereigns for rescuing Mona. Go to Don Frump's house in the northwest corner of town.

Talk to the Steward at the entrance. Talk to Don Frump and learn about the thieves at Mount Litmus. Get knife and leather suit from Don Frump. You can get items from the Item Shop, but the Weapon Shop won't sell to you yet. Do not waste time building up levels, for you will soon be reduced to Level 1.

MOUNT LITMUS

Enter Mount Litmus west of Squalor Hollow. Be sure you have several heal potions. Follow the winding path until you reach the thief, picking up items from the treasure chests along the way. Get the items from the four chests, then talk to the thief.

The thief reveals himself to be a demon, but no battle ensues. After the demon disappears, you'll be outside of Mount Litmus. Return to Squalor Hollow

DON FRUMP

Visit Don Frump's steward, where you learn that Frump went to the Nameless Village.

NAMELESS VILLAGE

Go north to the mountain pass. Talk to Larrouse and get the Magic Medal. Go through the pass to the Nameless Village. You'll get weaker and be reduced to Level 1. At first no one will talk or sell to you.

Speak with Don Frump in the north part of town. Follow Frump into the basement and talk to him. Frump turns into the demon Byrt. After the demon disappears, you can talk to the townspeople and buy items and weapons. Return to Squalor Hollow to collect your reward from the real Frump.

CLARA'S PLACE

Clara's place is southwest of the Nameless Village. Follow the mountains to get there. Rescue Clara from the wolf. You will now be able to rest here without paying whenever you return. Come back later to get a 100-sovereign reward from Clara's grandmother.

PRISCILLA'S PLACE: AFTER VISEL

Go south along the mountains until you reach Priscilla's place. Rescue Priscilla from the dwarves. Priscilla will tell you about Visel and the Mystic Marble. Exit the left door, go around the back, and enter the right door to find eight treasure chests. You may rest here for free whenever you return. Go to Dreadsden, northwest of Priscilla's place.

DREADSDEN

You'll meet the Dark Knight at the gate. The man in the lower-left building is looking for his Flammo Pocket Warmer. Get the Flammo Pocket Warmer from the jar in his house. Trade Flammo Pocket Warmer for 100 sovereigns. Before you enter the town, walk left around the wall (it's easier to use the arrow keys than the mouse). At the corner, walk up until you reach a staircase. Go down the stairs. Get the Mystic Marble from the Hermit. Go to Visel's cave, north of Priscilla's place.

VISEL CAVE

You'll automatically use the Mystic Marble to enter the cave. To find Visel, go north, east, north, west, north, and east to a wall). From the wall, head north, east, south, east, south, east, south, east, north, west, and north to Visel. Return to Priscilla.

PRISCILLA'S PLACE: THE MIRROR

Priscilla will give you the Magic Mirror for beating Visel. Go to Coventry, south of Dreadsden.

COVENTRY

You'll learn that Tymm is blocking the way to Phoenix. Talk to the Dark Knight in the hotel above the cafe. Exit Coventry and walk west to the cliffs. Walk south to a man standing by a sign. Talk to the man and read the sign for the Suicide Cliffs.

TYMM

Seek out Tymm, who is blocking the path to Phoenix, east of Coventry. With the Magic Mirror, you will automatically defeat Tymm. Now rescue Marie in the building. Go to Phoenix, which is east of Tymm.

PHOENIX

Talk to Kate, who is hiding in the trees in the southwest corner of Phoenix. Talk to Rolf, who is in a building north of the town entrance. If you already talked to Kate, he'll want to pack. Talk to Rolf, who'll be ready to go with you. Go into Desmond Tower, next to Rolf's home. On the top floor, open the chests in the following order to get a Desmond Action Figure: right, left, center. Check the cemetery stones for items and armor. Go to Nero's Retreat.

NERO'S RETREAT

Nero's Retreat is south of Phoenix. Go to the building in the northeast part of town. Talk to the man standing in front of a jar. Go up the left staircase to the top floor. Keep searching the jar. You'll get one sovereign and, after ten searches, will eventually find a diamond ring. This will enhance Luna's Blizzard Magic when she joins your party. Go back down and search the jars. Make sure you search the jar the man was standing in front of. It will contain rats. Go to Squalor Hollow.

SQUALOR HOLLOW: TWIG

Go north of Phoenix and have Rolf lift the rock blocking the path to Squalor Hollow. Talk to Larrouse, the only person left in town. You'll learn that the Falcon Sword is in the Castle of Kalist. Larrouse will give you the Magical Twig. Go to Carnage Corners.

CARNAGE CORNERS: ARENA PASS

Go west of Phoenix and over the bridge, where you learn that the Arena battles have been moved to the cemetery. In the large building in the north of town, buy the Arena pass for 1,000 sovereigns. Go to the cemetery north of town.

CEMETERY ARENA: PICTURE

Enter the cemetery. Go south to the bottom, west, and over the bridge.

Go up to get the items from the three chests. Go south to the bottom, then west. Descend the stairs. After exiting the tunnel, go west and south to get Sexy Drawing. Go back north, take the right ramp down, and go south to the stairs. Then head south, east, south, east, south, east, north, west, north, east, south, east, south, west, south, and down the staircase. You'll go through a series of stairwells. Go in the following order: left, center, right, left, center. You'll be kicked out of the cemetery at the last door when you step on the rocks. Go to Carnage Corners.

CARNAGE CORNERS: NUTS

Talk to the young man in the front of town and learn about Arcadia and Luna. Talk to the old man in the second building from the left in the northern part of town. The old man will give you the Transsexual Nuts in exchange for the Sexy Drawing. Go to Arcadia.

ARCADIA

Go east of Carnage Corners to the mountains and find a path slightly to the north. If you have the Transsexual Nuts and the Magical Twig, you will be able to get through the pass. Go east to Arcadia. Talk to Luna in the church in the northeast part of town, and she'll join you. Enter the long pathway in the southwest corner of town. Talk to the goddess Aquarina. Talk to the Princess in the building north of the town entrance. Get the Virgin Medal from the Princess.

LUNA'S GEMS

Luna initially possesses two half gems that she uses for spells. When you get a new gem, it will appear in the item section. Click on items and use the gem to give Luna the new spell power.

Go to Dreadsden (walk or use Luna's Warp spell). Talk to the man to whom you gave the Flammo Pocket Warmer. He'll give Luna the magma gem, which lets Luna use the Fire spell on an entire group of enemies. Go to the fountain in the east of town. Search the top-right-hand corner of the fountain. You'll get a single sovereign. Keep looking. After about four tries, Luna will find a snow gem, which gives her the Blizzard spell.

Go to Coventry. Trade your Desmond Action Figure to the man in the lower left hand corner for the crystal gem. This will give Luna the Earth spell for all of your party. Exit Coventry and go to the Suicide Cliffs sign.

After reading the sign, look around for the lightning gem: Go to Nero's Retreat and visit the building in the northeast part of town. Search the jar that had rats in it earlier. You'll find the lightning gem. This gives Luna the Thunder spell. Go to Carnage Corners. Buy the Cemetery Arena pass for Luna from the committee chairman, then go to the Arena.

CEMETERY ARENA: BATTLE

Return to the spot in the basement where you were teleported out of the Arena. Fight the two minor demons, then slay the demon Yrnie to get the Kalist Key. Talk to Mona, who will eventually give you a ruby pendant. Exit the dungeon; there will be no battles on the way out. Return to Carnage Corners and get your 5,000-sovereign reward from the person who sold you the Arena passes. Go to Mellions, northeast of Carnage Corners.

MELLIONS

Go east of Carnage Corners until you reach the mountains, then head north. Your next destination, the Castle of Kalist, has a nine-staircase puzzle. You can get part of the solution from the two feuding jar makers located in the basements of the furthermost buildings on the left and right side of town. Each one will tell you a partial solution to the nine-staircase puzzle, but if you talk to one, the other one will not talk to you. The complete solution is on the back of the signpost south of Mellions. Alternatively, you can get the full solution by saving the game, talking to one jar maker, then restoring the game and talking to the other jar maker.

CASTLE OF KALIST

Bring lots of heal potions because you will not have Luna's Earth spell for the main battle. Go east of Mellions to the trees, north around the mountains, then east to the Castle of Kalist. You'll be able to enter the castle if you have the Kalist Key and the Virgin Medal (and a virgin, of course).

In the castle, go south, east to a wall, north, east, north through the pillars, then east and south to stairs. Descend the stairs. Go east to the wall, north, and east to the stairs.

Descend the stairs. Go north and west to the nine-staircase puzzle. Take the upper-right-hand corner staircase, then the lower-left-hand corner staircase, and finally the middle bottom staircase. At this point, you will temporarily lose Luna. Go east, north, and down the stairs. You'll find the Falcon Sword in a chest — do not equip it because it is a fake.

Descend the stairs twice. Talk to Luna, who is lying on the ground. Fight the demon Haggis, who is impersonating Luna. Get the snow gem after the battle. Be sure to equip Luna when she rejoins your party.

Return to the top floor of the castle; you don't need to worry about the nine-staircase puzzle when going up. Go to the door west of the pillars. The door will now be unlocked. Enter the door. Get the Demonic Key from the chest. Exit the room.

Go all the way east to a big room with a face on the south wall. Walk up to the face; you should now be in a small room with a pentagon on the floor. Save the game. Walk into the pentagon to be teleported to the Wastelands.

Japanese-style graphics distinguish Knights of Xentar.

● ● ● ● ● ● ● ● ●

WASTELANDS

If you need items or rest, you can warp back to town and then warp back to the Wastelands. If you fight the Mad Hand, be sure to have Luna use spells; it will try to grab Luna and drain her hit points. If it succeeds in grabbing Luna, you will not be able to attack it anymore and will probably die. Follow the winding path to Moronvia in the south. When the path stops winding, go down one screen to Moronvia.

MORONVIA

Nothing is required here at this time, but you'll now be able to warp back later. Go back to the winding path and follow it to the northeast signpost. Take the westernmost path and go north until you reach the Feline Farms.

FELINE FARMS

You'll learn about the Tuna Liver Lumps stolen by the dogs. Go to the Cave of Doggies, north of Feline Farms.

CAVE OF DOGGIES

Go north, east, take the second south, and go east to a wall. Click the mouse by the stairs to automatically go through the hidden passage into the cave. Take the stairs down. Go south, east, north, west, and north to the skeleton.

Click on the east passage, and you will go through the hidden passage into it. Go east, north, west, north, and through the doorway. You will be in a dark hallway. Click the mouse at the top-center part of the screen, and you will move around the passageway. Keep doing this until a small room appears. Click on it to enter. After beating the dog leader, get the Tuna Liver Lumps from the chest and return to Feline Farms.

FELINE FARMS: LUMPS

Talk to Parrrtesia, the cat leader. She'll let you keep some Tuna Liver Lumps. Go to Moronvia.

MORONVIA: USE LUMPS

Give the Tuna Liver Lumps to the man guarding the stairs in the last building on the right. Leave town, then reenter. Go back to the guard, who should now be asleep.

Descend the stairs. Talk to the chief in the second building. His daughter will then hide. Go to the Lake of the Fairies, northwest of Feline Farms.

LAKE OF THE FAIRIES

Go up to the area of the Cave of the Doggies, then go west. After the screen changes, go north between the two groves of trees. Follow the northwest passage through the trees until you reach a lake. Enter the lake the same way you enter a town. The key to the Temple of Xentar is on display, but you will not be able to get it and will not need it. Go to Tristrap.

TRISTRAP

Leave the lake and go south until you are out of the trees. Go west until you reach the mountains. Go north until you reach the town of Tristrap. Talk to people; you'll be told that the "darkness" went southeast. Go to the Lake of the Fairies. Talk to the fairies. Go to Moronvia.

MORONVIA: PEARL

Go to the basement. Descend the stairs in the furthermost-left building to reach the subbasement. Talk to Alice. You'll eventually get the Pearl of Sorrow. Go to Tristrap.

BACK TO TRISTRAP

Talk to everyone. Buy as many heal potions as you can afford because you'll fight the last battle alone. Go to the Temple of Xentar. Go east until the screen changes. Continue walking east until you reach the mountains. Go south to the mountains. Walk east and then south at the mountains. Enter the Temple of Xentar.

TEMPLE OF XENTAR

After talking to the Dark Knight at the door, ascend the stairs and enter the doorway directly in front of the temple entrance. Go north, east, and south through the doorway. Go west and enter the door. Go north, east, and south down the stairs. Go south, east, and north to get the Genji Armor from the chest.

Go up the stairs. Go east to the wall, south, east, north, east, and south through the door. Go west and enter the second door to get the Falcon Sword. Exit the room, go east, and enter the first door. Go west, north, west, and south through the door. Go east to the first door and use the Pearl of Sorrow to unlock it. Go through the door, then go north through the passage until you finally exit in the clouds.

Go through the door and talk to the Goddess (Desmond's mom). You'll be teleported outside a mountain.

161

FINAL BATTLE

Enter the mountain. Walk down the passageway until you meet the Dark Knight. After talking with him, save the game and try to leave; you'll be stopped by Deimos. Keep healing during the battle — you will eventually win.

ENDGAME

After the battle, exit the mountain and rejoin Rolf and Luna. Look at the sign and find the Mirror of Illusion, which enables you to use the Photo Shop after watching the credits. Go to Arcadia. Talk to Aquarina. Talk to the Princess.

Watch the credits. Reload the game. There will now be an additional option on the menu: Photo Shop. This option will show you nudie pictures of all of the girls you visited during the game.

ORBS & STUFF

Object	See this Section for Location	Also See Section(s)
Magic Medal	Nameless Village	Location only
Flammo Pocket Warmer	Dreadsden	Location only
Mystic Marble	Dreadsden	Visel Cave
Magic Mirror	Priscilla's Place: The Mirror	Tymm
Desmond Action Figure	Phoenix	Luna's Gems
Diamond ring	Nero's Retreat	Luna's Gems
Magical Twig	Squalor Hollow: Twig	Arcadia
Arena pass	Carnage Corners: Arena Pass	Location Only
Sexy Drawing	Cemetery Arena: Picture	Carnage Corners: Nuts
Transsexual Nuts	Carnage Corners: Nuts	Arcadia
Virgin Medal	Arcadia	Castle Of Kalist
Magma gem	Luna's Gems	Location only
Snow gem	Luna's Gems	Location only
Crystal gem	Luna's Gems	Location only
Lightning gem	Luna's Gems	Location only
Arena pass for Luna	Luna's Gems	Cemetery Arena: Battle
Kalist Key	Cemetery Arena: Battle	Castle Of Kalist
Ruby pendant	Cemetery Arena: Battle	Location only
Snow gem	Castle of Kalist	Location only
Demonic Key	Castle of Kalist	Location only
Tuna Liver Lumps	Cave of Doggies	Feline Farms: Lumps, Moronvia: Use Lumps
Pearl of Sorrow	Moronvia: Pearl	Temple Of Xentar
Genji Armor	Temple of Xentar	Location only
Falcon Sword	Temple of Xentar	Location only
Mirror of Illusion	Endgame	Location only

THE LEGEND OF KYRANDIA 3

BY
PAUL SHAFFER

TYPE
Animated Adventure

SYSTEM
IBM PC (Required: 386/33, MS-DOS 5.0+, 4MB RAM, 15MB free hard disk space, CD-ROM drive, MSCDEX 2.2+, Microsoft-compatible mouse and driver. Supports: Sound Blaster, Sound Blaster Pro, Sound-Blaster 16, AWE32, 100% Sound Blaster compatibles, Pro Audio, Adlib Gold and Gold Standard, Audiotrix Pro.)

COMPANY
Westwood Studios

163

I N AN UNUSUAL PLOT TWIST FOR A SEQUEL, KYRANDIA 3 CASTS YOU IN THE ROLE OF MALCOLM. "MAD MALCOLM" WAS BLAMED FOR KILLING THE KING AND QUEEN IN THE FIRST INSTALLMENT OF THE SERIES. HIS WACKY JESTER SHOES WILL BE HARD TO FILL, BUT THAT'S YOUR ROLE AS YOU SET OUT TO PROVE YOUR INNOCENCE AND EXACT REVENGE ON THE FIEND WHO FRAMED YOU FOR THE MURDER. PUZZLES RANGE FROM SIMPLE TO PSYCHOPATHIC. MALCOLM, WHEN CONVERSING WITH OTHER CHARACTERS, MAY BE SWITCHED FROM HIS TYPICAL SARCASTIC MOOD TO A NICER GUY, OR TO A LIAR. A PUZZLE'S SOLUTION MAY HINGE ON MALCOLM'S ATTITUDE MORE THAN ON OBJECT MANIPULATION. GRAPHICS — THE 3D EFFECTS IN THE ANIMATED INTRODUCTION IN PARTICULAR — DELIVER A MORE CONVINCING SENSE OF FANTASY THAN CARTOON-STYLE ANIMATIONS OR EVEN FULL-MOTION VIDEO. A DIVERSE SCORE KEEPS YOU FROM TURNING DOWN THE MUSIC, AND VOICE ACTORS WERE MORE CAREFULLY SELECTED THAN IN MANY MULTIMEDIA GAMES. THEY LEND RESONANCE TO THE BIZARRELY HUMOROUS EXPERIENCE IN ONE OF THE BEST ADVENTURES OF THE YEAR.

THE SOLUTION

GENERAL

Random points can be scored by using your jester staff on different characters throughout the game.

GETTING STARTED

Search garbage for two nails, an empty flask, and a shoe (if you don't get them all the first time, exit this screen, return, and try again). Go to the town arena. Touch frog (it moves). Go east. At the city limits, take two pieces of firewood. Go to the town square. Use nail on lock. Enter toy factory. Go to the bedroom. Search the third drawer down (getting nut-on-a-string). Use bent nail on nut-on-a-string. Look under bed (getting jester's staff). Examine family album twice.

MAKING TOYS

Return to factory. Examine blueprint book (displays image of soldier). Save. Put firewood in toy machine. Push green button on wall (makes toy soldier). Get soldier. Move left lever on machine. Examine blueprint book (displays image of ball). Put shoe in machine. Push green button (makes ball). Get ball. Move left switch up and right switch down. Examine book (displays image of horse). Put firewood in machine. Push green button (makes horse). Get horse.

GETTING A FISH

While still in the toy factory, examine cellar hole. Enter cellar hole. Get flask. Use nail-on-a-string on water (catching eel). Take eel. You can also fish for eel at the boat dock.

GETTING CREAM

Go to the dairy. Get five sesame seeds from bag. Go to the town arena. Fill flask with water by using it on frog. Use flask on all five seeds (refilling the flask each time), changing them into sprouts. Return to dairy. Use all five sprouts on hopper (cows appear). Use nail on cream container. Use flask on cream.

GETTING A SQUIRREL

Still in dairy, take some more seeds. Go to the dump. Use seeds on post where squirrel sits. Use nail-on-a-string on squirrel (hypnotizing it). Get squirrel.

GETTING A FISH SANDWICH

Offer horse, soldier, or ball to boy who shows up in random locations. Repeat this until he trades you for his sandwich.

TALKING TO CATHERINE

Go to the crossroads. Use toy soldier on monkey jumper blossom (getting flower). If you gave your soldier away, go back to the toy factory and make another. Go to the graveyard. Use toy soldier on blossom there (getting second flower). Put both flowers on Catherine's grave. Talk to Catherine until she disappears.

GETTING MIME DISGUISE

Go to the town outskirts. When mime turns his back to you, put eel in his hood. Use squirrel on self (wears it as hat). Use nail-on-a-string on money box on fence (enter public baths). Set your mood dial to lying. Turn bath temperature dial to red hot. Take mime costume from window after everyone runs out. Exit. Use nail-on-a-string on self to get rid of squirrel hat. Wear mime disguise.

FISH-CREAM SANDWICH & STATUE

Repeat squirrel hypnosis trick at the dump, getting squirrel back. Go to town parlor with cream, more seeds, and another eel. Drop squirrel. Use nail-on-string with squirrel (de-hypnotizing him). Talk to bartender three times. Put cream, eel, and seeds in sandwich machine. Get sandwich. Go to the town hall. Use sandwich on statue. Talk to statue three times.

GETTING OUT OF JAIL

If you get caught while exploring and wind up in jail, there are two ways to get free. One is to follow the warden's directions and make 10 doilies to get out on parole. The other involves carrying a nail with you before you get caught. When you are caught, you will be asked to drop all your items; merely pick up the nail from your inventory to smuggle it inside with

165

you. Inside, use nail on lock on the box (reveals man). Put rope from machine in man's hands, then poke man with scissors. Activate the machine, and he'll make a frayed rope that you can use to climb down from window to freedom.

Should you be arrested a second time and taken to the rock quarry, put fertilized seeds on a load of rocks. Click on Malcolm until he sweats on the seeds.

ESCAPING KYRANDIA

The Cellar Method: Go to the cellar with seeds, eel, and flask. Examine loose bricks on wall. Use eel on seeds (making fertilized seeds). Use fertilized seeds on bricks. Fill flask with water and use it on seeds on bricks. Enter the new hole (catacombs). Open green bottle. Use flask on green bottle (getting potion). Go to the town arena and use Portal potion.

The Boat Dock Method: In your mime disguise, go to the docks. Talk to dog in lying mode. Give extra fish-cream sandwich to dog.

ISLE OF CATS: FLUFFY

If you reach the island by using the potion, exit the ruins into the dog fort. If you sailed to the island, click on the dog cart in nice mode twice (taking you to the beach). Talk to captain in lying mode three times (he asks for a magic weapon). Go to the dog fort via the cart.

At the fort, take the machete and as many seeds as you can carry. Enter the jungle by going west. Regularly pick fleas off yourself by clicking on you or occasionally bathing in the jungle pools. Clear jungle bushes using machete, and also use machete on randomly discovered snakes. If you want to map the jungle, use seeds as you go (dropped bones will disappear). Get bones off ground as you go. Go west, west, north. Talk to Fluffy in lying mode (getting mouse).

FIXING ALTAR, ESCAPING ISLAND

Go east. At the mouse altar, go west to statues. Use mouse on round statues. Return to dog fort by going east from altar, then go west, north and north. Save. Give bones to the dog. He'll bury each one, sometimes revealing a gem. His success at finding gems is random, so save and restore occasionally so you don't have to keep going back into the jungle for more bones.

When you have six gems, return to the altar. Place each gem on altar, noting symbol attached to that particular gem. Return to fort and enter hole to ruins. Go east. Examine statues and corresponding symbols. Return to altar and go west to the statues. Place a single gem in each of the statues in this order from left to right: diamond, topaz, amethyst, emerald, sapphire, and ruby. Get crystal mouse that appears. Go to the beach (from altar, go east, north, north, north). Use crystal mouse on Louie (man with crutch).

FALLS AT END OF EARTH

With the three gold coins you automatically receive, buy an insurance policy from first machine, an umbrella from the second machine (third button), and a pool toy from the second machine (fourth button). Use pool toy on self.

Enter water. At Under the End, use pump (from pool toy) on inflatable plant. Click on plant (you jump across gap). Enter cave. Enter water again. At Further Down, use umbrella on hook in waterfall (swings you across gap). Remove pool toy and use umbrella on self. Click on rocks beneath you (float down). At Way Down, enter cave. Click on rocks beneath you (still using umbrella). At Way Way Down, enter last cave.

Dust-bunny alert in Kyrandia.

•••••••••

FISHWORLD

Click on self (wakes you up), and you automatically exit. Go northwest (you're called back to the Queen). Play tic-tac-toe and lose on purpose. Talk to Queen twice in lying mode. Return to perch university. Use jester staff on lower-left fish (shoots spitball at teacher). Grab apple from desk when teacher's not looking. Go to the dump (again called back to Queen). Repeat losing at tic-tac-toe and lying to Queen. Return to dump. Talk to batfish. Eat apple twice, leaving you with worm.

Give worm to batfish, getting coin. Return to university and get another apple. Go west from university to waterslide (again called back to Queen). Repeat tic-tac-toe sequence.

Return to university for another apple (you should now have two). Go to the waterslide. Enter waterslide by yellow rail (click on it twice to enter). Pull round knob twice (takes you to fish dump, but you're now on top of dump). Search dump three times. You'll get kicked out of the dump but have two new items. Repeat process of riding slide into dump until you find a newspaper. Go to the fish ladder. Eat both apples, leaving you with two worms. Give both worms to lowest fish on fish ladder (cracks slide). Go to the waterslide entrance and ride slide to the underworld.

UNDERWORLD

Talk to woman in nice mode three times, until she tells you of ingredients for seance. You're taken back to Queen in Fishworld.

FISHWORLD II: SEANCE

Play tic-tac-toe until five mermen are on the board. Drop newspaper and use coin on newspaper (King arrives). Return to Underworld via the fish ladder approach, or save up five coins selling worms to the batfish or selling any three-of-a-kind items you find in the dump (you get one coin for every three items). Give the coins to the attendant at the waterslide and he will cannon you into the underworld.

UNDERWORLD II

In nice mode, talk to the man in line, taking his place in line. Talk to lady when Elvis gets dumped (takes you to lobby). Talk to lady until she removes your collar. Talk to couple until they leave. Talk to man with surfboard until he leaves. Explore lobby until lady sends you back to surface. Click on seat of bore machine (takes you back to Kyrandia).

THREE PATHS OF CONSCIENCE

There are three endings, depending on your choice here. Each is described.

BAD CONSCIENCE

Go to the castle. Talk to Louie until he tells you about getting the gems. Go to the cellar. Touch the green apple, then the red apple on carpet (takes you to Darm). Talk to Brandywine (the dragon) until she asks you for a squirrel. Return to Kyrandia and go to the bath house (now a pawn shop) and sell any item for seeds (exit and enter to change which items are being bought). Go to the dump and repeat squirrel hypnosis (will find nut-on-a-string in dump pile), getting squirrel. Return to Darm via the carpet and give squirrel to Brandywine (getting Portal potion). Note: To exit cellar, you can now go back through the hole in the factory floor. Go to the town arena and use potion.

ISLE OF CATS II

Take machete outside ruin. Go to Fluffy. Talk to Fluffy (getting cheesemaker). Go to the Cat Colossi (west of altar). Use cheesemaker on self. Get cheese and use it on mouse statue. Get all six gems. Return to Fluffy. Talk to Fluffy (getting empty tuna can). Use can on self.

ENDGAME: CLEARING YOUR NAME

Return to dump and get magic collar. Go to the castle and give any gem to Louie. Give collar to captain (Queen rings). Go to the pawn shop and sell enough items to get six seeds (five for cream and one for the sandwich machine). Also buy the crutch by using any gem. (The fastest ways to get seeds are selling flasks you find at the dump and buying toys with gems.)

Go to the Malcolm's bedroom. Get crumpled portrait from under bed. Catch an eel (from the cellar or boat dock). Make cream (five seeds with water in dairy hopper). Go to the parlor and use crutch on sandwich machine. Put eel, seeds, and cream in machine. Push button. Get sandwich. Go to the town hall via cellar and talk to statue (twice). Save. Use portrait on magic cabinet. Use portrait and sandwich on statue (should teleport you to parlor). Use portrait on magic cabinet.

CHOOSING THE GOOD CONSCIENCE

Get nail from dump. Go to the castle. Talk to Louie. In jail, use nail on chains (freeing self). Talk to others. Use nail on lock (freeing others). Get eel, seeds, and water flask from floor. Use eel on seeds. Use fertilized seeds on door. Use water flask on seeds in door (opens door).

Go to the castle and talk to Louie until he tells you about jewels. Go to the town hall via cellar. Talk to Zanthia (asks for horse ingredient). Make or buy toy horse and put it in Zanthia's mixing pot. Use empty flask on pot (getting Pegasus potion). Go to the Pegasus point and use potion on self.

Repeat jungle sequence as described when choosing the bad conscience. Repeat castle sequence, giving jewels and collar to pirates. Leave and return to castle entrance, (Brandon and Kallak will be behind the castle's drawbridge gate). Use cheesemaker on self. Give cheese to Brandon. Go to the parlor and use cheesemaker again. Give cheese to bartender. Exit and return (sandwich machine will be fixed). Get ingredients for fish sandwich and put in sandwich machine. Get crumpled portrait from under bed in bedroom. Catch an eel (from the cellar or boat dock). Make cream (five seeds with water in dairy hopper). Go to the parlor and use crutch on sandwich machine. Put eel, seeds, and cream in machine. Push button. Get sandwich. Go to the town hall via cellar and talk to statue (twice). Save. Use portrait on magic cabinet. Use portrait and sandwich on statue (should teleport you to parlor). Use portrait on magic cabinet.

CHOOSING BOTH GOOD AND BAD CONSCIENCE

The only difference to this ending is that you must pick the jail-door lock from the outside rather than from the inside. Enter the jail and free mice with the nail. Get the Pegasus potion from Zanthia or the Portal potion from Brandywine. At the Isle of Cats, you will need to find ten bones for Fluffy before he gives you the cheesemaker.

Return to dump and get magic collar. Go to the castle and give any gem to Louie. Give collar to captain (Queen rings). Go to the pawn shop and sell enough items to get six seeds (five for cream and one for the sandwich machine). Also buy the crutch by using any gem. (The fastest ways to get seeds are selling flasks you find at the dump and buying toys with gems.)

Go to the Malcolm's bedroom. Get crumpled portrait from under bed. Catch an eel (from the cellar or boat dock). Make cream (five seeds with water in dairy hopper). Go to the parlor and use crutch on sandwich machine. Put eel, seeds, and cream in machine. Push button. Get sandwich. Go to the town hall via cellar and talk to statue (twice). Save. Use portrait on magic cabinet. Use portrait and sandwich on statue (should teleport you to parlor). Use portrait on magic cabinet.

ORBS & STUFF

Object	See this Section for Location	Also See Section(s)
Nails	Getting Started	Making Toys, Getting Cream, Jail: Getting Out, Choosing the Good Conscience
Flask	Getting Started	Getting Cream, Escaping Kyrandia, Endgame: Clearing Your Name, Choosing the Good Conscience, Choosing the Good and Bad Conscience
Shoe	Getting Started	Making Toys
Firewood	Getting Started	Making Toys
Nut-on-a-string	Getting Started	Location only
Nail-on-a-string	Getting Started	Getting a Fish, Getting a Squirrel, Getting Mime Disguise, Fish-Cream Sandwich & Statue, Bad Conscience
Jester's staff	Getting Started	Fishworld
Toy soldier	Making Toys	Getting a Fish Sandwich, Talking to Catherine
Monkey jumper blossom	Talking to Catherine	Location only
Ball	Making Toys	Getting a Fish Sandwich
Horse	Making Toys	Getting a Fish Sandwich, Choosing the Good Conscience
Eel	Getting a Fish	Boat Dock, Getting Mime Disguise, Fish-Cream Sandwich & Statue, Escaping Kyrandia, Choosing the Good Conscience

Object	See this Section for Location	Also See Section(s)
Sesame seeds	Getting Cream	Getting a Squirrel Fish-Cream Sandwich & Statue, Jail: Getting Out, Escaping Kyrandia, Choosing the Good Conscience, Choosing the Good and Bad Conscience
Cream	Getting Cream	Fish-Cream Sandwich & Statue, Bad Conscience, Choosing the Good Conscience
Squirrel	Getting a Squirrel	Getting Mime Disguise, Fish-Cream Sandwich & Statue, Bad Conscience
Mime disguise	Getting Mime Disguise	Escaping Kyrandia
Sandwich	Getting a Fish Sandwich	Fish-Cream Sandwich & Statue, Escaping Kyrandia, Endgame: Clearing Your Name, Choosing the Good and Bad Conscience
Potion	Escaping Kyrandia	Bad Conscience, Choosing the Good Conscience, Choosing the Good and Bad Conscience
Machete	Isle of Cats: Fluffy	Isle of Cats II
Bones	Isle of Cats: Fluffy	Fixing Altar, Escaping Island, Choosing the Good and Bad Conscience
Mouse	Isle of Cats: Fluffy	Fixing Altar
Six gems	Fixing Altar, Escaping Island	Isle of Cats II, Choosing the Good Conscience
Crystal mouse	Fixing Altar, Escaping Island	Falls at End of Earth
Insurance policy	Falls at End of Earth	Location only
Umbrella	Falls at End of Earth	Location only
Pool toy	Falls at End of Earth	Location only
Apple	Fishworld	Location only

172

Object	See this Section for Location	Also See Section(s)
Coin	Fishworld	Fishworld II: Seance
Newspaper	Fishworld	Fishworld II: Seance
Cheesemaker	Isle of Cats II	Choosing the Good Conscience, Choosing the Good and Bad Conscience
Can	Isle of Cats II	Location only
Magic collar	Endgame: Clearing Your Name	Location only
Crutch	Bad Conscience	Choosing the Good Conscience, Choosing the Good and Bad Conscience
Portrait	Bad Conscience	Choosing the Good Conscience, Choosing the Good and Bad Conscience

MENZOBERRANZAN

BY
CLANCY SHAFFER
& FRED PHILIPP

F YOU'VE BEEN DOWN SO LONG THAT IT LOOKS LIKE UP TO YOU, THEN MENZOBERRANZAN IS YOUR KIND OF GAME. THIS IS ONE OF THE MOST EXTENSIVE, MOST INTENSIVE DUNGEON CRAWLS SINCE RAVENLOFT. (NOT COINCIDENTALLY, IT WAS CREATED BY THE SAME DESIGNERS, DREAMFORGE.) BASED ON R.A. SALINGER'S NOVEL *THE LEGACY*, IT PITS YOUR FOUR-MEMBER PARTY AGAINST THE DROW, MALEVOLENT DWARVES WHOM YOU MUST TRACK DOWN TO RESCUE THE HUMANS THEY HAVE CAPTURED. YOUR CHARACTERS CONSIST OF CONVENTIONAL AD&D-TYPE FIGHTERS AND MAGIC USERS, THOUGH MAGIC PLAYS A LESS IMPORTANT ROLE THAN IN MOST ROLE-PLAYING GAMES. AS YOU MIGHT EXPECT, COMBAT AND DUNGEON DELVING — WITH THE EMPHASIS ON THE LATTER — MAKE UP MOST OF THE ACTION. A CONVENIENT AUTOMAP SIMPLIFIES KEEPING YOUR BEARINGS AS YOU EXPLORE ONE SUBTERRANEAN MAZE AFTER ANOTHER; YOU CAN EVEN "WRITE" NOTES ON THEM, AS IN ULTIMA UNDERWORLD. THE MOST INVITING ASPECT OF MENZOBERRANZAN IS THE VAST ASSORTMENT OF GRAPHICS USED TO DEPICT THE DUNGEON WALLS. THAT WON'T

TYPE
Fantasy Role-playing

SYSTEM
IBM PC (Required: 386/40+, 4MB RAM, VGA monitor, DOS 5.0+, 13MB hard drive, double-speed CD-ROM drive, mouse. Recommended: 486/33+. Supports: Aria, Sound Canvas (music only), Soundscape, Wave Blaster, Soundman, Sound Blaster family (except AWE32), 100% compatibles; keyboard.)

COMPANY
Strategic Simulations, Inc.

BE ENOUGH TO SATISFY ANYONE SEEKING A SUBSTANTIAL ROLE-PLAYING EXPERIENCE, HOWEVER, FOR THE STORY AND CHARACTERS REMAIN UNDEVELOPED. IF YOU ENJOY DUNGEON CRAWLS AND SLAYING DWARVES, HOWEVER, MENZOBERRANZAN IS RIGHT UP YOUR COBBLESTONE ALLEY.

THE SOLUTION

GENERAL

If you don't use the two pregenerated characters, create a Paladin and a female half-elf who has Cleric, Mage, and Fighter powers. The latter character, after earning enough experience points, enjoys the powers of all three classes. You may add up to two nonplayer characters to the party.

Print out maps as you proceed and mark your route. Always print out a map before leaving each level. Orange spots on the map indicate loot, large orange spots indicate an enemy, and blue spots represent nonplayer characters. Due to the nature of the Underworld topography, you must rely on the automap and object-oriented directions. After locating the Great Orb of Omo, for example, your next direction will be described in reference to the Great Orb of Omo.

THE FIRE DOWN BELOW

Your first mission is to put out the fire in the storeroom in the southeast part of the village. To do so, collect about ten empty buckets and fill them at the well in the center of the village (by clicking on them). Go to the fire and click the buckets to put out the flames. Slay any Drow raiders who arrive.

Then talk to Baldassar, the Captain of the Guard, who will join your party. Visit each orange spot in the village area and collect scrolls and gear. Look for the scroll case and bags, which are essential to carrying the gear you need. You will also be invited to enter the guard house and take any gear you want.

The mage cannot use her Magic powers with armor on, but she can wear it and use the Cleric powers until the Magic is needed. Go back to the Innkeeper. He will give you a Helmet that is necessary to complete the game.

FOREST NEXT TO VILLAGE

Go east while collecting all the orange items seen on the map. Next, visit the house and speak with Vermulean, who suggests you get four gems, which he will enchant. If you're using the

CD-ROM version, do not enlist the Centaur because he won't go underground. (The Centaur is not in the floppy version.) Leave Vermulean and go east.

ICE DALE PLAINS 1

Proceed east to a small alcove in the rocks. Wipe out the veeburg giants and get the Ring of Feather Fall and a suit of ring-mail armor.

Combat is frequent in this area, so watch your lifeline and rest if necessary. You can rest at Vermulean's cottage or any corner. You may also run away from a fight. Go to the cave in the east wall; it's about one-third of the way down from the top line.

LEUCROTTA'S LAIR

Save frequently, for the beasts here are tenacious. Inside, immediately turn right and head for the northeast corner. The four gems are in four separate rooms: the two top rooms, the one directly south of the east room, and in the room just west of the latter. You will need the Jump spell or potion to get into the northwest room.

Make your way to Vermulean so he can enchant the four gems. This lets you see radiation and protects you from it. He will also give you any scrolls you find lying around.

Return to Dale Plains 1 and get all the orange items you can find. Then go to the south-central area, where you'll be attacked. A Drow kills the attacker; it's Drizzt, who will join if asked. You must accept him because he's the best NPC in the game.

ICE DALE PLAINS 2

Again search out all the orange spots and get all the scrolls and other useful gear. In particular, look for a Mage Scroll of Melf's Acid Arrow and a Scroll of Improved Identify. When you locate Vonar, ask him to join (ask Baldassar to leave). Vonar, a fighter, thief, and mage, is the second best NPC in the game (after Drizzt).

The entrance to the Underdark in the southeast section of the south wall. Save before entering.

UNDERDARK: LEVEL 1

You begin in the northeast area, where you will be attacked by gnolls, Drow fighters, cloaker lords, jellies, and leucrottas. From your initial position, you want to get to the southwest area and access the stairs down to the next level. To do so, head south and west until you find a crossbow, then continue south and west again until you meet a barbarian named Manahath.

177

He will help by giving you a piece of map. (He will want to join the party, but this is not advised.) Use his map in conjunction with the regular map to see how much farther you must go to reach the ladder. Move west and south from the barbarian to find a Mage Scroll of Spook. Then continue south and west until you reach the wall furthest to the south. The ladder is located just a little west of the final map's center, but almost in the southwest corner of your present map. Descend.

UNDERDARK: LEVEL 2

You arrive in the southwest corner and must reach the northwest corner to get back to Level 1. Foes here include Drow fighters, troglodytes, gnolls, jellies, and leucrottas. Initially head west and north because you will find either a Mage Scroll of Fireball and a Passweb potion. If you find the scroll first, get the potion from the chamber west of it; if you find the potion first, reverse the procedure. Your route to the scroll or potion will not permit you to travel north, so you must move southwest until you are able to go north. There is a spell trap nearby so be careful.

Once headed north again, you will find a Mage Scroll of Passweb almost directly north of where you found the potion. However, you cannot get there directly. Go east a little, then north to an overhead passage. Use the Jump potion or spell to reach the passage.

Continue north, staying a little to the east. You will soon find a Levitation potion. Then go north, also moving a little to the west as you proceed, and you will soon see a door covered by a web. Use the Passweb potion or scroll to get through. Next go slightly northwest to the top of this chamber, from which you can return to Level 1 of the Underdark. Save your game.

UNDERDARK: LEVEL 1 AGAIN

You now are seeking to return to Level 2, whose entrance, in reference to your current position, is in the extreme southwest corner. Investigate any orange dots because you need all of the scrolls you can find.

Go south along the west side until you find the Cloak of Piwafwi. A little farther south you will find a Sling of Seeking. Stay as close to the western wall as possible, and you will also locate a spear. Defeat the monsters and pick up the True Seeing spell they drop. You can use this spell a little to the south to locate an illusionary wall if you can't find it otherwise. Go through the wall, then south and west. (The Jump potion or scroll will be necessary.) A glance at your map will show that you're now in a new area on this level. Continue to the ladder in the extreme southwest corner, then go east to find a pickaxe that is also essential to finishing game. Take the entrance down to Level 2 of the Underdark.

UNDERDARK: LEVEL 2 AGAIN

You begin in the south-central part of this level and again must go to the northwest corner. To the east, and about halfway to the corner, you'll find a mace in an alcove. North of the mace is a Scroll of Passweb. Take it and go north. Eliminate any black elves you come across. Keep an eye out for a Passweb potion to the southeast.

When you enter a room from which there seems no exit to the north or west, seek out two illusionary walls on the west side of the room. The southern illusionary wall contains several items and a few troglodytes. The northern wall contains a web and will require you to use the Passweb spell or potion to get by it. After passing through the wall, go north to a dwarf who has been poisoned. You may recruit and heal him later if you wish, but don't replace Drizzt at this time. Go northwest from the dwarf to an underground lake.

UNDERGROUND LAKE

Save your game because you may be poisoned if you get too close to the Aboleth, and you can't be cured until you reach the Healing Waters.

Use ranged weapons and spells to slay the Aboleth. In the lake, go directly south and get the elven golden armor. Take the nearby exit and emerge into Level 2 for the third time.

UNDERDARK: LEVEL 2 YET AGAIN

Bring up your map to see your location. Head south and east through a stone archway. Then go south and west through another archway. You should find a Cleric Scroll of Spiritual Hammer, a Mage Scroll of Darkness, and an Extra Healing potion. Then go back through the archway and south again. Stay as far west as you can. Be sure and get the Passweb potion just northeast of the ladder. Go south, then east to a ladder. Go down to the dwarvian level.

DWARVIAN LEVEL

You begin in the south part of this level. Take the first west turn and go past some large bins. Go north at the western wall (you must pull the nearby chain). Turn east and enter the first door to the south, which is the also the first room you find in the Eastbound Hall. Get the Healing potion and wipe out the derros. Leave, then head west to a door covered with runes. Click on it. If you have the Learning spell, click again and read the runes. Then go to the end of the hall. Turn south and, near the end, pull the chain on the east wall. Enter the west door.

Do in the derro and go into the next room to the west (you must pull two chains here, one on each side). Enter the southern room and get the Wand of Paralyzation, then go into the room just to the north and get a Cleric Scroll of Flame Blade. Retrace your steps, and where the hall turns west, go north through the door. Push the button on the wall. Go west through these rooms and into the second room. Be prepared to dodge north to avoid a fireball. Step on the pressure plate in the floor to open the doors here.

You must dispatch the derro dwarfs and get the Bag of Holding that one of them drops. In the room containing the fireball, enter the north door, go north, then enter the first door to the west and follow the right wall around to the end. Head north and follow the left-hand wall around to a Shield of Lightning. If you check your map, you'll see that you're in a miniature maze.

At some time during this phase, you will encounter a pretty maid who is really a yochlol — do not take her into your party. When you turn to leave, she transforms into a monster. The Wand of Paralyzation is very useful to kill this monster.

Keep your eyes peeled for a shield as you traverse the maze and go north from where you find it. About three or four steps west of the east wall is an illusionary wall leading north. Pull the east chain and enter the room to the east. You will encounter a hook horror guarding a Mage Scroll of Stoneskin. Get it, then return to the hall and head north to the first west door. Enter the first door north and search this room for a Longsword.

Exit this room and go west, then north to another room. From here, head east to another room, and then another until you enter a hall that runs north to south. Go south, pulling all the chains you pass. Push the button on the wall to enter the next east door. Inside this room, save the game and rest. You will note two large doors on the north wall. Enter the eastern door and head north to the Temple of Dumathoin.

TEMPLE OF DUMATHOIN

You start in one of the southern rooms. Go west through three rooms, a hall, and another room at the west side of the temple. You will find a Scroll of Cloud Kill in the first room and a pickaxe in the second (get this if you don't have one — you'll need it). Return to where you started on this level and take the east door that leads into a hall. Go north in the hall and enter the second door to the east (you must push the button on the wall). Inside this room you will find the Silver Moon Key; while getting the key, you overhear a conversation through a hole in the wall.

Leave the room and go north to a room with four pillars. Turn right (east) and enter the door to the south. Use the Silver Moon key to open this door, then discard the key, deal sudden death to the disgusting derro and get the Silver Star Key. Go back to the room with four pillars. Observe the two projections from the north wall into the room. To get past the spinner trap as you advance toward the north wall, put your party into Step mode.

The east side of the east projection has an illusionary wall. Enter and push the oval button, which turns off the trap and opens a door elsewhere. Now go to the west side of the west projection and enter through the wall. Go east and get the Holy Symbol of Dumathoin. Leave the main room through the west door, cross a large room, and use the Silver Star Key to enter the northwest door in the next room to the west. The stairway will take you to Level 2.

TEMPLE OF DUMATHOIN: LEVEL 2

You start in the northwest corner. Go through the door to the east and stride east until you run into a spinner trap. After being spun around, take three or four steps backwards, and you will be headed in the correct direction. Continue east until you reach a door with a hall running south. Go south to a large room with many columns in it.

Exit through the southern door and use the button to open the door and continue south. When you hit another spinner, use the backwards steps described previously to pass it. Go into the third door on the east side and slay more derros.

On the east side, you will run into a prisoner named Vlkakverdling. Free him and let him join the party because Drizzt will soon be captured. Vlkakverdling is a Level 6 thief who is promoted rapidly. You must nurture him until you find the Fountain of Healing. Otherwise, he is very useful if equipped with a Longsword.

After Vlkakverdling joins the party, proceed down the hall to a door. The button is concealed in some carvings there but is easy to find. Use it and enter the door. Pass through the next room to a hall running east and west. Go west to a north-south hall and follow it north. Go into the first east door and get the Silver Circle Key. Exit and go north up the hall. Enter the next room by pressing the button on the west wall. Do in more derros, leave the room, and proceed north until you arrive at an east-west hall. Go east in the hall and open the east door by pressing the button. Enter the room and go to the northwest corner. Use the Silver Circle Key on the keyhole to open the wall on the west. Enter, and you are teleported west into another area. Look for a button on the south side. Press it and proceed west. Press the button near the next door to the west. If attacked by umber hulks, use Lightning on them.

Inside, get the dwarven horn and go to the northwest area, where you will teleported to a large room in the south. You will be attacked by derros and derro mages.

Exit through the door to the south, cross the hall, and press the button hidden in the carvings. The door to the west will open, and you'll see a statues in the room. Find the one with the Chalice in his hand and use the dwarven horn on him to get the Chalice. (You must have this Chalice and the Holy Symbol to enter Level 3 of the Temple.) Go out the southeast door along the hall, east through another door, and down the steps to Level 3.

TEMPLE DUMATHOIN: LEVEL 3

You start this level in the southeast corner. Go out the west door, then head south in the hall until you have to turn west. Go west along the south wall. As you pass a hall on the north side, a lightning bolt trap fires down the east-west hall; duck north to avoid it. Then continue west. Turn north at the corner and go as far as possible, then turn east. This hall contains another lightning trap to dodge.

Just a hair south of the east end of the hall is a door leading east. Use the lever to open the door, then leave the room by the south door and get the Silver Axe Key. Go about halfway back west the way you came and take the hall leading south. When you come to a door on the west side, pull the lever and enter. Once inside, you can use the pickaxe to pry a diamond from the wall. You must use the diamond as a sacrifice to the Healing Fountain. Drop the pickaxe. Search the room and get the Shield of Lightning Protection.

THE HEALING FOUNTAIN

Go north in the same hall you used before. Turn west, go through a door leading south and take the Iron Circle Key. Leave and continue west in the hall. Turn south at the end and enter the first hall on the east side that is blocked by a door. Use the Silver Axe Key and go east in the hall on the other side of the door. Dodge the fireball as before. When you reach the first door to the east, use the Iron Circle Key.

Enter the room and go to the Fountain of Healing. Use the diamond as a sacrifice; put it in your left hand and click on it. The fountain and the dwarven hero will speak to you. Take the Axe of Hurling from near the fountain. Heal any member of the party by using the Chalice.

Leave this room through the south door. The first room to the south contains a Ring of Regeneration. Just south is the door leading up to Temple Level 1. Save your game now, for you will meet two bad monsters on this level; use long-range weapons and spells on them.

Just south of this room is the entrance to the dwarvian mine level. You will be attacked by drows, and Drizzt will be captured if he's still in the party. Go to the next room to the south and use the mine cart. It crashes, and you will find yourself in the northeast corner of the Cavern of the Myconids. (If playing the floppy version, the Cavern of the Myconids is not in the game; proceed directly to the Cavern of the Galeb Duhr section.)

CAVERN OF THE MYCONIDS

You start this level in the northeast corner. Just to the west is a jade spider. Attach it to the Helmet you got from the Innkeeper. You will now have the ability to throw lightning bolts once a day. Return to the previous room and go south. Look for a hidden button on the south wall. It opens the west wall. Go through this door, head west and south, and then back north to acquire an adamantite-chain helmet. From here, go south and west to a door. Use the chain on the east wall to open a door to the south. A wall drops behind you, and you must battle a group of Fungi Skeletons. You will find a Dagger of Throwing and a Mage Scroll of Hold Monster. Then head south from this room.

Continue south, staying as far west as possible. When you can go no farther in either direction, look for a hidden button on the north wall. Push it, then enter the north room. Go south to a door. Push the button on the south wall, which will open the door. Guards from the Myconid King will allow you to pass south to speak with the King, who asks you to kill an umber hulk that is eating the Myconids. Go through the west door that opens automatically, then find and kill the umber hulk. Return to the King, who will give you three doses of antivenom. If Vlkakverdling is in the party, one dose will cure him. Afterwards, the king opens another wall to the south. Go west and south, pick up the Scroll of Vampiric Touch, and go west to leave this level and enter the Cavern of the Galeb Duhr.

CAVERN OF THE GALEB DUHR

You start in the southeast corner. Go south, then back up and around to the north and get a Plate Helmet. Go north and west to a Scroll of Darkfire and a Scroll of Cone of Cold. From here, move north and east to a Mage Scroll of Wizard Eye and a Flying potion. Just west along the wall is a Passweb potion.

Go north from the potion and meet Galeb Duhr, who is a part of the west wall near the potion. He wants a necklace and will open a wall to the north. Go north and immediately turn east, then turn around to the south, east, and north. Use a spell or potion to get past the webbed door. Go north and west and find a flask of Oil of Fiery Burning. Go east and north to a Scroll of Spidercloak Armor, then make your way north and west to an opening high in the wall. Use one of the scrolls or potions of Levitate or Flying to get through the hole. Go to the northwest corner of this level to get the necklace. There is a lot of loot here, so take what you want.

Not far south is a white robe. Southeast are Flying and Passweb potions. Go through the webbed door to the south. Continue south to another Passweb potion. From here, head west to a blue candle, which can fire lightning bolts. Get it and the Borgner Stone, then go north to find a broadsword. In the room north and east of the broadsword is a Scroll of Acid Bolt. Return to where you found the broadsword. This time, turn east and south to find a Flying potion. Next, move north around a corner, then go south through the hall (a Flying potion is necessary). Go south to Galeb Duhr. Once you give him the necklace, he will open the second wall to the southwest.

Go southwest and proceed south to a shield. Go south, then around to the west to get the mage Scroll of Disintegrate. Southeast of this is a blue gem. You will need two of these. Now go to the southwest corner of the level. You must fly or jump. As you reach the southwest section, a disruption of the ground takes you to Cavern of the Driders.

CAVERN OF THE DRIDERS: LEVEL 1

You must move from Level 1 to Level 2, then back to 1. Beginning in the southwest corner, go west and north to a Flying potion in the corner. Just north is a Passweb potion. Go southeast from this potion to a Scroll of Passweb, then east to Flying potion. From here head to the southeast corner, where a teleporter will move you east to a door.

Open the door and go east, then north and east to an Ivory Scroll Case. Go southeast and get another Blue Gem, then return to the door just north of where you found the ivory scroll case.

Go north through the door, then west to a Rod of Antilevitation. Search to the southeast for a Scroll of Lightning Bolt and go south, then east to a door leading east. You need Passweb to get past the door. Go east through another door and around the corner to the north, where you encounter a carrion crawler. Get rid of it, then go north through a door and around to the west to a teleporter.

You emerge in a room. Search to find a Passweb potion, then go east and north to another door. Move thorough this door and go north as far as possible to find a Scroll of Ice Storm. Go west to a door, which requires a Passweb scroll. You will find yourself in the lair of some Uropygui. Slay them and get the Wand of Magic Missiles. Beyond the wand, a teleporter takes you to another part of this level.

Move north and west to a suit of adamantite-chain mail. Go east from here, then north and get a Flying potion. Now go east and north for a Scroll of Fireseed. Go west across the area to a Web Door; open it by using a nearby button and go west through the door into a tunnel leading to the Cavern of the Driders.

CAVERN OF THE DRIDERS: LEVEL 2

Immediately go north and west to a point high in the wall. Use Jump or Flying to get through. Grab the throwing knife here. If Vonar the Kenku did not join previously, you'll get a second chance to pick him up now. Proceed north and east to Maznafein, a drider, who wants some help and will provide you with a Scroll of Spider Shape. Go east to find a Scroll of Stinking Cloud and Gauntlets of Stone Giant Strength. Also get the nearby Stone of Infravision (which is vital if Vonar has just joined the group). Go south and east to reach Level 1.

RETURN TO CAVERN OF DRIDERS: LEVEL 1

Move north to a door. Go through the door and head west a short distance, then go north again. When you hit an impassable chasm, use the Scroll of Spider Shape to cross it.

Next move north, east, then south to a Flying potion. From here, go further east for a Scroll of Flame Strike. A bit south and west of the scroll is the second blue gem. An exit in the east wall leads to the Underground River.

THE UNDERGROUND RIVER

You meet a boney ferryman and must pay him two Blue Gems to cross the river. On the other side, take the south exit.

APPROACH TO MENZOBERRANZAN

You begin in the northeast corner of this area. Zigzag south, then northeast to a suit of banded-mail armor. Go south, then west to the southwest corner of the area. There you will find the Menzoberranzan interface. Check the map on page 27 of your manual, which is correct except that the two Mantle Caves must be switched: Mantle Cave 1 is on the top right corner.

You can choose The Merchant Bazaar, Tower of Sorcere, Carpathian's Tavern, Gllvelius Tavern, House Fey Branche, House Do'Urden, Mantle Caves 1 and 2, and House Baenre, which will not appear until you have gotten the Scroll of Drider Wish.

THE MERCHANT BAZAAR

You start this level in the southwest corner. Enter a small shop called Galentha's Goods and trade the Helmet you got from the Innkeeper for Galentha's music box and some candles. You will need the music box in the Tower of Sorcere.

Go to the southwest shop, where you will meet Ssar Tarell the Drow, who was mentioned by Maznafein. Ssar will ask you to contact Jalynfein in the Tower of Sorcere. She tells you that he has a scroll that will return Maznafein to his original form, and only after this has been accomplished will she talk about the prisoners. Go back to the interface and then to the Tower of Sorcere.

TOWER OF SORCERE

Press the button, which opens a door to the north. Go north to a green levitation tube and use it to get farther into the tower. Go south, then west past a spinner trap to the wall. Very carefully turn and face south. Just in front of the door to your south is a teleporter. Save your game. To deactivate the teleporter, take one step forward and then one back. This activates a hidden pressure plate. Now proceed south through the door.

Inside is Jalynfein the Spider Mage, who offers to trade the Scroll of Drider Wish for your music box. Return to the interface and select the House Baenre, and the computer takes over briefly. Once you return to the interface, you must recover the Helmet, so go to the Merchant Bazaar.

THE MERCHANT BAZAAR AGAIN

Return to Galentha's Shop. You see an assassin strike Galentha and flee with the Helm. Visit with Ssar Tarel. Maznafein, who has been restored, is with her. Tarell tells you that the people they seek to free are in House Do'Urden and suggests that you see Grumsznar, the House Fey wizard. Return to the interface and on to the House Fey Branche.

HOUSE FEY BRANCHE

You begin in the northwest corner. Go south, then east to a door. Press the button and enter the door. Go south to a door leading south. Enter and talk with Grumsznar. The Wizard unwittingly reveals an important piece of information about Loth and the Helmet of Spiders you are seeking. You are asked to see Rizzen Do'Urden, who will assist you. Use the word sanctuary. The party is turned into Drow.

Visit Ssar Tarell and ask for assistance. Ssar will put you in contact with the Old Druid Vermulean, who informs you that one of your gems is actually the Gem of Loth, which will complete the Helm of Spiders. The Helm and Crest portion are in the hands of the House Do'Urden. Return to the interface, then proceed to the Carpathian Tavern.

CARPATHIAN TAVERN

Click on the door and enter. In the back room you will meet Rizzen Do'Urden, who provides the party with the password for entering House Do'Urden, as well as allowing the party to enter a part of the house. Rizzen says you must get the House Do'Urden insignia. These can be obtained from Jarlaxle, leader of the Bergan D'Aerthe. He can be found at the Gollvellius Tavern. Go back to the interface and click on Gllvellius Tavern.

GLLVELLIUS TAVERN

Speak with Jarlaxle, who agrees to help — but says you must first retrieve a necklace hidden in a chest in Mantle Cavern 2. Return to the interface and click on Mantle Cavern 2. Remember that these are the caves that are switched on page 27 of the manual.

MANTLE CAVERN 2

From the northwest corner, go south and west to a mace. From the mace, go south a short distance until you find a hidden button on an east wall. This button deactivates traps along your path. By moving northeast and east, then south in a slight curve, you will be able to go north. Go through the illusionary wall, avoiding a fireball trap south of you. A Wand of Fireballs and the necklace are in this area.

Return to Jarlaxle and give him the necklace. He tells you where to get the insignia. Leave the Tavern and go to the interface. Go to Mantle Cavern 1.

MANTLE CAVERN 1

From your arrival point, go west as far as possible, turning south when necessary. You will find a Javelin of Lightning in a corner. Go around a bend slightly east, then move south as far as possible. In the southwest corner, you will find a Drow patrol. Do them in and get the insignia from them. Go back to the interface and now click on House Do'Urden Commoner's Area.

HOUSE DO'URDEN COMMONER'S AREA

When you enter, you must have the insignia and password. Go past the guards and the first crossroads, then turn north. Go north to the second door leading east and enter. Inside is an illusionary wall to the north. Walk through it and press the button on the east wall. You will find a shrieker, a longsword+1, and a Ring of Wizardry.

Leave the room and go south down the hall you just came up, then head west at the first crossing. You will trigger a fireball trap at the next crossing. Duck the fireball and proceed north in the hall.

Enter the second door leading east and take the Gold Key with Red Gem inside. Leave the room and go south back down the hall. Use the Gold Key with Green Gem to open the third door going west. Enter the hall beyond and enter the north door.

Inside this room is an illusionary wall leading west. Go through this wall and take the White Circle Key from the room beyond. You will have to fight an ochre jelly.

Once you have the key, go back to the north-south hall. Go south down the hall and open the second door leading west, using the Gold Key with Green Gem. Speak with the guard in the hall about the prisoners. Mark this spot on your map.

Go west and use the White Circle Key to open the door at the west end of the hall. Go through this door and down to the next level.

HOUSE DO'URDEN NOBLES: AREA 1

Enter this area from the east and go west down the hall. Soon you will meet guards who inform you that only the key in possession of Rizzen Do'Urden can open the door to the west. Return east to a door leading north. Open the north door and enter the hall. At the end of the hall go west. Go to a door leading south. Enter the room and use the levitation tube to go to Area 2.

HOUSE DO'URDEN NOBLES: AREA 2

From the starting point, go north through a door and into a room. Leave this room through the door going west. Go west down the hall to the end, then turn south and enter the room. Leave this room via a door going south. You are attacked by Uropygi. Kill, kill, kill. Once in the hall outside, turn west through the archway. Enter the second room to the north.

Leave this room through a door going west. Go west as far as possible. Explore the north-west corner of this area. One of the walls is illusionary. Go through the wall and slay the Drow

Priestess, then take the Wand of Frost. In the northwest corner of this room is a teleporter that sends you to the southeast corner of this level.

Use the button on the south wall of the room to open a door going west. Go through it and head north to the door in the northeast corner of the room. Enter the door there and take the Scroll of Flame Arrow.

Leave this chamber and go west to a room to the north. Get the Extra Healing potion. Leave this, go southwest to another room, and get the Bracers of Protection.

Leave the room, go west to a door, and get another Extra Healing potion. Leave this room, go west to a door, and enter. Inside this room is an illusionary wall to the west. Go through the wall and turn north. Here you will see the Helmet of Spiders, but it vanishes as you approach.

Simultaneously, you are attacked by Rizzen Do'Urden and some Drow fighters. After killing them, go through another illusionary wall to the east. Inside the room is the Helmet of Spiders and the Gold Key with Black Gem (owned by Rizzen). Just beyond, in the chest, is a teleporter that takes you back to the northeast corner of this level. Make your way back, going west and south to a levitation tube and on to the next area.

HOUSE DO'URDEN NOBLES AREA: LEVEL 1 AGAIN

Consult your map and make your way back to the locked door leading west. Use Rizzen's Gold Key with Black Gem to open the door, then go south. When you reach the corner, turn west and go to a door leading west. Enter the door, take the Gold Circle Key and press a button on the north walk to open a door going west. Inside this room you find Drizzt Scimitars and a Javelin of Lightning.

Leave these two rooms the way you came. Go back east. Halfway there is a hall leading north; go as far north as possible. You will be in an east-west hall. Go west and use the Gold Circle Key to open a door in the northwest corner. In this room you find Keoghton Ointment, Extra Healing potion, and Fire Resistance potion. Go south into another room and get the Scroll of Cause Critical Wounds and the Scroll of Harm. In the southeast is an illusionary wall leading to a room with a Ring of Wizardry, a Wand of Magic Missiles, and a Gold Key with a Blue Gem. Go back to the door requiring the Gold Circle Key. From here, go south to down the hall to a door leading south. Use the Gold Key with the Blue Gem to open the door. Save your game before entering. Defeat the Priestess inside.

Prepare your party for the fight of their lives, then use the Teleporter in the west-central wall. You'll see Malice preparing to kill Drizzt. At Malice's side is a Yolchol and some spiders. Do not fight head-on. Use a Scroll of Flying to get on the other side of the Yolchol, which enables you to avoid the Malice's Lightning Bolts. Use Disintegrate to slay everything but the spiders.

ORBS & STUFF

Object	See this Section for Location	Also See Section(s)
Helmet	The Fire Down Below	Cavern of the Myconids, The Merchant Bazaar, Tower of Sorcere
Four gems	Forest Next to Village	Leucrotta's Lair
Centaur	Forest Next to Village	Location only
Ring of Feather Fall	Ice Dale Plains 1 Location only	
Second map	Underdark: Level 1	Location only
Cloak of Piwafi	Underdark: Level 1 Again	Location only
Pickaxe	Underdark: Level 1 Again, Temple of Dumathoin	Temple of Dumathoin: Level 3
Elven golden armor	Underground Lake	Location only
Wand of Paralyzation	Dwarvian Level	Location only
Bag of Holding	Dwarvian Level	Location only
Longsword	Dwarvian Level	Temple of Dumathoin: Level 2
Silver Moon Key	Temple of Dumathoin	Location only
Silver Star Key	Temple of Dumathoin	Location only
Holy Symbol of Dumathoin	Temple of Dumathoin	Temple of Dumathoin: Level 2
Silver Circle Key	Temple of Dumathoin: Level 2	Location only
Dwarven horn	Temple of Dumathoin	Location only
Chalice	Temple of Dumathoin	The Healing Fountain
Silver Axe Key	Temple of Dumathoin: Level 3	The Healing Fountain
Diamond	Temple of Dumathoin: Level 3	The Healing Fountain
Iron Circle Key	The Healing Fountain	Location only
Fountain of Healing	The Healing Fountain	Location only
Ring of Regeneration	The Healing Fountain	Location only
Centaur	The Healing Fountain	Location only
Jade spider	Cavern of the Myconids	Location only
Adamantite chain helmet	Cavern of the Myconids	Location only
Antivenom	Cavern of the Myconids	Location only

189

Object	See this Section for Location	Also See Section(s)
Plate helmet	Cavern of the Galeb Duhr	Location only
Necklace 1	Cavern of the Galeb Duhr	Location only
Necklace 2	Mantle Cavern Two	Gllvellius Tavern
White robe	Cavern of the Galeb Duhr	Location only
Blue candle	Cavern of the Galeb Duhr	Location only
Borgner stone	Cavern of the Galeb Duhr	Location only
Broadsword	Cavern of the Galeb Duhr	Location only
Blue gems	Cavern of the Galeb Duhr, Cavern of the Driders: Level 2	The Underground River
Ivory scroll case	Cavern of the Driders: Level 1	Location only
Adamantite chain mail	Cavern of the Driders: Level 1	Location only
Scroll of Spider Shape	Cavern of the Driders: Level 2	Return To Cavern Of Driders: Level 1
Stone of Infravision	Cavern of the Driders: Level 2	Location only
Banded-mail armor	Approach to Menzoberranzan	Location only
Galentha's Music Box	The Merchant Bazaar	Tower of Sorcere
Candles	The Merchant Bazaar	Location only
Gem of Loth	House Fey Branche	Location only
House Do'Urden insignia	Mantle Cavern One	Carpathian Tavern
Gold Key with Red Gem	House Do'Urden Commoner's Area	Location only
Gold Key with Black Gem	House Do'Urden Nobles: Area 2	House Do'urden Nobles Area: Level 1 Again
Gold Key with Blue Gem	House Do'Urden Nobles: Level 1 Again	Location only
Gold Key with Green Gem	House Do'Urden Commoner's Area	Location only
White circle	House Do'urdreden Commoner's Area	Location only
White Circle Key	House Do'Urden Commoner's Area	Location only
Helmet of Spiders	House Do'Urden Nobles: Area 2	House Fey Branche
Gold Circle Key	House Do'Urden Nobles: Level 1 Again	Location only

NOCTROPOLIS

BY
PAUL SHAFFER

TYPE
Graphic Adventure

SYSTEM
IBM PC (Required: 386/33, 4MB RAM, CD-ROM drive, MS-DOS 5+, and SVGA, 256-color, VESA compliant monitor. Recommended: 486/33, Microsoft compatible mouse. Supports Music: Sound Blaster family, MPU-401 General MIDI or 100% compatibles. Sound and speech: Sound Blaster or 100% compatible, ProAudio.)

WINNING A SWEEPSTAKES DOESN'T ALWAYS LEAD TO A LIFE ON EASY STREET. FOR COMIC-BOOK FAN PETER GREY, IT LEADS TO NOCTROPOLIS, A CITY AT THE MERCY OF VAMPIRES AND DARK MAGICIANS. NOCTROPOLIS IS ALSO THE HOME OF GREY'S FAVORITE COMIC BOOK HERO, DARKSHEER, LONG SINCE RETIRED. GREY SOON DISCOVERS THAT HE IS DESTINED TO ASSUME THE ROLE OF HIS FORMER HERO AND DISPATCH A SERIES OF COMIC BOOK-STYLE VILLAINS WHO CONTROL THE CITY. DISTINGUISHED BY SOME OF THE MOST HIGHLY STYLIZED ART AND PROSE SEEN IN RECENT ADVENTURE GAMES, NOCTROPOLIS ENJOYS A CLEARLY ORIGINAL LOOK AND FEEL — THE KIND OF COMIC ART SEEN IN HEAVY METAL, NOT KIDS' CARTOONS. GRATUITOUS SEX AND VIOLENCE, DELIVERED WITH STYLE, ARE THE TICKET, AND YOU'LL FIND ENOUGH OF BOTH IN NOCTROPOLIS FOR THE PUBLISHER TO DESIGNATE IT FOR "AGES 17+." PUZZLES ARE TYPICALLY OBJECT oriented, and the necessary items are usually handy. A simple interface enabled the designers to devote the entire screen to graphics throughout the game. Full-motion video dramatizes some scenes, but only a line or two of a character's dialogue is spoken, forcing you to read the rest. Lacking the heft of a Legend or Sierra adventure, Noctropolis is an originally illustrated work of comic art worth every comic fan's attention. With a more intriguing story and at least one plot twist, it could have been worth every adventure gamer's attention.

THE SOLUTION

GENERAL

You may obtain different information by using various dialogue options. The choices listed here provide the basics needed to finish the game.

GETTING STARTED

Get bills on counter. Open office door. Enter office. Get letter from desk, notices from floor under desk, and divorce papers to the right of the lamp. Examine all inventory. Get comic from ottoman. Read comic. After dream sequence, go to front door: 2, 1, 4. Get package (getting comic, silver token, and gold token). Read rest of comic. Use silver token.

NOCTROPOLIS

Talk to newspaper dealer: 1, 2, 1. Offer comic (getting newspaper). Ask about all. Travel to Cathedral (scroll up on travel map).

THE CATHEDRAL AND THE GARGOYLE

Talk to boy: 1, 1, 1, 1, 1, 1, 1, 1. Get wire beside left lamppost. Get fence spar from left fence. Open panel on right lamppost. Open access panel. Use wire. Use fence spire. Enter church. Enter confessional booth. Save game. Move window: 2, 2, 1, 1, 1, 1 (getting jawbone). Travel to Main St.

FINDING THE SUCCUBUS

Enter Hall of Records. Use jawbone. Ask about all. Travel to Stiletto's apartment. Open door: 1, 2, 1. Travel to Mausoleum. Open gate on right. Open door on right. Enter. Look at coffin. Move cover on right corpse. Get coffin key. Use key. Save game. Enter coffin: 3, 3, 1. Move statue. Get lace from wall column. Use stairs. Move pillow in front of Holy Virgin statue. Look at diary. Get spear from cherub statue to the right. Use spear. Exit chamber. Travel to Cathedral.

SUCCUBUS SHOWDOWN

Enter Cathedral. Talk to Father: 1, 3. Move pillow in front of altar. Get detonator. Get chalice from altar. Use chalice (gets holy water). Succubus enters. Wait for Stiletto to arrive. When Stiletto asks for help, use chalice with holy water on Succubus.

SHADOWLAIR

Talk to Stiletto: 2, 2, 2, 2, 4, 2, 3, 2. Ask about all. Move panel on column to right of statue. Look at compartment. Get book and noctroglyph. Move panel on column that is furthest right. Look at compartment. Get Darksheer uniform and liquidark grenade. Talk to Stiletto. Travel to Bornick Mansion.

BORNICK MANSION

Go to front door. Talk to Widow Bornick: 1, 2, 3, 3, 3, 2, 1. Ask about all. Travel to Sunspire Tower.

SUNSPIRE TOWER

Look at truck. Talk to security guard: 2. Talk to Stilleto: 1. While Stilleto distracts guard, go to lift. Move stack of bricks on lift. Move motor (takes you up). Look at bucket. Take glass shard from bucket. Move motor. Get off lift. Get glass cutter from lumber pile. Talk to security guard: 1, 2, 3 (gives you name: Sam Jenkins). Travel to Cygnus.

CYGNUS: GETTING TO THE TOP

Enter building. Talk to secretary: 1, 3. Get elevator passcard on floor (right side of desk). Talk to secretary: 2, 1, 2, 1. Enter room on right. Talk to Leon: 1, 3. Talk to Stiletto: 3. Move red

193

switch. Return to lobby. Talk to secretary: 1. Enter room on left. Talk to Jenkins: 1, 1, 1, 1. Ask about all. Take clock. Exit. Talk to secretary: 3. Go to elevator. Use elevator passcard. Talk to Shoto: 1, 3, 1, 1, 1. Reenter elevator. Use passcard. Exit building. Travel to Incarnate Technologies.

INCARNATE TECHNOLOGIES

Talk to guard: 1, 1, 1, 1, 3, 2. Talk to guard again. Ask about all (getting location of Jim Drake). Go to neon noose (rear of screen). Talk to Drake: 3, 1, 1, 2. Talk again. Ask about all. Exit. Travel to Main St.

GREENHOUSE AND THE PLANT MAN

Talk to newspaper dealer. Ask about greenhouse. Travel to greenhouse. Go to truck. Get seeds and quick-grow solution. Exit. Use glass cutter. Enter greenhouse: 1, 1. Use liquidark grenade. Get Stiletto. Outside, get poster that blows across screen. Look at poster. Return to Shadowlair. Go to pool. Return to Main St.

FINDING THE OPERA HOUSE

Enter Hall of Records. Talk to clerk (small black silhouette below monitor). Ask about Opera House. Travel to Opera House.

TOP HAT

Enter: 3, 2, 1. Travel to Observatory. Use noctroglyph. Go to Observatory entrance. Use seeds (plant formula is used along with it). Enter crack. Watch spotlight paths; time it right to avoid being seen. Save game. Because it is extremely easy to be caught by the spotlight, save after getting each item on the ground floor. When you restore, you will be back by the entrance door. Walk along the wall until you are directly north of the screwdriver. When the timing is right, get the screwdriver. Save game. Go to bottom of screen just below where spotlights intersect, then get oil can. Save game. Go to log book on ramp. Get log book. Use oil can. Use screwdriver. Get lens. Move platform. Save game. Return the way you came. Travel to Opera House. Enter: 3, 1. To janitor: 2, 1. Save game. Return to Shadowlair and enter pool. Travel to Opera House. Get throwing knives. Get brick. Stand on trapdoor. Use brick (takes you below stage). Get jewelry box and make-up kit. Move costumes. Go to door. Get screwdriver from boiler. Use screwdriver. Move valve above hose. Get hose. Use hose. Enter door. Talk to gang: 2, 3, 1, 2. Offer knives. 2, 3. Offer jewelry. Return to dressing room. Move switch. Travel to Main St.

FINDING STILETTO

Ask newspaper man about butcher. Travel to butcher shop. Talk to butcher: 3, 2, 1. Offer newspaper (getting sausage). Go to freezer door. In freezer, get meat hook. Move two carcasses on wall (exposing stairs). Go to stairs.

MASTER MACABRE AND THE MAZE

Choose: 1, 2, 3, 2, 1. Move beaker of acid on cart. Move left cart (frees Stiletto). Get beaker from shelf. Go to door (Stiletto stabs Macabre). Enter door. Use beaker (getting acid). Go east, north (walk to fan and go to adjacent room just when the blade passes). Get valve wheel by junk to the left. Use shard of glass (getting rope). Pass through fan again. Use rope. Go east. Use acid. Go to exit on other side of stream. Go north. Get rebar from ground. Exit. Use rebar. Cross bridge, go west. Use valve. Get net. Return to acid room. Use net (catches rat). Get rat. Return to rebar room. Enter now-dry drain. Go north (through curtain). Talk to mutant: 2, 3, 1. Offer make-up kit: 1, 1. Save game. Examine door. Note arrows on the edge of the door. Move colored balls to align each color with their corresponding arrow. Using the diagram below as a guide to ball position:

```
        1           4
          2       5
          3   6
            7
            8
          9           10
```

Each number represents a ball in a hole. Click on them in this order: 9, 2, 6, 3, 8, 5, 2, 8, 4, 1, 9, 10.

DREAM PARK

Return to Shadowlair and enter pool: 1, 1. Get paint bucket to the left of Jack's Funhouse. Talk to Drealmer. Go to Mr. Smile's mouth. Enter mouth of clown with big red nose. Get dental pick. Exit. Enter tower. Get oil lamp horn. Exit. Enter Funhouse door frame (takes you back outside). Use pick. Enter Funhouse. Get matches. Exit. Go to Mr. Smile's mouth. Move rolled-up screen to the left of the clown. Enter screen doorway. Use oil lamp (match is used automatically). Get egg sack. Get web (above egg sack). Exit. Reenter tower. Use egg sack. Get diamond. Exit. Go to Funhouse. Use diamond. Move pepper shaker. Get pepper. Exit. Return to Mr. Smile's mouth and go to red-nosed clown's mouth. Use pepper. Get paint brush. Exit. Use paint brush (on canvas). Enter canvas door. Use web. Go to top of web (climbs up). Move carpet. Get key (door opens). Enter door. Talk to Drealmer. Talk to Stiletto: 2, 2. Travel to Cygnus.

WHISPERMAN

Enter building. Go to elevator. Use elevator passcard. Talk to Shoto: 1, 1, 1, 1, 3. Exit building. Outside, get shaft from fence around lamppost. Use shaft. Enter manhole. Open furnace door. Get broken chair from rubble pile. Use chair. (Repeat two more times.) Enter pool. Talk to Whisperman: 1, 1, 4, 1, 1, 1, 1, 1, 2, 1, 3, 1. Reenter pool. Exit furnace room. Reenter Cygnus. Enter elevator. Use log book (takes you to roof).

GETTING INTO SUNSPIRE TOWER

Use meat hook (swing into Sunspire Tower). Get duct tape. Get rope from stair. Go up. Get broom. Go up. Use rope (ties to sausage). Use broom (attaches to meat hook with tape). Use rope and sausage (dog falls). Use broom and hook.

FLUX AND ENDGAME

Choose 3, 2, 1, 1, 1, 1, 1, 2, 1. Use gold token: 1.

ORBS & STUFF

Object	See this Section for Location	Also See Section(s)
Comic	Getting Started	Noctropolis
Silver token	Getting Started	Location only
Gold token	Getting Started	Flux and Endgame
Letter (ticket)	Getting Started	Location only
Newspaper	Noctropolis	Finding Stiletto
Wire	The Cathedral and the Gargoyle	Location only
Fence spar	The Cathedral and the Gargoyle	Location only
Jawbone	The Cathedral and the Gargoyle	Finding Succubus
Coffin key	Finding the Succubus	Location only
Spear	Finding the Succubus	Location only
Chalice	Succubus Showdown	Location only
Book	Shadowlair	Location only
Noctroglyph	Shadowlair	Top Hat
Liquidark grenade	Shadowlair	Greenhouse and the Plant Man
Darksheer uniform	Shadowlair	Location only
Glass shard	Sunspire Tower	Master Macabre and the Maze
Glass cutter	Sunspire Tower	Greenhouse and the Plant Man
Elevator passcard	Cygnus: Getting to the Top	Whisperman
Seeds	Greenhouse and the Plant Man	Top Hat
Quick-grow solution	Greenhouse and the Plant Man	Top Hat
Screwdriver	Top Hat	Location only
Oil can	Top Hat	Location only
Log book	Top Hat	Whisperman
Lens	Top Hat	Location only
Throwing knives	Top Hat	Location only
Brick	Top Hat	Location only
Jewelry box	Top Hat	Location only

197

Object	See this Section for Location	Also See Section(s)
Make-up kit	Top Hat	Master Macabre
Screwdriver	Top Hat	Location only
Hose	Top Hat	Location only
Sausage	Finding Stiletto	Getting into Sunspire Tower
Meat hook	Finding Stiletto	Getting into Sunspire Tower
Beaker	Master Macabre and the Maze	Location only
Acid	Master Macabre and the Maze	Location only
Valve wheel	Master Macabre and the Maze	Location only
Rope	Master Macabre and the Maze	Location only
Rebar	Master Macabre and the Maze	Location only
Paint bucket	Dream Park	Location only
Dental pick	Dream Park	Location only
Paint brush	Dream Park	Location only
Oil lamp horn	Dream Park	Location only
Diamond	Dream Park	Location only
Matches	Dream Park	Location only
Pepper	Dream Park	Location only
Egg sack	Dream Park	Location only
Web	Dream Park	Location only
Key	Dream Park	Location only
Shaft	Whisperman	Location only
Broken chair	Whisperman	Location only
Duct tape	Getting into Sunspire Tower	Location only
Rope	Getting into Sunspire Tower	Location only
Broom	Getting into Sunspire Tower	Location only

RAVENLOFT: STONE PROPHET

BY
CLANCY SHAFFER
& ALFRED GIOVETTI

TYPE
Fantasy Role-Playing

SYSTEM
IBM CD-ROM (Required: 386/33+ MHz, 4MB RAM, VGA, 25MB hard disk, CD drive with 300K transfer rate, 320 ms access time, and MSCDEX 2.2+. Recommended: 486/33, uncompressed hard disk. Supports: Sound Canvas, Soundscape, WaveBlaster, Soundman Wave, SW 32/GW 32, Sound Blaster family and 100% compatibles.)

COMPANY
Strategic Simulations Inc.

HE SEQUEL TO STRAHD'S POSSESSION, ALSO DESIGNED BY DREAMFORGE (WHOSE PREVIOUS WORK WAS MENZOBERRANZAN), THIS FIRST-PERSON PERSPECTIVE ROLE-PLAYING GAME (RPG) TAKES PLACE IN TSR'S AD&D SECOND EDITION GAME WORLD RAVENLOFT, WHERE THE UNDEAD RULE LANDS OF MYTH AND MYSTERY. PEOPLE BANISHED TO RAVENLOFT BECOME MERE TOYS FOR THE UNDEAD. TRAPPED IN A DESERT LAND INHABITED BY MUMMIES AND THE GODS OF ANCIENT EGYPT, YOUR GROUP OF TWO ADVENTURERS SEEKS TO ESCAPE THE LANDS OF THE UNDEAD AND RETURN TO THE WORLD OF THE FORGOTTEN REALMS. ALONG THE WAY, YOU MAY ADD UP TO TWO NONPLAYER CHARACTERS (NPCS) AT A TIME TO THE PARTY AS ALLIES. EXPECT INTENSE REAL-TIME COMBAT WITH AN ENORMOUS VARIETY OF CREATURES. BATTLES ARE DEPICTED IN ANIMATED, 3-D SCENES THAT FILL MOST OF THE SCREEN. PUZZLES FALL INTO THE TREASURE HUNT CATEGORY: FIND THE APPROPRIATE OBJECT, AND YOU'RE ABLE TO ACCESS DEEPER RECESSES OF RAVENLOFT. TWO convenient features will be welcomed by all: You can "write" on the automap to record discoveries, as in Ultima Underworld, and automated note-taking records vital conversations and clues. Both the automap itself and the automated notes can be printed on all major printers. Even without such handy features, Ravenloft would be among the toughest, most entertaining RPGs of the year.

THE SOLUTION

GENERAL

The difficulty setting affects the monsters you will encounter, but not the difficulty of the puzzles.

CHARACTER CREATION

Use multiclass Mage/Fighter/Cleric Half-Elf characters with magic and charm resistance, since these characters can attain Level 20. Transferring characters from Strahd's Possession will bring characters into the game at as high as Level 20, but freshly rolled characters enter the game at Level 6. Use the Modify feature to increase or change statistics to make your characters as strong as you can.

NONPLAYER CHARACTERS

There are over 30 NPCs. Two NPCs at a time can join the original two player characters on the quest. Initially you will need one additional NPC, Trajan Khet. A Ranger-Cleric, he is just northeast of the well and northwest of the Temple of Set (which is in the far southeast corner of the desert map).

THE DESERT

You begin in the south-central portion of the map and emerge from a wall of heat that will kill all who enter it. Check your map continually to avoid this area.

Characters must possess water at all times. They will automatically drink available water to survive the heat, or use a magic Create Water spell to restore themselves. Automatic drinking or Create Water spells restore the waterline to 100 percent.

THE DESERT MAP

The Temple of Set is in the southeast. The Vistani woman's tent is in the south-central edge of the desert. The well is between the Temple of Set and the Vistani woman's tent. In the center of the map just north of the well is the Tent Village. The obelisk is north of the Tent Village. The burial catacombs are in the northeast portion of the map, north of the Temple of Harvest. The Temple of Harvest is at the west-central edge of the desert. The Sphinx is in the northeast on the eastern edge of the map.

GETTING AROUND

To reach the Temple of the Desert Trolls, go north at the north edge of the desert and then move west and north.

To reach the Temple of Ra, go to the outstretched hands, go to the large rock just south, go south of the rock about four paces, then directly east to another rock. Move south from this rock about eight paces. When you are at the entrance you will fall right through into the Temple of Ra. (The hands projecting from the sand are on a line north and a little west of the Temple of Set.)

TELEPORTING

When you find two small obelisks right next to one another, these form a teleport nexus. You will also find stones with icons identical to the plaques on the small obelisks (Teleport Tiles), in various areas of the game. When you click on them, the stones will teleport the party to that particular dungeon area. Don't discard these stones. There is at least one stone for each dungeon, usually found in the dungeon itself or in a dungeon close to the obelisks.

On the automap, type the name of the location (for example, "Set"). Then type dashes (- - - -) on each side for several inches, as this makes it much easier to find your notes on the map.

Once you have the Teleport Tiles, you can use these anywhere to reach the pylons of that particular location. You do not have to use them between the obelisks. As an example, if you have finished a dungeon, just click on the Teleport Tile in your hand and you will be transported at once to the location. This is a convenient way to exit any dungeon.

THE DUMB AND THE BLIND

After the introduction, pick up the dagger in the sand. Enter the tent northwest of your party and talk to the dumb and blind Vistani woman. Click on the Vistani's hand to bring up a

201

drawing in the sand. The drawing refers to the well to the east of the tent, which should be the first dungeon you tackle.

Now go north to the Tent Village for additional help. But do not add another character to the party until you have completed the well maze, or you will have to let them go in order to save the woman with the hurt ankle. (You may take on Piotra, from the southeast tent; he'll curse you when you drop him, but you can add him again later; he will drop all of his gear when you let him go, so you must salvage it and then give it back to him.)

TENT VILLAGE

Befriend the young boy outside the tents near the village square, where the two small obelisks (teleport nexus) are found. He will give the party a map of the desert that shows most of the major dungeons and locations, including the obelisks mentioned previously.

Leave the Tent Village and go to the well. At some point later, return to the tent and talk to everyone. The lady who has lost her husband will reward the party for retrieving her husband's things from the desert. (Many other useful items will be found lying around bones in the desert.)

THE WELL

Walk right through the well, and the party will climb down the rope and into the first level. Just to the left of the entrance is a woman with a hurt ankle. Speak with her, but don't add her to your party now, because she is too weak to help explore the well.

Stay alert for traps, which consist of holes in the floor. You will be constantly attacked by fire toads and spitting cobras. Do not enter the wells without a number of Nullify Poison spells.

The well has two subterranean levels. Completely explore the well until you find the two eyes of Nefertiti, a Helm of Telepathy, and the first piece of Anhktepot's Seal. A scroll explains about Nefertiti and how the eyes were made for her.

There are at least 22 scrolls here. You can also find a map of the well, and a teleport symbol with a mark like a letter "O." The broken piece of the Seal is in the southwest corner. You can find a Stone of Good Luck and a Wand of Magic Missiles in a false wall.

You can see into a room full of loot here, but cannot enter it. After searching this level and finding the first eye, return to the room you couldn't get into previously. You can get another eye inside the room, through a hole in the wall — but not until you have the first eye.

Other things to find in the well include a Teleport Key for the well and the Tent Village, and The Helm of Brilliance, which enables the party to explore dark areas without the light spells or torches.

After acquiring the items mentioned above, add the woman with the hurt ankle to your party and return to the village. Do not give her anything you found while exploring, for they may disappear. When she leaves the party, you'll gain one Good Judgement point.

THE VISTANI TENT

Return to the blind Vistani woman's tent and wear the Helm of Telepathy so you may communicate with her. Allow her to use the eyes of Nefertiti, which will enable her to see.

Then go to the obelisk. Take the blind Vistani seer, who will open the obelisk for you. Inside the obelisk, the seer will depart. Return and recruit the Vistani male from the tent on the southeast edge of the Tent Village. Give the dagger to the him and equip him for the journey.

THE OBELISK

A deadly dungeon, the obelisk is lined with floating death heads that attack with fireball or lightning attacks, as well as manscorpions that attack with melee weapons and stingers.

Once inside, speak to the guardian of the Stone Prophet. The Stone Prophet is found in the anteroom of the obelisk. Explore the lower levels of the obelisk to find chests with pieces of two parchments, which you need in order to understand the Stone Prophet's words. Keep an eye out for a map, which tells how to reach the lower levels of the obelisk.

Locate the second piece of Anhktepot's Seal on the first level. Combine the pieces as you find them. Then return to the Stone Prophet, who will translate the puzzle.

INSIDE THE OBELISK

There are many buttons to push here to open doors (for some doors, you will need to press two). Watch for bright yellow spots on the map, indicating where loot may be found. Watch for the holes in the floor and examine all four sides of the columns for buttons that will open the doors.

To reach Level 2, find the hall that runs around the perimeter of Level 1 and follow it to the center at the bottom. Then proceed north to a set of stairs that will bring you out in the center of Level 2. At the south end of Level 2 are a number of teleport units. Save the game and try them all to reach the stairs down to Level 3.

(Save often on Level 2; if you fall down a hole, it may be necessary to restore a saved game. To close all the holes in the floor, use trial and error to find corresponding buttons on the wall.)

THE OBELISK: LEVEL THREE

Use fireballs to defeat the Minotaurs, saving frequently. If you clear a room of them, you can rest and restore your spells. You will find a very useful Wand of See Enemy on this level.

You must search every room for valuable items. Use wall switches to turn off all the hole traps. When you leave, use the parchments you found to decipher the writings on the wall.

TEMPLE OF SET

To locate the Temple, go to the southeast corner of the map until you find two arms projecting from the sands. (A teleport nexus is also in this location, and the Temple of Ra is underground here.) The Temple of Set is west of these. (It's a little south and west of the place where you found Trajan Khet.)

On the ground floor of the temple, speak to the temple priestess for background information. Go east to the center of a large hall and find a key to the locked door in the southwest corner. Take the steps behind the locked door to reach the first of two more levels. You will arrive in the southwest corner of the first level. A little to the north, on the east side of the outer wall, are steps to the second level up. You must battle spitting cobras and dark nagas here, so carry a lot of Fireball and Cone of Cold spells.

When you arrive on the second level up, enter the first large room to the west. You must go north, then south at the first opening, and then west into a large room. Here you will find the Helm of True Seeing, which enables you to see all the illusory walls and invisible watchers of Set. Now enter the teleport in the center of the floor and teleport from here to a room, and from this room to another, until you have covered the entire floor in this manner. You will find four or five Iron Snake Idols. Take them; you will need a total of nine.

Wearing the Helm of True Seeing and return to the second floor, where you will now find many illusory openings. Do not leave these floors until you have found a total nine of the idols.

You'll need many Fireball spells; Ice Storm and Cone of Cold spells are also helpful. Note that your map will show four large areas on the first level up, which you have not entered. Three of these can be opened with buttons on the wall on or near these areas that look like stone.

Return to the first level and save the game. (If you should fall into a hole on the first or second level, you will go to Senmet, whom you cannot kill at this stage in the game.) With the Helm of True Seeing, you can see a pedestal and a serpent outside each of nine doors on the temple's ground level.

Place each one of the nine Iron Snake Idols of Set on the pedestals next to the nine doors, and the serpent will allow you to enter the main door, which will then be opened. In one room you will find the magical watering vase, necessary for the Temple of Harvest.

In another area you will find a key that will open a door on this level. On the west wall is a button that opens another door; you will need the ninth idol to go farther. The idol enables you to descend to a lower level, which consists of prison containing snakes and bones. Teleport to the outside by using the Teleport Tile.

Visit the pyramids and sphinx in Ravenloft 2.

● ● ● ● ● ● ● ● ● ●

TEMPLE OF HARVEST

Go to the Temple of Harvest. Use the Neutralize Poison spell in the poisoned areas, which are green on the automap. Enter the temple from the south and explore until you find the Mask of Hathor, which is in a poisoned area in the center of the temple's southeast portion.

The mask enables the party to communicate with animals. Use it to speak with the cat in the western part of the maze. Get the cat to retrieve the key to the door she is guarding. Kill the occupants of the room beyond the door and retrieve the cat statuette. Use the key to open the door in the center of the temple, which opens a hallway to the north-central area.

Give the magical watering vase from the Temple of Set to the old priest in the north-central area of the Temple of Harvest. He will give you the key to the lower levels of the Temple of Harvest.

Before entering the lower levels, get air spores for each member of your party (from the north part of the garden; they are white in color). They enable you to breathe fresh air in the unbreathable areas below the temple.

Go to the east side of the temple grounds and look for a stone and two regular switches to throw. You are then enable to enter the northeast part of the grounds, where you must throw another switch, then enter and push the stone button.

The priest will ask you to retrieve a small girl that left her father and mother. When you do so, you will have to have Piotra leave the party. Leave Piotra's gear there. Take the girl home via teleport; her tent is south or southeast of the teleport obelisks. Return to the southeast tent and have Piotra rejoin you, then collect his gear back at the Temple of Harvest.

BELOW THE TEMPLE OF HARVEST

In the large room south of the garden, look for a button in the northwest corner (it is a stone). Push it, then proceed to the lower levels. You will fight caterwauls, fire beetles, and shadows.

To make progress, you need five different statues of animals, which may be acquired as you proceed. However, the last two rooms cannot be entered until you go to the southwest corner room. In this room are two plates in two of the north alcoves. Step on each, and a wall will open to the south. Enter, and you will find a statue. Then go through the teleport to the lower end of the room.

Go to the northwest and use the statue on the guard. Now use the air spores, one for each party member. You will find weapons and other useful items here.

In the areas filled with green mist, collect the Special Scroll of Retirement, a large chain, a scroll that reveals the true name of the Sphinx, and the Coffer of Ra. You will have find two maces in these areas, and you already have a sword+1. Use Enchant Weapons on all weapons until you have most of them up to +2, and one or two to +3. This may require several rest periods.

There are two figures in the north room. Speak with the male figure. Place the Coffer of Ra in your hand and click on it. A cinematic sequence will show the figure being blown apart, and you get the third piece of Anhktepot's Seal.

Take the animal statue you find into the next room to the south and search it.

BURIAL CATACOMBS

The burial catacombs are in the northeast section of the desert. To get there, go north in a large opening in the wall there until you reach a fanged opening in the wall.

Before entering, be sure you have +3 or +2 weapons and some Fire spells to destroy the Trolls. Get the lute on the first floor of the burial catacombs; it is behind the hole in the floor on the west side. To close the hole, go to the three alcoves on the east side directly across from the hole.

(There is also a hole in the center alcove.) Throw the switch in the east alcove to close it, then throw the other two switches. Now go to where the first hole was located and enter the alcove, where you will find another switch, which opens the door so you can get the lute.

You must also locate the undead Paladin. Go to the north end of the long hall. Turn right through a false wall and go to the end, where you may get the Paladin to join the party. If you have Piotra, you must release him; collect his armor so you can return it to him after the undead Paladin leaves the party.

You must also go through all the holes in the floor to locate the first piece of the Hierophant's Seal. First you must locate a silver key and use it below; the seal piece is located in the south end of the lower level. You can now leave the area. Be prepared for a number of Trolls awaiting you at the entrance.

Go to the ghost that wanders the sands just north of the Tent Village. On the map, it appears as a zigzag portion of a building with a green dot near it. Click on the lute as you approach the ghost. Draw closer and reclick on the lute, then click on the ghost, which will turn into the Talk symbol. At this point, a cinematic sequence reveals a keyword, which is the son's name in the song. This word will activate a stone statue that opens a tomb, enabling you to enter the royal burial hall.

TEMPLE OF SET REVISITED

Return to the Temple of Set and jump down the pit in the ground level floor. Fight and kill Senmet. Save the game. Cast the Scroll of Return over Senmet's dead body, killing him for good and preventing his return. The undead Paladin will leave the party, leaving her armor, and you will gain two Good Judgement points.

From here, use the Tent Village emblem and teleport to the Tent Village. Go to the southeast tent and return Piotra's gear, and he will rejoin the party.

STONE MAN

The Stone Man is due west of the obelisk. Get and put the chain in your hand, then click on it and use the boy's name: Tekhen. (You must have obtained the name from the song in the cinematic sequence or it will not work.)

Use the chain on the stone statue guarding the stone slab in front of the royal burial hall. The stone guardian will pull the stone slab door from the front of the royal burial hall. Enter the teleporters in this order: north, south, west, then east. Explore the four associated areas. Collect the second piece of the Hierophant's Seal and the Gold Whistle from these areas.

The west teleportal area is the most difficult one. It is full of holes in the floor. When you enter, turn carefully and look at the top of the wall behind you to see a broken tile. Press it and move farther south. Continue pressing tiles. When you find one that will not press in, bypass it. Look at the automap and go toward the column. Press the tile here, and press again when you reach a dead end.

Return to the tile that would not operate previously and press it. Work your way to the columns and go between them to the next column (moving north from east to the side of the door). Press the tile here, then enter the door. Use the key to open the secret door near the stairway where you entered. Descend into the royal burial hall. Go beyond the door, where you will be judged. As long as the party has collected Good Judgement points and no Bad Judgement points, the party will pass.

A cinematic sequence shows the party talking to a dead adventurer. The dead adventurer reveals the location of a Scroll of Return that will let them leave Ravenloft and return home. The location is east of the Temple of Ra, just beyond the wall of Ra.

THE SPHINX

You must have the scroll from the Temple of Harvest, which provides the Sphinx's true name. Move very close to the Sphinx, and you'll enter via a cinematic sequence. Read the books and scrolls to fully understand the conflicts within the land of Ravenloft's desert. Find the Thought Bottle and talk to the five magic mouths to learn the command word that activates the bottle. Put the Thought Bottle in your hand and click on it.

Inside the Sphinx, you can also find the third piece of the Hierophant's Seal and a map showing the buried Temple of Ra's hidden entrance. This is a rather large dungeon guarded by doom guards and mimics. Click on all the jars with the right mouse button, and you will be surprised at what you will find. You must descend five flights of steps to get to the final level.

TEMPLE OF RA AGAIN

Inside the temple, search for the Eight Tears of Ra. Put all eight tears on the wall murals in the room with the handmaidens. The wall will open. The fourth and final piece of the Hierophant's Seal is found beyond the open wall.

Put all pieces of the Hierophant Seal together. Enter the large adjacent room, where the Hierophant appears to be dazed or in a dream. Find a place in wall where you can put the now-assembled Hierophant Seal, which in turn transforms the Temple of Ra. Blow the Gold Whistle (click on wall mural) on the wall mural of a falcon at the Pharaoh's Rest. The falcon will become the Falcon of Ra, a living falcon who can talk to the party through the Mask of Hathor, or with animals through the Speak skill. The Falcon of Ra will retrieve the heart of Ra for the party in another cinematic scene.

ENDGAME

You must ensure that the seals are intact and in place in both the Temple of Ra and the Pharaoh's Rest, thus reestablishing the links between the two that were destroyed as revealed in the scrolls in the Sphinx.

Retrieve the mallet from the Crypt of the High Priest. Search the crypt for the fourth and final piece of Anhktepot's Seal. Assemble Anhktepot's Seal. Use the Seal on the depression in the gate in the Pharaoh's Rest. Stick Ra's heart into the door with the picture of a hero on it, which opens the door.

Thoroughly search and map the area and passages between Anhktepot's gong and the gateway in the Pharaoh's Rest. Save the game. Strike the gong with the mallet, awakening Anhktepot. Save the game. Anhktepot will attempt to kill you. Go to the gateway, and he will follow. When you reach the teleport point, which is where you assembled the seal into the wall, Anhktepot will also be teleported to the Temple of Ra.

Enter the gateway with Anhktepot just behind the party. The party and Anhktepot will teleport to the buried temple of Ra, where Anhktepot and the Hierophant fight. (If Anhktepot does not follow the party, restore the game and try again.) While Anhktepot is fighting, he must release his grip on the Red Desert. Leave the temple quickly, head east, find the Scroll of Return, and use it before the time runs out.

209

ORBS & STUFF

Object	See this Section for Location	Also See Section(s)
Dagger	The Dumb and the Blind	The Vistani Tent
Eyes of Nefertiti	The Well	The Vistani Tent
Anhktepot's Seal Piece	The Well	Below the Temple of Harvest, The Obelisk, Endgame
Hierophant's Seal	Burial Catacombs, Sphinx, Temple of Ra	Temple of Ra
Stone of Good Luck	The Well	Location only
Helm of Brilliance	The Well	Location only
Helm of Telepathy	The Well	The Vistani Tent
Helm of True Seeing	Temple of Set	Location only
Snake Idols	Temple of Set	Location only
Magical Watering Vase	Temple of Set	Temple of Harvest
Mask of Hathor	Temple of Harvest	Temple of Ra Again
Special Scroll of Retirement	Below the Temple of Harvest	Location only
Sphinx's True Name	Below the Temple of Harvest	The Sphinx
Coffer of Ra	Below the Temple of Harvest	Location only
Lute	Burial Catacombs	Location only
Gold Whistle	Stone Man	Temple of Ra Again
Thought Bottle	The Sphinx	Location only
Mallet	Endgame	Location only

SHADOWS OF CAIRN

BY
FRED PHILIPP AND
CLANCY SHAFFER

TYPE
*Action
Role-Playing*

SYSTEM
*IBM PC
(Required:
386+, single-
speed CD-ROM
drive, 4MB
RAM, Windows
3.1 and/or
DOS 5.0.
Recommended:
double-speed
CD-ROM
drive, 486+.
Supports:
Sound Blaster,
AWE32, and
compatibles.)*

COMPANY
*Masque
Publishing Inc.*

F OR A WALK ON THE WILD SIDE, STEP INTO THE SHOES OF QUINN, A THIEF ON THE VERGE OF GETTING BOOTED OUT THE THIEVES GUILD BECAUSE OF HIS CHARACTER FLAW — HE'S TOO HONEST TO STEAL! THIS LEADS TO SOMEONE PLANNING TO FRAME HIM FOR THE MURDER OF THE DUKE OF CAIRN, WHICH PROPELS QUINN INTO A DUNGEON CRAWL THROUGH SEWERS, DUNGEONS, AND A HEDGE MAZE FULL OF MONSTERS AS HE STRIVES TO WARN THE DUKE AND SAVE THE DAY. THE ACTION IS SHOWN FROM A PROFILE VIEW, SO YOU SEE QUINN'S FULL FIGURE FROM THE SIDE AS HE MOVES LEFT OR RIGHT ACROSS THE STREET OR ALONG A CORRIDOR, AND THE GAMEPLAY RESEMBLES PRINCE OF PERSIA. ROTOSCOPED ANIMATION OVER HAND-DRAWN CINEMATIC SEQUENCES IS EMPLOYED THROUGHOUT THE THOUSANDS OF SCREENS. BUT MOST OF THE TIME YOU'RE LOOKING AT DUNGEONS, HALLS, AND WALLS, WHICH ARE NOT THE MOST SCINTILLATING SUBJECT MAT-TER, AND EVEN THESE GRAPHICS ARE UNINSPIRED. PUZZLES INVOLVE LOOKING FOR TRAP DOORS, USING SKILLS, ROUNDING UP ASSORTED ITEMS, AND COMBAT. THERE ARE THREE SKILL LEVELS, FROM NOVICE TO EXPERT, providing extra replay value in an otherwise ordinary dungeon crawl. (It can be played completely from the CD, saving disk space.) With a weak plot that shows little depth, Cairn offers nothing out of the ordinary.

THE SOLUTION

GENERAL

Ratty scrolls may be found throughout the game. There are eight, and each adds one life point. Refer to the "Outside City" map provided with the game for a sense of direction and the order in which you will proceed through the quest.

THE SEWERS

From the Tower, jump down to the lower level and into Shambles North. Go west and enter the tavern. Go through the tavern to the sewers. Talk to the crazy old guy. Go east to the thug and knock him out. Get the rat. Return to the old guy, who'll give you a pair of knives.

Proceed west to the end, north to the end, then east to a door in the north wall and enter.

THE FENCE'S WAREHOUSE

Enter and talk to the fence. You must perform a number of errands for him before he'll help. For each assigned errand, you'll see the appropriate location's area displayed in the upper-left corner. Click on that icon to travel there.

THE DAGGER

Exit the warehouse and travel to the Weapons Shop. Enter and get dagger. Return to the fence. Exit and travel to the Alchemist's Shop.

THE POTION

Go to the Alchemist's Shop, get the potion, and return it to the fence. Travel to the dungeon.

THE DUNGEON

From this point on, all interior areas consist of corridors running east-west. Doors, trapdoors and secret doors lead off from them to the north or south, or to another east-west corridor. Secret doors may be discovered by their lack of moss. All areas contain miscellaneous traps that you can avoid by jumping over or running past them, or by sidestepping trigger plates on the floor. Portcullis traps look normal, except that the groove at the back side is slightly darker.

Proceed through Level 1 to Level 2, then on to Level 3. Except for combat, traps, and chests, these levels are fairly straightforward.

Continue to Level 4. Enter the first secret door and get the Skull Dagger. You will need this to kill the guard in the next room. Go to Level 5, then Level 6.

LEVEL 6

Follow these directions to the end of each corridor. Go W, S, E, S, W, S, E, S, W, then exit to Level 7. Go E, N, W, N, E, N, W, N, E, then exit to Level 8. Go W, S, E, S, W, S, E, S, W and exit to Level 9.

LEVEL 9

Follow these directions to the end of each corridor except where noted. Go four steps N, E, S, S, E, N, N, E, three steps S, E, two steps N, E, then three steps S to the exit to Level 10.

LEVEL 10

Go W, W, N through the secret door. Pick up the Ring of Invulnerability. Go W, W, get scroll. Go four steps E, then N through a secret door and exit to Level 11.

LEVEL 11

Go S, four steps W, and pick up Amulet of Levitation. Go N through the secret door, three steps W, S, and pick up Ring of Strength. Go S, E, then exit to Level 12.

LEVEL 12

Go W, N, W, S, W. Go N, E, N, W, N, E, then N. To continue through this room to the west, take small steps backward until your back is up against the right wall. Then jump twice to the west. Go W to end, open the chest, and get Ancient Book.

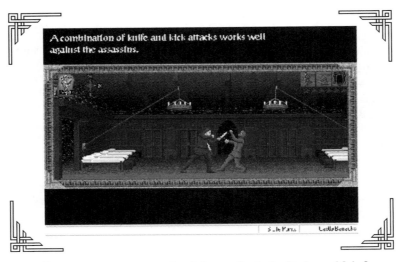

A combination of knife and kick attacks works well against the assassins.

Have you ever seen your mother, baby, standing in the Shadows of Cairn?

● ● ● ● ● ● ● ● ● ●

STRATEGIES FOR GETTING ANCIENT BOOK

1. Run past or jump through guards falling from ceiling trapdoors to the Elevator Room. Entering this room will automatically save your game.

2. Move slowly into room and try to take out the guards one at a time.

When you have the book, climb on the Elevator and continue up to Level 1 and out. Return to Fences Warehouse and talk to Fence. You must now deliver the book to the Wizard.

WITH THE BOOK

When you have the book, go north, climb on the elevator. Continue up to Level 1 and exit. Return to the fence's warehouse and talk to fence. You must now deliver the book to the Wizard.

HEDGE MAZE

Click on destination and travel to Hedge Maze. Proceed north, west, north, east, north, then west to the gates leading to the Wizard's Tower. Enter Tower.

WIZARD'S TOWER

This is a teleporter maze. Doors in rooms are actually teleporters. The following instructions will simplify getting through: "T" means enter teleporter and teleport to next the room; "TR" and "TL" mean to use the right or left teleporter in a room with more than one.

T, E, T, E, E, TR, T, E, T, TR, W, T, TR, T, T, T, T, T, TR.

W, N, T, T, W. Jump. W, T, T, TR, TL, T, T, N, N, T, E, E.

Get scroll. W, W, TL, TR, T, T, TR, T, N, E. Get scroll. W, T, E, N, T, S, S, T (to exit the Tower and enter the Hedge Maze).

HEDGE MAZE

There are six areas in the Hedge Maze. You begin in Area 1. Go W to second door and enter. Enter next door. This will take you to Area 3a.

Go N through three doors. E, run past Medusa, N through door. W to end, go through door to Area 3b.

E, enter door, W, enter door, E, enter door, enter next door, pull lever to return to Area 1.

W to second door, enter, N through new door, enter door to travel to Area 4a.

N, N, W, N, E, N, W to end. Enter door to continue to Area 4b.

E, N, W, N, E, N, W, N, E. Get scroll. S, S. Pull lever. N, E, N. Exit through door.

THE DUKE'S KEEP

Climb the east wall of the Duke's Palace to enter the Main Keep. Cross the alley and climb the Keep wall to enter the Duke's Keep.

There are five locations in the Keep, each requiring combat. Proceed down through the Keep until you reach the Duke's Bedroom. The first location is the Castle Guard Post. Enter and kill the guard. Go through the rear door into the Castle Barracks.

Kill guard and go through door at rear to arrive at the Castle Study. Kill guard and go through rear door into the Main Hall. Kill guard and go through rear door to reach the final room in the Keep, and the confrontation with your Master in the Duke's Bedroom. Kill your Master.

ORBS & STUFF

Object	See this Section for Location	Also See Section(s)
Rat	The Sewers	Location only
Pair of knives	The Sewers	Location only
Dagger	The Dagger	Location only
Potion	The Potion	Location only
Ring of invulnerability	Level 10	Location only
Amulet of levitation	Level 11	Location only
Ring of strength	Level 11	Location only
Ancient book	Level 12	Strategies for Getting Ancient Book, With the Book

UNDER A KILLING MOON

BY
PAUL SHAFFER

TYPE
*Animated
Mystery
Adventure*

SYSTEM
*IBM PC
(Required:
386/25+, sin-
gle-speed
CD-ROM
drive, 4MB
RAM, 2MB free
hard disk
space, SVGA
(VESA),
mouse.
Recommended:
486/33+, SVGA
(VESA), 16MB
RAM, 10MB
free hard disk
space, double-
speed CD-ROM
drive, 16-bit
sound card.
Supports: all
major sound
boards.)*

COMPANY
*Access
Software Inc.*

ONCE AGAIN WE PLUNGE INTO THE FUTURISTIC WORLD OF PRIVATE DETECTIVE TEX MURPHY, LAST SEEN IN MARTIAN MEMORANDUM. FOLLOWING A NUCLEAR WAR, HIS HOME BASE OF SAN FRANCISCO HAS BEEN DIVIDED INTO OLD AND NEW SECTIONS. MUTANTS DWELL IN THE OLD SECTION, AND "NORMS" IN THE NEW. ALWAYS THE ICONOCLAST, TEX FEELS MORE AT HOME IN THE OLD PART OF TOWN, WHERE A SERIES OF CASES LEAD HIM TO DISCOVER A SECRET SOCIETY PLOTTING TO WIPE OUT THE MUTANTS. THE ENTIRE WORLD OF KILLING MOON, AND EVERY OBJECT IN IT, ARE DISPLAYED WITH 3D GRAPHICS SO REALISTIC THAT YOU CAN ZOOM IN AND OUT ON ANY OBJECT OR PART OF THE ROOM, ALMOST AS IF YOU WERE ACTUALLY THERE. FULL-MOTION VIDEO IS NOTHING NEW TO ADVENTURE GAMES, BUT ACCESS PUT HOLLYWOOD ACTORS SUCH AS BRIAN KEITH, MARGOT KIDDER, AND RUSSELL MEANS IN FRONT OF THE CAMERA, AND THE RESULTS ARE STUNNING. (TEX IS PLAYED BY THE GAME'S PRODUCER, CHRIS JONES, WHO TURNS IN A SURPRISINGLY GOOD

PERFORMANCE.) YOU'LL ALSO APPRECIATE A PLETHORA OF MUSIC, SOUND EFFECTS, AND SPOKEN DIA-LOGUE. HUMOR ABOUNDS, ALTHOUGH IT IS OFTEN ADOLESCENT AT BEST. THE PUZZLES ARE FAIR, CHARACTER INTERACTION IS STRAIGHTFORWARD, AND THE POINT-AND-CLICK INTERFACE MAKES UNDER A KILLING MOON AMONG THE MOST ENJOYABLE MULTIMEDIA ADVENTURES EVER — ONE EVERY "CD DETECTIVE" WILL WANT TO INVESTIGATE.

THE SOLUTION

GENERAL

While you're in movement mode, everything you see is at eye level. Throughout the game it may be necessary to raise or lower your view. To look in drawers or boxes, for example, you may have to lower your view (use the Ctrl key and/or the arrow keys and the "D" key). To look at things on a high shelf, you may need to raise your eye level (use the left Shift key). To return to eye level, press Tab or "E."

DAY ONE

STARTING OUT

Get stamp from the lower-right drawer of desk. Get pen from lower-left drawer. Look at phonograph, then play it. Look at ex-wife's photo on desk. Look at fax machine on top of file cabinet. Look at crime-link computer behind desk. Take gun from credenza. Take both pieces of mail (sales flyer and surgery gift certificate) from beneath door. Examine all mail (getting credit card application). Combine pen and stamp with credit card application (getting ready-to-mail application). Go to street.

FINDING WORK

Look at mailbox. Use ready-to-mail application on mailbox. Talk to Chelsee at the newsstand: C, C, B, A. Ask her about the robbery (noting two clues). Go to pawnshop (next to newsstand). Talk to Rook: C, C, B, C, A, B, C (takes you to alley). Pick up glass shard from under window. Examine shard (clue).

Move trash can, getting key. Examine footprint (clue). Get basketball. Move staircase. Climb staircase. Look at painted door. Get radio from side of dumpster. Examine radio (getting batteries). Examine chocolate cans on ground. Open and look in dumpster. Move boards on fence. Exit back to street and go left. Get newspaper on street in front of Brew 'n Stew. Examine newspaper. Read all articles. Go to police station.

MORE CLUES

Talk to Mac: B, A, C (getting three more clues). Return to Chandler Avenue and visit Golden Gate Hotel. Talk to Ardo: B, B, B, A. Ask about all. Return to alley. Talk to bum: B, B. Go to Brew 'n Stew. Talk to Louie: B, C, A. Ask about chocolate (getting pie). Return to alley. Talk to bum: C. Offer pie from inventory. Ask about burglary (getting last two clues).

COMBING THE CLUES

Return to office. Use computer. Enter clues: caucasian, mutant: no, male, 60-64, 281-320 lbs., red hair, two eyes, green eyes, AB-, 14 shoe, anchor tattoo. View suspect file.

TRACKING THE BAD GUY

Go to street. Talk to Chelsee. Ask about Beek and Rusty. Go left toward Golden Gate Hotel. At hotel, go left and through fence to Coit Tower. Talk to Beek: A, C, A. Offer surgery certificate from inventory. Ask about all.

Go to Rusty's. Move doormat. Get key to Rusty's. Use key to unlock door and enter. Get suction dart crossbow from cabinet. Turn on TV. Go behind counter. Move crate. Get Rusty doll. Combine batteries with Rusty doll (getting live Rusty doll). Get Inspector Burns' mask from shelf. Get stacking (ring toss) ring from bottom of wall with plastic weapons. Get ring toss from wall. Get key to back room taped on wall support. Look at employee's door. Use key to back room on employees' door.

Enter back room. Get suction dart from wall and balloon from sink. Open acid vat (to find out what happened to Rusty). Return to front room. Look at nozzle on giant Rusty face on wall. Use balloon on nozzle . Combine dart with crossbow (getting loaded crossbow). Leave Rusty's.

CATCHING THE BAD GUY

Go around the corner to the right. Go to warehouse. Open door. Save. Enter warehouse. Climb stairs. Get key from post on wall. Use Rusty doll on ceiling pulley hook. Go back down stairs. Open crate. Get fireman's uniform from crate.

Use key on wall box. Hide behind crates (crouch). After Flemm runs, get keys and bracelet from table. Use Flemm's keys on locked wall box. Get strongbox. Combine key from alley with strongbox. Examine strongbox (getting jade). Combine mask with fireman's outfit (getting Inspector Burns disguise). Exit.

DAY TWO

FINDING MORE WORK

Get mail (credit card) on floor by door. Examine it. Go to electronics shop (across the street from pawnshop). Use credit card on electronics shop door. Enter. Talk to Hamm: B, B. Use credit card on blue box special. Get fax machine. Return to office. Take fax. Examine it. Go to countess' mansion.

BLACK MARKET

After countess encounter, go to newsstand. Talk to Chelsee: A, A. Ask Chelsee about statuette. Go to police station. Ask Mac about Franco. Go to pawnshop. Ask about jade and Franco. Go to alley. Open and search recycling trash can. Get and examine the Jewelry Weekly trade paper.

Go to Alhambra Theatre. Talk to Franco: C, C, A. Offer jade from inventory. Ask about artifact. Return to office. Get fax. Examine it. Go to police station. Ask Mac about Knickerbocker and Eddie Ching. Go to Ching's.

BREAKING INTO CHING'S

Go to electronics shop. Talk to Hamm: C, C, B, A (tells you how to beat security system). Use credit card on blue-light special. Get laserblade. Return to Ching's.

In library, open closet door (left of Buddha). Get trap and fish food. Open aquarium. Use fish food on aquarium. Use ring toss on aquarium (getting filled ring). Get book on top of bookshelf. Examine book (getting Eddie Ching's key). Enter hall. Examine laser beams. Use loaded crossbow on lasernets. Use filled ring on lever. Enter study.

CHING'S STUDY

Get geigger chow from behind obelisk next to Venus. Get fax from under table. Examine it (birthday fax). Combine geigger chow with trap (getting baited trap). Look at geigger in terrarium. Use baited cage on geigger. Move painting (exposing safe).

220

Look at safe. Open Ultrasafe 8000. Click Start. Click 101412 (from birthday fax). Click enter. Take bidder list and security card from safe. Examine both. Get capture noose behind ugly thing in corner of room to the right of the safe. Move mirror (above noose). Use Eddie Ching's key on switch lock. Return to library.

CHING'S SECRET ROOM

Enter secret room. Examine statuette. Move crate. Take bandana from statue of David. Look at display case. Do not pull lever unless you save first (you'll lose 20 points and destroy all the valuables). Use bandana on dirty sign above pull lever. Move painting (exposing security card slot). Use security card on slot. Use capture noose on statuette. Return to office.

DAY THREE

THE NEXT JOB

Go to pizza shop. Talk to Francesca: A, C, A (gives you note). Examine coded note. Go to Brew 'n Stew. Ask about Sal. Outside, open trash can beside Brew 'n Stew. Get note scraps. Assemble scraps (first line reads: Regency Escort Service; second line: YV UZNV SIAKWB-HUG.) Combine note from Francesca with assembled note. Examine encoded note. Change letters until each is red, and note will be readable: "We have confirmed your appointment with Chastity at the suite in the Golden Gate Hotel at usual time. The password today is silicon." Go to Golden Gate Hotel.

GOLDEN GATE HOTEL

Use Burns' disguise (you must have inflated balloon). Enter hotel: A, A. Type "Silicon." In suite entry, get foil off tabletop. Move Mishap on High Seas painting. Look at Twistee board game. Move picture to right of bedroom door. Look at list of female names. Enter piano room. Get deodorizer (magnet) from door. Move piano. Go to bedroom.

HOTEL BEDROOM

Open closet. Get champagne glass. Open left nightstand cabinet. Look at Playbub magazine. Look at desk. Look at locked drawer. Open left-middle drawer and look at Gideon Bible. Open bottom-left drawer and look at camera. Open top-right drawer and look at change. Go to hot tub room.

HOT TUB

Move towel. Examine grate. Examine vase with cork in it. Use champagne glass on pool. Use filled glass on vase (getting cork). Examine cork (getting wire). Return to bedroom.

GETTING EVIDENCE ON SAL

Examine locked drawer. Use wire on locked drawer. Get shoelace. Combine shoelace with magnet. Return to hot tub room. Use magnet-on-a-string on grate (getting screwdriver). Use screwdriver on grate. Get film.

Go to electronics shop. Use credit card on blue-light special. Get developing kit. Combine kit with film. Examine photos. Return to pizza shop: C. Offer photos. Ask about mugging and Pug.

TRACKING A MUGGER

Go to Coit Towers: A. Ask Beek about Pug (takes you to Pug). Talk to Pug: A, A, C, A, B, B. Go to Colonel's. Talk to Oriental woman (Eddie Ching): A, A, B, C, A.

DAY FOUR

SEARCHING THE COLONEL'S PLACE

Go to Colonel's office. Move bottom-right vase on bookshelf. Get disc. Move picture frame on table by window. Examine it. Open bottom-left drawer of desk. Get and examine greeting card. Open bottom-right drawer and get envelope. Examine it. Turn on computer. Use disc on computer. Read through computer file. Go to Melahn's apartment: A, C, B, A. Offer greeting card to her. Ask about Chameleon, Colonel, and Colonel's key (getting key). Return to Colonel's office. Use Colonel's key on cabinet. Open cabinet and get coded documents. Examine documents. Move painting to the left of file cabinet, revealing safe. Examine safe.

SEARCHING THE COUNTESS' MANSION

Go to Countess' mansion. Examine eagle on chandelier. Use foil on eagle (drops case). Get cigarette case. Examine cigarette case (getting cigarette). Move newspaper to reveal ashtray. Look at ashtray to see cigarette butts.

Get note scraps from wastebasket. Examine scraps and assemble them. ("...circum-stances—/are progression smoothly/delighted to hear that Murphy was able/the final piece of our puzzle. He probably doesn't/...") Do not be concerned if the note does not "stick" after putting it together. Get watch from fireplace mantle.

San Francisco of the future — hasn't changed much, has it?

• • • • • • • • • •

BACK AT THE COLONEL'S

Return to Colonel's. Move mail by door. Get and examine UPEX receipt. Return to Melahn's. Ask her about UPEX receipt (gives you paper with numbers). Return to Colonel's. Open safe with combination from paper (5-7-1). Click left knob five times, click middle knob seven times, click right knob once. Get code book. Combine code book with coded documents. Examine coded documents. Go to Roadside Motel (talk to Alaynah). Go to GRS.

GRS: SECURITY

While walking around GRS, you are observed by a roving security eye. When you are in the hallway, it is best just to avoid it. In each of the four rooms, a designated hiding spot is indicated below. Constantly save in each room. If the warning signal is heard and you are not near the hiding spot, you won't have enough time to get there. When you hide, crouch down (using Ctrl key) as low as possible. The game does not alert you to when it is clear. The first time you hide successfully in each room, you get one point, so watch your score. When the score changes, it is safe to get up. The time spent crouching can be anywhere from one to three minutes. If points are not important to you, or you visit later, this can be avoided by restoring a saved game as soon as you hear the warning message. This resets the amount of time you have to explore the room.

GRS: CONFERENCE ROOM

If security arrives while you're in the conference room, hide behind desk. Open lower-left drawer and get laserdisc player. Open top-left drawer and look at Playbub magazine. Go to R&D office.

GRS: R&D OFFICE

If the security eye shows up while you're here, hide behind Paul's desk or the wall by the trashcan. Take wrench on floor. Take miniature TV from desktop. Combine TV with laserdisc player (getting audio-visual equipment). Take pennant from wall and examine it (getting computer card). Look at Paul's desk. Look at computer. Turn computer on. Use card on computer. Read all files. Go to Eva's office.

GRS: EVA'S OFFICE

If the security eye pops in, hide behind office divider. Use wrench on air vent, then use geigger on opening. Enter security section and get minidisk from table top. Look at memo on desk. Open lower-left drawer of desk and get passkey. Open upper-left drawer and get laserdisc. Exit security area and get Eva's computer card from beneath her desk. Turn computer on. Use her card on computer. Use minidisk on computer. Go to Tucker's office.

GRS: TUCKER'S OFFICE

If security eye comes, hide behind plants. Look at access panel by door. Use passkey on panel. Open door and enter office. Open lower-right drawer and get match. Open lower-left drawer and read tape (142235). Return to Eva's office.

GRS: EVA'S SAFE

Open wall safe (using tape combination: click on 142235 and Enter). Get viral powder. Return to Tucker's office.

224

GRS: TUCKER'S SAFE

Look at door to safe. Look at safe panel. Turn on safe panel. Combine laserdisc with audio-visual equipment (TV and laserdisc player). Save. Use loaded audio-visual equipment with safe panel. Enter safe. Get statue, videocassette, and shredded paper from wastebasket, then get out as quickly as possible.

Immediately hide behind plant in office; get into a position from which you can see the safe panel and safe. Wait for security eye to enter safe. Quickly turn off safe panel to close door and trap security eye in safe. Examine statue (getting Winter chip). Combine chip with watch. Examine shredded note. Assemble note ("Brother Marcus: We are seekers of purity who will abide no defect in..."). Go to conference room.

GRS: VIDEO IN CONFERENCE ROOM

Turn on remote-control pad on the tabletop. Look at video screen. Get cabinet key off rail along wall. Use key on cabinet. Look at VCR. Turn on VCR. Use videocassette on VCR. Combine viral powder with cigarette (getting lethal cigarette). Return home.

DAY FIVE

225

THE CHAMELEON

Go to Bastion of Sanctity. Look at Chameleon. Look at Alaynah. Do not enter main room because Chameleon will kill you immediately. Follow right passage. Get clamp on right wall. Look at gargoyle in small alcove to the right. Get gemstone from gargoyle. Get bungee cord from left wall. Look at vase.

Combine bungee cord with clamp (forms slingshot). Combine gemstone with slingshot. Combine match with lethal cigarette. Save. Use loaded slingshot on vase above gargoyle. Immediately go to opening on other side of passage and enter main room. Use lit cigarette on cigarette in ashtray. After Chameleon's death, move shield on wall. Move switch: C, A, B, A.

HEADING INTO SPACE

Go to Broken Skull: A, C, C, B. Offer $100 bill (appears in inventory): B, B. Go to Roadside Motel. Ask Alaynah about token. Go to pawnshop. Ask Rook about silver dollar. Examine silver dollar.

Return to Broken Skull: A. Offer silver dollar (takes you to Ferrel Plus): A. Save before picking each ball. (Tickets are typically in this order: upper-right, middle, lower-right, lower-right ball.) Talk to bartender: A, B, A.

DAY SIX

ESCAPING ARBORETUM

Get rock from rock wall by fountain (on path to the left). Just beyond is a door. Open it and get lighter fluid. Get flint on top of rock wall next to windows. Get rake. Walk to pile of leaves.

Look at pile of leaves. Look at door but do not open. Look at smoke detector above door. Combine rock with flint (getting sparks). Use rake on leaves. Use lighter fluid on leaves. Use sparks on leaves.

EXPLORING MOON CHILD

Follow map to residential entrance. Get pipe. Backtrack to stasis room. Enter. Turn machine on.

Phase 1: Raise temperature to 60 degrees. Raise oxygen to 12. Use epinephrine. Use electric shock.

Phase 2: Raise temperature to 90 degrees. Use pentathol. Use epinephrine. Raise oxygen to 14.

Phase 3: Raise temperature to 98.6 degrees. Raise oxygen to 16. Use epinephrine. Use bicarbonate. (Eva gives you mission paper and Eva's key.)

DAY SEVEN

ENDGAME

Examine mission paper. Go to observation deck. Unlock panel door with Eva's key. Move software. Get linkup computer. Examine computer. Combine Winter chip with computer (getting computer virus linkup). Get glass. Examine it (getting straw). Move plant (revealing floor panel). Look at floor panel. Use pipe on floor panel.

Get computer cord. Combine computer cord with computer (getting virus linkup connection). Look at recessed button on wall next to door. Use straw on recessed button (reveals panel). Examine panel. Use virus linkup connection on panel.

ORBS N STUFF

Object	See this Section for Location	Also See Section(s)
Stamp	Starting Out	Location only
Pen	Starting Out	Location only
Sales flyer	Starting Out	Location only
Surgery gift certificate	Starting Out	Tracking Bad Guy
Credit card application	Starting Out	Finding Work
Glass shard	Finding Work	Location only
Key from alley	Finding Work	Catching Bad Guy
Radio	Finding Work	Location only
Batteries	Finding Work	Tracking Bad Guy
Newspaper	Finding Work	Location only
Chocolate pie	More Clues	Location only
Key to Rusty's	Tracking Bad Guy	Location only
Suction dart crossbow	Tracking Bad Guy	Location only
Rusty doll	Tracking Bad Guy	Catching Bad Guy
Inspector Burns mask	Tracking Bad Guy	Catching Bad Guy
Ring toss	Tracking Bad Guy	Breaking into Ching's
Key to back room	Tracking Bad Guy	Location only
Suction dart	Tracking Bad Guy	Location only
Balloon	Tracking Bad Guy	Golden Gate Hotel
Loaded crossbow	Tracking Bad Guy	Breaking into Ching's
Wall box key	Catching Bad Guy	Location only
Fireman's uniform	Catching Bad Guy	Location only
Flemm's keys	Catching Bad Guy	Location only
Bracelet	Catching Bad Guy	Location only
Strongbox	Catching Bad Guy	Location only
Jade	Catching Bad Guy	Black Market
Burns' disguise	Catching Bad Guy	Golden Gate Hotel
Credit card	Finding More Work	Breaking into Ching's, Getting Evidence on Sal
Fax	Finding More Work	Black Market, Ching's Study

227

Object	See this Section for Location	Also See Section(s)
Fax machine	Finding More Work	Location only
Jewelry Weekly paper	Black Market	Location only
Laserblade	Breaking into Ching's	Location only
Trap	Breaking into Ching's	Ching's Study
Fish food	Breaking into Ching's	Location only
Filled ring	Breaking into Ching's	Location only
Book	Breaking into Ching's	Location only
Eddie Ching's key	Breaking into Ching's	Ching's Study
Geigger chow	Ching's Study	Location only
Baited trap	Ching's Study	Location only
Geigger	Ching's Study	GRS: Eva's Office
Bidder list	Ching's Study	Location only
Security card	Ching's Study	Ching's Secret Room
Capture noose	Ching's Study	Ching's Secret Room
Bandana	Ching's Secret Room	Location only
Coded note	The Next Job	Location only
Note scraps	The Next Job	Location only
Foil	Golden Gate Hotel	Searching the Countess' Mansion
Magnet	Golden Gate Hotel	Getting Evidence on Sal
Champagne glass	Hotel Bedroom	Hot Tub
Cork	Hot Tub	Location only
Wire	Hot Tub	Getting Evidence on Sal
Screwdriver	Getting Evidence on Sal	Location only
Shoelace	Getting Evidence on Sal	Location only
Film	Getting Evidence on Sal	Location only
Developing kit	Getting Evidence on Sal	Location only
Disc	Searching the Colonel's Place	Location only
Greeting card	Searching the Colonel's Place	Location only
Envelope	Searching the Colonel's Place	Location only
Colonel's key	Searching the Colonel's Place	Location only
Coded documents	Searching the Colonel's Place	Back at the Colonel's

<u>Object</u>	<u>See this Section for Location</u>	<u>Also See Section(s)</u>
Cigarette case (cigarette)	Searching the Countess' Mansion	GRS: Video in Conference Room, The Chameleon
Note scraps	Searching the Countess' Mansion	Location only
Watch	Searching the Countess' Mansion	GRS: Tucker's Safe
UPEX receipt	Back at the Colonel's	Location only
Paper with numbers	Back at the Colonel's	Location only
Code book	Back at the Colonel's	Location only
Laserdisc player	GRS: Conference Room	GRS: R&D Office
Wrench	GRS: R&D Office	GRS: Eva's Office
Mini TV	GRS: R&D Office	Location only
Audio-visual equipment	GRS: R&D Office	GRS: Tucker's Safe
Pennant	GRS: R&D Office	Location only
Computer card	GRS: R&D Office	Location only
Minidisk	GRS: Eva's Office	Location only
Passkey	GRS: Eva's Office	GRS: Tucker's Office
Laserdisc	GRS: Eva's Office	GRS: Tucker's Safe
Eva's computer card	GRS: Eva's Office	Location only
Match	GRS: Tucker's Office	The Chameleon
Tape combination	GRS: Tucker's Office	GRS: Eva's Safe
Viral powder	GRS: Eva's Safe	GRS: Video in Conference Room
Statue	GRS: Tucker's Safe	Location only
Shredded paper	GRS: Tucker's Safe	Location only
Videocassette	GRS: Tucker's Safe	GRS: Video in Conference Room
Winter chip	GRS: Tucker's Safe	Endgame
Cabinet key	GRS: Video in Conference Room	Location only
Clamp	The Chameleon	Location only
Gemstone	The Chameleon	Location only
Bungee cord	The Chameleon	Location only
Silver dollar	Heading into Space	Location only
Rock	Escaping Arboretum	Location only

Object	See this Section for Location	Also See Section(s)
Lighter fluid	Escaping Arboretum	Location only
Flint	Escaping Arboretum	Location only
Rake	Escaping Arboretum	Location only
Pipe	Exploring Moon Child	Endgame
Mission paper	Exploring Moon Child	Endgame
Eva's key	Exploring Moon Child	Endgame
Linkup computer	Endgame	Location only
Glass (straw)	Endgame	Location only
Cord	Endgame	Location only